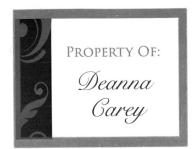

PROPERTY OF:

Deanna
Carey

The Women in
Lincoln's Life

The Women in Lincoln's Life

By H. Donald Winkler

Rutledge Hill Press®

Nashville Tennessee

A Division of Thomas Nelson, Inc.

For Azile, my loving wife and
cheerleader since 1956.

For our sons, Don and Jim, who make us
proud to be their parents.

And for our grandchildren, Ben, Jason,
Jessica, and Michelle, whom Ann Rutledge
would have enjoyed knowing
as her first cousins, seven times removed.

Published by Rutledge Hill Press, a Division of Thomas Nelson, Inc., P.O. Box 141000, Nashville, Tennessee 37214.

www.ThomasNelson.com

Library of Congress Cataloging-in-Publication Data

1-55853-922-0

Printed in the United States of America

01 02 03 04 05—5 4 3 2 1

I want in all cases
to do right, and most
particularly so, in all
cases with women.

ABRAHAM LINCOLN, 1837

*M*r. Lincoln had a heart [like] a
woman's—filled to
overflowing with sympathy
for those in trouble, and ever ready to relieve
them by any means in his power.

G. W. HARRIS,
a law student in Lincoln's office
in Springfield, Illinois

Contents

Acknowledgments

The following persons and institutions are respectfully acknowledged for their important services in the development of this book:

Genealogists: Charlotte Bergevin, Peoria, Illinois; George R. Rutledge, Hanover, Pennsylvania; Sharon Schirding, Petersburg, Illinois; Irene Wilson, San Diego, California; and Ralph E. Winkler, Lakeside, California.

Agencies and Libraries: Darlene Epperson and Linda Wilson, Beaufort County Library, Hilton Head Island, South Carolina; Joelle Bertolet, Haverford College Library; Linda Hallmark, Henderson County Historical and Genealogical Society (KY); James T. Murphy and Iver F. Yeager of Illinois College, Jacksonville, Illinois; New Salem Lincoln League; David Blanchette, Illinois Historic Preservation Agency; Illinois State Historical Library; Library of Congress; Carol Jenkins, Mary Ann Russell, and Charles Starling, Lincoln's New Salem State Historic Site; Menard County Historical Society (IL); and Emily Jansen, New England Quarterly.

Individuals: Webb Garrison, Lake Junaluska, North Carolina; Mabel Gunn, Stone Mountain, Georgia; Georgia Leinberger and Raymond H. Montgomery, Petersburg, Illinois; Susan Hatton McCoy, Peoria, Illinois; Mohamed Danawi and Dan McGregor, Savannah College of Art and Design; and Lisa Winkler, Mililani, Hawaii.

I am indebted to all historians, journalists, and genealogists of present and earlier generations who have taken a special interest in the Ann Rutledge mystery and have contributed informational gems that, linked together, provided a treasure chest of rich resources. I thank them all.

Introduction

*I*t took a postcard to prime my interest in this subject.

I remember it falling to the ground from the pile of bills and junk mail I pulled from the mail box. The postcard was from my brother Ralph, our family's genealogist. There was a photo of a log home on one side and a simple message on the other: "Congratulations! You are a first cousin of Ann Rutledge! More information will follow." From my school days in southern Illinois I remembered Ann Rutledge's name. She was somehow connected with Lincoln, perhaps as a girlfriend. At the time, however, I was busily engaged in a high-level administrative position at a college in central Virginia, and there was little time to ponder genealogy.

While I savored a bowl of chili in the college dining room a few days later, a history professor sat down at my table. "What do you know about Ann Rutledge?" I asked. "Oh," he said, "she was once thought to be Lincoln's sweetheart, but most historians think the story is pure nonsense. Why do you ask?" I reported my recent news. "Her paternal grandparents were my five-times great grandparents. Should I be ecstatic?" I laughed. "Well, it's interesting," he replied, "but if it's only folklore, it's not worth talking about. I suggest you read J. G. Randall's book on Lincoln."

Randall, I learned, was an imposing Lincoln scholar of the 1940s—a scholar so respected that when he called the romance "a great myth" everyone assumed that it was. Randall repudiated the love story revealed by William H. Herndon, who was Lincoln's longtime law partner and early biographer. Herndon discovered the romance during his twenty-five-year search for information about the martyred president—a search that produced a voluminous collection of letters, interviews, and statements. According to Herndon, the Lincoln-Rutledge romance and her tragic death were keys to Lincoln's greatness and to his chronic melancholy. Historian Randall regarded Herndon's rambling accounts as unreliable, however, and suggested that Herndon had created his account of the romance because he so disliked Mary Todd Lincoln. Who was I to question J. G. Randall's conclusions? So I forgot about my cousin Ann for the next three years. In January 1991 my wife's brother-in-law, Webb Garrison, called. He had written numerous books on the Civil War and was aware of my relationship to Ann Rutledge. "I've got two articles in front of me that I think you'll find interesting," he said. "Both were published this past year. One is in the *Journal of the Abraham Lincoln Association*; the other is in *Civil War History*. Both shed new light on the romance."

The first, by Lincoln scholar John Y. Simon of Southern Illinois University, was based on his exhaustive study of Herndon's source material. Simon acknowledged Herndon's "misuse of the romance to settle scores with Mary Lincoln" but also noted serious problems in Randall's work. "All the primary sources—the testimony of witnesses—support the romance," Simon argued, "and the reality of the story appears certain."

The second article, by Douglas L. Wilson, director of the Center for Lincoln Studies at Knox College, added more substance. Wilson found statements from twenty-four witnesses in Herndon's documents. They included Ann's teacher, siblings, and relatives and Lincoln's friends and associates. Wilson considered these witnesses to be "straightforward and reliable" and "with no purpose to deceive."

Significantly, no witness denied Lincoln's love for Ann. Fifteen knew about the Lincoln-Rutledge engagement; twenty-two knew that Lincoln courted Ann; and seventeen knew that he grieved excessively after her death.

The reports from Simon and Wilson were so convincing that I began my own research, reading everything I could find on Lincoln and Ann Rutledge. The work intensified after my retirement in 1995. I secured and read more than one hundred books and articles, and even retraced Lincoln's travels down the Mississippi River (although I chose an elegant steamboat over the kind of flatboat he used).

Research of Herndon's materials at the Library of Congress was next on my agenda, but I was spared that tedious work by the publication of *Herndon's Informants* (edited by Wilson and Rodney O. Davis) in 1998. It contained not only all of Herndon's materials but also items collected by his collaborator, Jesse W. Weik. Other recent works also reinforced the revived theory about the romance, especially *The Shadows Rise* by John E. Walsh.

Even with all these resources, the complete story of Ann's life and relationship with Abraham Lincoln remained untold. With the material I had accumulated from persistent research, I felt I could do so. In my bulging files were stories from obscure sources apparently seen by few historians—family genealogy from the New Salem community where Lincoln and Ann lived; testimony from daughters of Ann's cousin, John Miller Camron; Camron family scrapbooks of period newspaper reports; and accounts of Ann's early life in White County, Illinois, by Margaret Land, a family historian.

Further investigation into the Camron and Rutledge families uncovered a 195-page manuscript, *Camrons, Westward They Came*, by Charlotte Bergevin, Daisy Sundberg, and Evelyn Berg, which provided valuable information. Of special help were the papers of descendants of Ann's siblings and relatives: James Rutledge Saunders, George Rutledge, C. Vale Mayes, Pauline Warthen, and Captain Keith F. Brown. My brother Ralph also provided substantial information.

Culminating my search for the real Ann Rutledge I explored Rutledge and Lincoln sites in Illinois and participated in a workshop at New Salem addressed by historian Michael Burlingame. He graciously shared with me some new research about Ann. Through New Salem volunteer Georgia Leinberger I met genealogist Sharon L. Schirding, who is a distant cousin of John Camron's wife and the niece of Julia Drake, one of Camron's biographers. Mrs. Schirding provided background material used by her aunt in writing the biography. It contains interesting anecdotes about Ann and the relationship between Camron's daughters and Lincoln. The people of central Illinois were unusually hospitable to me. When I asked for directions to Ann's original gravesite, Mrs. Leinberger shook her head. "It's impossible to tell you. You could never find it. But Mrs. Schirding and I will be happy to guide you there." And they did. A few miles from Petersburg, they turned off a state road into a space between corn fields. It felt like a deeply rutted tractor path overgrown with weeds. About a half mile down the trail a flag pole marked the Old Concord Burial Ground. Many headstones were hidden by knee-high weeds, but near the middle of the cemetery was Ann's original grave. Here Ann lay buried for fifty-five years before her remains were reinterred at Oakland Cemetery in Petersburg, Illinois. Here, at Old Concord, Lincoln wept for days. I stood there and absorbed the historical significance of this obscure location.

During preceding months I had also researched Mary Todd. I found remarkably diverse opinions about her marriage to Lincoln—and about their courtship. The differences led me to look deeper into Lincoln's relationship with his wife. Especially helpful were biographies of Mary Todd and works by Burlingame (*The Inner World of Abraham Lincoln*) and Wilson (*Honor's Voice*).

The more I studied, the more I discovered other women who had influenced Abraham Lincoln. I became so intrigued that I expanded my work to examine the way women affected Lincoln's life, as well as the impact he had on many of them.

For me, closure on this subject finally came when I signed a contract with Rutledge Hill Press to publish this book. Ironically, the signing occurred at a meeting in the palatial Charleston Place Hotel in Charleston, South Carolina, where the first shots of the Civil War were fired in the opening days of Lincoln's presidency. As my wife and I were driving back to Hilton Head Island from Charleston, she asked me, "Do you think Lincoln would like this book?"

No, I started to say, because he was a very private person, and this book pokes into private matters. But, on further reflection, I replied, "I think he might, but only if he knew his wife would never see it!"

1

"All That I Am or Ever Hope to Be I Owe to Her."

*T*he prettiest, smartest, and sweetest girl around was dead.

Her name was Ann Rutledge, and she was the fiancée of Abraham Lincoln.

"He sorrowed and grieved, rambled over the hills and through the forests, day and night. . . . He slept not, he ate not, joyed not. This he did until his body became emaciated and weak. His mind wandered from its throne. . . . It has been said that Mr. Lincoln became and was totally insane at that time and place." So spoke Lincoln's friend, law partner, and biographer, William H. Herndon, in a lecture delivered the year after Lincoln's death. "Lincoln loved Ann Rutledge better than his own life," Herndon said. He loved her "with all his soul, mind, and strength," and "she loved him dearly. . . . They seemed made in heaven for each other."

The untimely death of Ann Rutledge appears to have made a phenomenal impact on Abraham Lincoln's life. Herndon claimed that "the love and death of this girl shattered Lincoln's purposes and tendencies" and that "he threw off his infinite sorrow by leaping wildly into the political arena." Had she lived and married Lincoln, would he have been content as a lawyer outside the political arena? Would he ever have become president? The answer remains elusive, but without question Abraham Lincoln's life was dramatically shaped by a succession of remarkable women—beginning with his mother.

From all accounts, Lincoln was ashamed of his mother. In his auto-biographical musings he said little about Nancy Hanks. He visited her grave only once and never had it marked with a headstone. In a letter written in 1836, he matter-of-factly recorded a callous description of his mother's "want of teeth [and] weather-beaten appearance." Yet he apparently believed that to her noble bloodline he owed much of his success. His fierce ambition—his driving desire to be someone—came, he confided to Herndon, from his mother.[1]

"My mother was the illegitimate daughter of Lucy Hanks and a well-bred Virginia planter or farmer," Lincoln reportedly confided to Herndon. "My grandmother was poor and credulous, and she was shamefully taken advantage of by the man. My mother inherited his qualities, and I hers." According to Herndon, Lincoln was convinced that from this unknown grandfather he acquired his "power of analysis, logic, mental ability, ambition, and all the qualities that distinguished him from . . . the Hanks family."[2]

Lincoln made his comments to Herndon as the two shared a buggy ride en route to a distant court case about 1851. As the buggy jolted over the country road, Lincoln added ruefully, "God bless my mother. All that I am or ever hope to be I owe to her." He then lapsed into silence and was "sad and absorbed," Herndon said. Finally, Lincoln spoke again, telling Herndon: "Keep it a secret while I live."[3]

Lincoln knew that his mother, with all her limitations—including the inability to write—was a strong woman. She was strong-minded and had "remarkably keen perception," according to her maternal cousin Dennis Hanks. These were uncommon traits within the Hanks family, which was notable for notorious philanderers and numerous cases of illegitimacy. Lincoln's own grandmother, Lucy Hanks, was charged with "fornication" by a grand jury in Mercer County, Kentucky. No wedding certificate was ever found for her.[4]

Nancy Hanks may have continued the family's illicit tradition. An Indiana neighbor who was Lincoln's age, Laurinda Mason Lanman, told an interviewer: "My mother . . . liked [the Lincolns] but she always said that not only was Nancy Hanks an illegitimate child herself but that Nancy was not what she ought to have been herself. Loose." Lincoln may have known about her disgraceful reputation, according to Herndon. Lincoln told Herndon that "his [relatives] were lascivious—lecherous not to be trusted."[5]

In early childhood Nancy was taken from her mother—afterwards married to Henry Sparrow—and sent to live with her aunt and uncle, Thomas and Elizabeth Hanks Sparrow. Then in late 1805, when Nancy was twenty-two, she drifted to Elizabethtown, Kentucky, and lived briefly with her uncle, Joseph Hanks.

Thomas Lincoln, described by a neighbor as "an uneducated . . . plain unpretending plodding man," walked into Hanks's carpentry shop that winter and asked to be an apprentice. The rapidly growing frontier town needed carpenters, and Hanks needed help, so he hired Thomas. Soon, Hanks introduced Thomas to Nancy, and he began courting her.[6]

Like Thomas, Nancy "cared nothing for forms, etiquette, and customs," according to Herndon. He further described her as "a bold, daredevil person who stepped to the very verge of propriety." At five feet ten inches and about 140 pounds, she was tall and athletic. "In a fair wrestle, she could throw most of the men who put her powers to test," a local townsman would recall. "A reliable gentleman told me he heard Jack Thomas, clerk of the Grayson Court, say he had frequently wrestled with her, and she invariably laid him on his back."

Abraham Lincoln was born in this primitive cabin near
Hodgenville, Kentucky, on Feb. 12, 1809. AUTHOR'S COLLECTION.

Thomas Lincoln may never have wrestled with Nancy Hanks, but he did propose to her, and she accepted. Thomas was twenty-eight, and Nancy was twenty-three. They were reportedly married on June 12, 1806, in Washington County, Kentucky, and afterwards set up housekeeping in a log cabin in Elizabethtown, where their first child, Sarah, was born on February 10, 1807.[7]

In December 1808, Thomas paid two hundred dollars for a farm on the south fork of Nolin Creek, about two miles south of Hodgenville. It was called Sinking Spring Farm after a bountiful spring at the bottom of a deep cave on the property. On a knoll near the spring, Thomas built a one-room log cabin, eighteen by sixteen feet, with a dirt floor and a door that swung on leather hinges. In that little cabin on a snowy winter evening Nancy went into labor. Soon after dawn on February 12, 1809, upon a bed of poles, cornhusks, and bearskins, Abraham Lincoln was born.

Childbirth for Kentucky pioneers of the day could be frightening as well as joyful. With few doctors, a midwife was necessary, but was often not called until the last moment. When his wife went into labor, Thomas Lincoln hurried to fetch the midwife. He ran into Abraham Enlow, one of his nearest neighbors. Enlow volunteered to find a midwife and advised Thomas to stay with Mrs. Lincoln. Enlow returned with his mother, who oversaw the birth. Afterwards, Enlow said the baby was named for him to honor his "neighborliness." In later life Lincoln acknowledged that was partly true. "The Enlows were good to us, and Mother gave them the pattern of the quilt that covered me." He was also named for his grandfather, whom Thomas, at age eight, had seen killed by an Indian. There had not been a generation of Lincolns without an Abraham since the late seventeenth century.[8]

As a child, Lincoln undoubtedly heard gossip about his possible illegitimacy. When he ran for president in 1860, his political opponents zeroed in on the old stories and spread them with vicious abandon. To counter the political damage, Lincoln wrote to Samuel Haycraft, clerk of the court in Hardin County, Kentucky, and asked him to locate the marriage record. Haycraft, a local historian and loyal Union supporter, had grown up in Elizabethtown and known Thomas Lincoln. But whatever search he conducted apparently failed to turn up the requested document.

Lincoln's longtime friend Ward Hill Lamon would later claim that there was no marriage license. Thomas Lincoln's marriage was a common law agreement with "no evidence but that of mutual acknowledgment and cohabitation," Lamon wrote in his biography of Lincoln. In 1878, however, W. F. Booker, clerk of the court in Washington County, made a remarkable discovery. While rummaging through piles of loose documents in the county courthouse, Booker said he found the marriage papers—a June 10, 1806 marriage bond signed by Thomas Lincoln and Richard Berry, guardian and uncle of Nancy Hanks, and an April 22, 1807 "marriage return" by Methodist circuit rider Jesse Head certifying he performed their marriage. Most Lincoln scholars accept the documents as genuine even though the bond was simply a standard form with the signatures added. The actual marriage certificate was never found.[9]

In the nineteenth century, an out-of-wedlock birth was scandalous. A worse sin was adultery, and in Lincoln's day rumors persisted that Nancy Hanks had adulterous relationships. Was someone other than Thomas Lincoln possibly the father of Abraham Lincoln?[10]

Upon what were the rumors based? Thomas Lincoln was five feet ten inches tall and stout, weighing 195 pounds, with a round face and a barrel chest. He was not likely, some suggested, to produce a slender son who would grow to a height of six-feet-four-inches. Thomas was also said to be sterile, according to the rumors. "Nancy Hanks was a rather loose woman," said Alfred M. Brown, a respected judge who lived most of his life in Hodgenville. According to some claims, as many as seven men other than Thomas Lincoln have been credited with fathering Abraham Lincoln. Prominent sources in or near Elizabethtown claimed that either George Brownfield or Abraham Enlow was Lincoln's father.[11]

Author William E. Barton, who investigated Lincoln's paternity for his 1920 book, concluded that all the charges were nonsense. But were they? Sometime between mid-May and early June 1808—when Abe was conceived—Thomas, Nancy, and toddler Sarah moved to Brownfield's farm, where they lived as tenants on the property. Thomas served as a hired laborer on the farm until that fall when the family settled at their Sinking Spring farm. Brownfield, then a thirty-five-year-old property owner, was a good-natured intellectual who resembled Lincoln in looks, height, and temperament. Enlow also had notable Lincoln features—long arms and ears, a large nose, and very large feet. When Enlow was an old man, he denied fathering Lincoln. However, Presley Haycraft, a staunch Lincoln supporter, said Enlow privately claimed Lincoln as his son for his entire life. "Enlow [was] as low a fellow as you could find," reported John B. Helm, a local merchant and lawyer. Enlow lived with his sister Polly, whom Helm called "a notorious prostitute." One of Polly's grand-daughters, Lizzie Murphy, claimed she often heard her mother and grandmother refer to Enlow as Lincoln's real father. Helm reported that Enlow once publicly bragged that he was Abe's father, prompt-ing a fight with Thomas Lincoln, who bit off a chunk of Enlow's nose. "I remember [Enlow and his maimed nose] as one of the insti-tutions of our county for some thirty years," Helm said. One reason Thomas Lincoln left Kentucky, Helm claimed, was "to get clear of Abe Enlow."[12]

Skeptics argued that Enlow could not have been Abe's father because he was only fourteen or fifteen at the time Abe was con-ceived, and that in early May 1808 the Lincolns were still living in Elizabethtown. Enlow was big for his age, however, and could have worked or visited relatives there. Also, some uncertainty exists about where the Lincolns actually resided just before joining the Brownfields. Adding to the conjecture about Lincoln's paternity was the fact that widower Thomas Lincoln, forty-one, married a thirty-one-year-old healthy and fertile woman in 1819, yet the couple never had children—proof, some said, of Thomas Lincoln's sterility. Herndon was convinced that Thomas Lincoln was incapable of fathering a child and that his fight with Enlow occurred after Thomas caught Enlow committing adultery with Nancy.[13]

In 1816 Thomas gave up on Kentucky—motivated in part by land-title problems and reportedly his dislike of slavery—and moved his fam-ily to Indiana. As little Abe grew he became more like his mother than his father—mild, tender, and athletic, with a strong memory and acute judgment. Her face, sharp and angular like his, projected a marked expression of melancholy. The same would be said of Lincoln after the death of Ann Rutledge and throughout the rest of his life. As a child Abe suffered experiences that could have emotionally scarred any youngster.

He was poor. He was continuously subjected to hard work and was often punished just for talking, asking questions, or studying.

Nancy had little time for her son. She and Sarah cooked, churned, cleaned, milked cows, hoed corn, dried beans, prepared tallow for candles, and made clay lamps. From Nancy's loom came clothes for the children and woolen blankets for the beds. She washed clothes in a large kettle by adding lye soap to the water and stirring the pot with a long-handled paddle. Survival in the wilderness required endless hours of tedious labor, so men prayed for sons, and mothers prayed for daughters—the more the better—to share the workload. But Thomas would have no more children—perhaps because he could not. His family was unusually small for his day.

At age eight, Abe was given an axe and required to clear trees, grub stumps, and split rails for fences—work usually reserved for older boys and men. He also had to carry heavy pails of drinking water about a mile—from a spring to the cabin. Usually, settlers built cabins near a spring or stream, but for reasons unknown, Thomas did not do that in Indiana. Twice Abe nearly died, and both instances may reflect the nature of his relationship with his mother.

Abe's playmate was Austin Gollaher. One day as the two boys were hunting partridges, Abe crossed Knob Creek on a narrow log, lost his footing, and fell into the swollen stream. Neither boy could swim. Austin hurriedly found a long pole and held it out to Abe, who was struggling to stay afloat in the deep water. After several attempts, he finally grabbed it, and Austin pulled him out of the creek. "I thought he was almost dead," Austin would later recall, "and I was badly scared. I rolled and pounded him in good earnest. Then I got him by the arms and shook him . . . and the water [began] pouring out of his mouth. . . . He was soon alright."

Then both boys became worried about what their mothers would do to them if they came home with wet clothes. "They would have whipped us hard," Austin would recount. "We dreaded their whippings from experience, and we were determined to avoid them." So they shed their clothes and dried them in the sun before returning home. Strangely, Abe seemed more afraid of his mother than his father.[14]

The other close call of Lincoln's childhood occurred at the local gristmill on a fall day in 1818. Abe hitched an old mare to the arm of the gristmill as was customary in grinding corn. It was late and he wanted to get home before dark, so with each revolution, he yelled, "Get up, you old hussy," and applied the lash. The horse responded with a fierce kick which struck Abe's forehead. It sent him sprawling to the earth, bleeding and unconscious. The mill owner summoned Thomas Lincoln, who loaded the seemingly lifeless child into a wagon and took him home.

The nine-year-old lay unconscious all night, but near daybreak he awoke and blurted out the words, "You old hussy!" finishing the phrase interrupted by the horse's kick. His mother seems to have been unconcerned about the injury. It was enough for her to leave matters in God's hands. She reportedly told Abe he did not die because it was "not his time," that Providence had "other designs" for him. "Nothing can hinder the execution of the designs of Providence," she said. "What is to be will be, and we can do nothing about it." Was Nancy Lincoln's untroubled response an admirable expression of faith or a lack of interest in her son?[15]

Abraham Lincoln's lifetime preoccupation with dreams and superstitions also appears to have come from his mother. A bird flying in the window, a horse's breath on a child's head, a dog crossing a hunter's path—all meant bad luck to Nancy Lincoln and her frontier neighbors. The moon had enormous influence. Fence rails could be cut only in the light of the moon, and potatoes planted in the dark of the moon. Trees and plants that bore their fruit above ground could be planted only when the moon shone full. Soap could be made only in the light of the moon, and it had to be stirred in only one direction and by only one person. Nothing was to be started on Friday, lest an endless chain of disasters occur. When a baby was due, an axe placed under the bed and a knife under the pillow supposedly eased the pain. Listening in boyish wonder to the legends his mother told him, Abe was led to believe in the significance of dreams and visions. Throughout his life, he would be puzzled and troubled by dreams and would hold a conviction that he was guided by forces beyond his control.[16]

His mother also influenced him in a positive manner. She introduced him to the Bible. In the winter the family gathered around the fireplace, and Nancy recited Bible stories. Those episodes produced

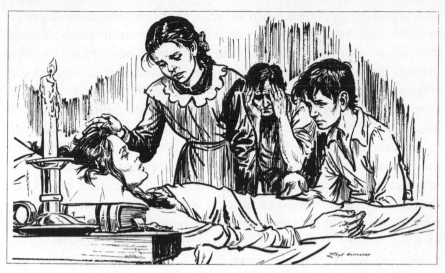

Abe, 9, and his sister Sarah, 11, were devastated with grief and a feeling of abandonment when their mother died at age 35. COURTESY OF LLOYD OSTENDORF.

Lincoln's warmest memories of his mother. His personal values, Lincoln would later claim, came from Scripture. "The fundamental truths reported in the four gospels . . . that I first heard from the lips of my mother," he would say, "are settled and fixed moral concepts with me."[17]

What Nancy did not do, or was unable to do, was restrain Thomas Lincoln from what Herndon called "cold and inhuman treatment" of Abe, treatment that may have been due primarily to Thomas's doubts about Abe being his son. Thomas, for example, physically abused Abe for asking childlike questions of neighbors, sometimes striking him with blows that knocked him to the ground. The boy did not cry, according to Abe's cousin Dennis Hanks, "but dropped a kind of silent, unwelcome tear, as evidence of his . . . feelings."[18]

Abraham Lincoln's greatest childhood pain occurred in the fall of 1818 when his mother died. A year earlier, Nancy's uncle and aunt, Tom and Elizabeth Hanks Sparrow, had moved into the Lincolns' neighborhood along with Dennis Hanks, Elizabeth's eighteen-year-old talkative and likeable nephew. In the fall of 1818, the Sparrows became ill from the deadly scourge called "milk-sickness" that swept through the Little Pigeon Creek community. The illness originated with a poisonous plant known as white snakeroot, which was grazed by cows and transmitted through their milk. In humans, the disease began with dizziness, nausea, and stomach pains. Then the skin turned clammy, breathing became irregular, and victims slipped into a coma. Death quickly followed—usually within a week. Tom and Elizabeth were among the first to die. Nancy nursed them in their last hours, and then she, too, became ill. Abe and his sister nursed their mother and read Bible passages to her. Near death, she called the children to her side. Placing a feeble hand on Abe's head, she told him to be good and kind to his father and sister and to worship God. Later that day she died. She was thirty-five (some historians say thirty-four). Herndon would later write: "Groping through the perplexities of life, without prospect of any betterment in her condition, she passed from earth, little dreaming of the grand future that lay in store for the ragged, hapless little boy at [her] bedside."[19]

As Abe watched his mother endure agony and then die, he was devastated. "I'll never forget the mizry in that cabin," Dennis Hanks would recall. As Nancy's body lay in the same room where they ate and slept, "Abe an' me helped Tom make the coffin. He took a log left over from makin' the cabin, and I helped him whipsaw it into planks an' plane 'em. Me 'n Abe held the planks together while Tom bored holes an' put 'em together with pegs Abe'd whittled. . . . Abe never got over the mizable way his mother died." When the coffin was ready, the family placed Nancy Lincoln's body on a sled and took her to a hillside near the cabin. They buried her next to her aunt and uncle. The burial was not accompanied by a funeral service because there was no church in the remote neighborhood.

Dennis Hanks, with no place to go, moved in with the Lincolns and became an extra field hand for Thomas and an "older brother" for Abe. The Lincoln children were miserable that winter. Deprived of their mother's care, they craved encouragement and compassion, but Thomas was capable of neither. Sarah, eleven, cooked and kept house but was lonesome and sad. Dennis and Abe got her a baby coon and a turtle, and tried to get a fawn, "but we couldn't ketch any," Dennis would recall. In a remarkable gesture for a nine-year-old, Abe wrote to the family's former pastor in Kentucky and asked him to come and conduct proper burial rites for Nancy Lincoln. In the spring of 1819, the Baptist parson, David Elkins, rode one hundred miles on horse-back to conduct the service. On a bright Sunday morning, two hundred people gathered around Nancy's grave. As Parson Elkins said a final prayer, all the mourners fell upon their knees. Abe's wish for a proper burial had been fulfilled. Despite problems and peculiarities in his relationship with his mother, the boy was left with an empty heart—a feeling his mother had abandoned him. Historian Michael Burlingame, who used the tools of psychobiography to analyze Lincoln's attitudes and feelings, concluded that the death of his mother and his relationship with her may have convinced him "that women are untrustworthy and unreliable." In the years ahead Lincoln would face more "abandonments" by women he loved. Each episode would deepen his emotional scars and perhaps make it more difficult for him to relate to women.[20]

That summer Abe and Sarah again may have felt abandoned when Thomas Lincoln returned to Kentucky to search for a new wife. He was gone nearly six months, and the children eventually assumed that he, too, had died. Left to live in squalor, they became hungry, ragged, and dirty. After almost half a year without parental support, Abe reportedly feared they would soon all be dead.[21]

2

"She Was Doubtless the First Person Who Ever Treated Him Like a Human Being."

While young Abe and his sister Sarah were barely surviving in Indiana, their father returned to Elizabethtown, Kentucky. There, Thomas Lincoln eventually called upon a thirty-one-year-old widow named Sarah Bush Johnston. She was a tall, sprightly, and talkative woman who had once declined Thomas's marriage proposal before he had met Nancy Hanks. Known as "Sally," Sarah was ten years younger than Thomas. Like Thomas, she was illiterate. Her former husband, the town jailer, had died of the cholera in 1816. Before his death, she had helped out by cooking for the prisoners while rearing three children. After her husband's death, Sally had moved her family to a modest cabin, where Thomas found her.[1]

"Mrs. Johnston," he told her, "I have no wife and you no husband. I came [with] a-purpose to marry you. . . . I know you from a gal and you know me from a boy. I've no time to lose; and if you're willin' let it be done straight off."[2]

She could not marry him immediately, she explained, because she had debts to pay. "Give me a list of them," he told her. He got the list and paid the debts. The following day, December 2, 1819, Thomas Lincoln and Sally Johnston obtained a license and got married.[3]

Back in Indiana, meanwhile, Abe, his sister Sarah, and cousin

Dennis assumed they were now on their own. Then one day in late December, a four-horse wagon arrived at their cabin carrying their father and four strangers. Besides the new Mrs. Lincoln, there were her three children—Matilda, John, and Sarah Elizabeth—ranging in age from eight to thirteen, and a load of Mrs. Lincoln's furniture.

The little cabin would now be home to a family of eight. John slept with Abe and Dennis Hanks in the loft. The three girls slept in one corner of the main floor. The newlyweds slept in another corner. "Mrs. Lincoln soaped, scrubbed, and washed the children clean, so they looked pretty [and] neat," Dennis would later recollect. "She sewed and mended their clothes, and the children once more looked human."

A resourceful woman, she immediately began to improve her home. She cleaned it thoroughly, then had Thomas add a wood floor, a door, and a window. Abe could not have hoped for a better stepmother.

Sarah and Abe meet their new mother.

Warm and loving, Sally Lincoln reared him like her own child. "She was doubtless the first person that ever treated him like a human being," recalled merchant John B. Helm. She won Abe's heart by replacing his hard, lumpy cornhusk bed with a soft feather mattress. She smiled a lot; hugged him often; and offered kind words and encouragement—something he never heard from his father. "Abe was a good boy, the best boy I ever saw," she would later attest. "I never gave him a cross word in all my life. His mind and mine seemed to move in the same channel. He never told me a lie, and he never quarreled, swore, or used profane language in my presence nor in others that I know of." Lincoln would later describe this period of his life as "a joyous, happy boyhood," a time when "there was nothing sad nor pinched and nothing of want."[4]

Abe called his stepmother "Mama." From her he received the softening influences of a mother. Through Sally's encouragement, the Lincolns enrolled Abe and the other children in a newly opened school—a one-room log schoolhouse where pupils sat on rough wooden benches and repeated their lessons aloud. For two brief periods Abe had attended a school in Kentucky where, according to a relative, he was sent "more as company for his sister than with the expectation that he would learn much." Now at Andrew Crawford's subscription school, they learned to prepare essays. When that school closed, they were enrolled in another that opened four miles away. Abe, however, attended only sporadically. Thomas Lincoln wanted the boy to stay home and work the fields and tend the livestock. A year later a closer school opened, and apparently through Sally's influence, Abe was allowed to attend for six months. That school term concluded Abe's formal education. He was fifteen. He would later say that he had attended school "by littles"—a little now and a little then—and that "the aggregate of all his schooling did not amount to one year."[5]

Perhaps through his stepmother's efforts, he developed the ability to think creatively and became sensitive to the mistreatment that was common on the frontier. He was annoyed by the boyhood practice of placing hot coals on the shells of terrapins, for instance. "He would chide us," Nat Grigsby would later recall, "tell us it was wrong and would write essays against it."[6]

Abe's stepmother wanted Abe to make something of himself. She encouraged him to read and study. Thomas, on the other hand, continued to belittle education. "It's enough for a boy to work hard and be strong," he allegedly proclaimed.

Sally brought books with her from Kentucky, and she encouraged Abe to read them. Exciting new worlds were revealed to him in John Bunyan's *Pilgrim's Progress* and Daniel Defoe's *Robinson Crusoe*. In the *Life of Benjamin Franklin*, Abe found the poor boy who became great, and in Mason Weems's *Life of Washington* he discovered the hero who fathered a republic. *Arabian Nights* was another of Abe's favorites. "Abe'd lay on his stummick by the fire and read out loud to me 'n Sairy, an' we'd laugh when he did," Dennis Hanks would recollect. "I reckon Abe read the book a dozen times, and knowed those yarns by heart." He kept a book in his loft—stuck in a crack in the logs—to read at daybreak. When working the field, he would rest the horse at the end of each row—while he leaned on a fence and read. When Abe came across a passage that struck him, he wrote it down on a plank and kept it until he had paper. Then he would rewrite it, look at it, repeat it. He had a copybook, a kind of scrapbook, in which he wrote. "I never saw Abe after he was twelve that he didn't have a book in his hand or in his pocket," Dennis would recall. "It didn't seem natural to see a feller read like that." "My best friend," Abe would declare, "is the man who'll get me a book I ain't read." Sally Lincoln appears to have been the female figure who stirred Lincoln's imagination, promoted his education, and fueled the critical thinking of the man who would become the sixteenth president.[7]

As a teenager, Abe discovered the opposite sex. With male friends he pondered the Biblical references to sexual activity, focusing most likely on the Old Testament's Song of Songs, which celebrates the joys of marital intimacy. Lincoln's curiosity about the opposite sex may have been further whetted by the presence of three teenage girls in the Lincoln cabin. Although Lincoln certainly became interested in girls, most girls apparently were not attracted to his gaunt, lanky figure and somewhat homely face. "Girls found him repelling," Polly Richardson, a female acquaintance of young Abe, would later admit. "Abe took me to church and to spelling bees," she would later claim, "and even wanted to marry me, but I refused." Her recollection of the teenage Lincoln depicts an awkward, unpopular youth. "All the girls my age made fun of him," she would recall. "They'd even laugh at him right before his face." Even frontier damsels thought young Lincoln's manner of dress was odd: his buckskin pants were always too short. "Six or more inches of Abe's shin bone was bare and naked," one classmate would remember. "He tried to go out with some of the girls," Polly would recall, "but no sir-ee, they'd give him the mitten every time, just because he was so tall and gawky. It was mighty awkward trying to keep company with a fellow as tall as Abe was."[8]

Beautiful and amiable Hannah Gentry, daughter of the community's richest man, refused to court Abe because "he was too fond of onions, and I could not endure them." Another girl found Abe to be "quiet and awkward and so awful homely that girls didn't much care about him." "Abe took me home from church once," an acquaintance of Sarah Lukens would relate, "and I could a'been his wife if I'd wanted to, but I didn't. He was just too peculiar."[9]

Abe took a special "likin'" to pretty Elizabeth Wood, who lived on a farm about a mile and a half north of the Lincoln cabin. His opportunity to attract her attention came after an ox that Thomas Lincoln had bought from her father broke loose and returned to the Woods' farm. Abe went to fetch the ox—named Buck—and Mr. Wood offered him a rope to lead the animal home. "No, thank you," said Abe, who intended to impress Elizabeth. "I'll ride him home and make him pay for his action." As Elizabeth watched, Abe leaped onto Buck's back and kicked him on both sides. Buck bolted and bucked—and disappeared down the road with Abe doing his best to stay on the beast. Elizabeth and her father laughed at the spectacle of the lanky Lincoln boy straddling the stampeding ox. Abe rode him home and proudly told his father, "I gentled him, Pap." Despite the triumph, Abe's daring feat failed to impress Elizabeth. "I know he wanted to become better acquainted with me," she would say later, "but I wasn't interested in him. He was so awkward, and his feet were awful big."[10]

Elizabeth Tuley was Abe's first "regular company." According to Elizabeth she and Abe "kept company for several months"—until she could no longer bear the "unmerciful" teasing from her friends, who joked about Lincoln's "coat sleeves and pant legs always being too short." Elizabeth soon broke off the relationship. Abe also become infatuated with one Julia Evans, an attractive girl who bowed to him one day as they passed on the street. At the time he was visiting Princeton, Indiana, where he had gone to have some wool carded. "My heart was in a flutter," Lincoln would later confess. "I was so thoroughly captivated by this vision of maidenly beauty that I wanted to stop in Princeton forever." To his teenage dismay he never saw her again. Once, Abe's sister Sarah scolded him for "bothering girls" when they were playing. "You ought to be ashamed of yourself, Abe. What do you expect will become of you?" He promptly responded: "I reckon I'll be president of the United States."[11]

Occasionally, Abe's interest in books and girls merged. When the schoolmaster asked Anna Roby, an attractive fifteen-year-old, to spell "defied," she began "d-e-f" and then stopped, debating whether to proceed with an "i" or a "y." She saw Abe with his index finger on his eye and a smile on his face. She took the hint and added "i-e-d."

"He was the learned boy among us unlearned folks," Anna would recall. "He took great pains to explain; he could do it so simply." On an evening stroll alongside a river, Anna and Abe sat on the bank, dangled their feet in the stream, and watched the moon slowly rise over the neighboring hills. Ignoring the romantic opportunity, Abe turned to a scientific discourse on the movement of heavenly bodies. "I did not suppose that Abe, who had seen so little of the world, would know anything about it," Anna would later say, "but he proved to my satisfaction that the moon did not go down at all; that it only seemed to; that the earth revolving from west to east, carried us under, as it were." "We do the sinking," Abe explained, "while to us the moon is comparatively still. The moon's sinking is only an illusion." Abe had improved Anna's intellect but had ignored her heart. "What a fool you are, Abe!" she exclaimed. Their relationship was short-lived.[12]

"As he got older, Abe seemed to develop a dislike for girls," Anna would later observe, "and didn't go out much with them." That view was confirmed by Abe's stepbrother John Johnston who said Abe was so busy studying he "didn't take much truck with the girls." Having been consistently rejected and often insulted by the fairer sex, Abe became even more bashful and uncomfortable around girls. "He wasn't very fond of them," his stepmother would later note. However, he became a popular figure among the farm boys of the community due to his collection of colorful jokes and barnyard stories. He fished, wrestled, ran races, and became the best athlete in the neighborhood. He never missed a horse race or a fox chase, a sugar-boiling or a wool-shearing. He excelled at cornhuskings, where men and boys were divided into two groups, each striving to shuck the most corn. Cornhuskings were often followed by an all-night dance for young people, but Abe was usually without a female partner. Participants shuffled and kicked to the sounds of a cracked fiddle and swaggered home at daybreak to the tunes of Dennis Hanks's festive lines: "Hail Columbia, happy land / If you ain't drunk, I will be damned."[13]

Cornhusking Bee. *HARPER'S WEEKLY*, Nov. 13, 1858.

Once, while attending a cornhusking with his friend Green Taylor, Abe drew the red ear of corn—which entitled him to kiss the girl he liked best. Being more honest than discreet, Abe kissed Green's girlfriend. Green was furious and a fistfight erupted. The fight ended when Green hit Abe with an ear of corn, causing a deep wound. Abe learned to stay away from other boys' sweethearts.

Abe and his stepsister Matilda—known to Lincoln as 'Tilda'—developed a frisky interest in each other when she was thirteen and he was sixteen. Once, Tilda sought to accompany Abe when he left home in the morning to clear a stand of timber, but her mother firmly forbade it. A few days later Tilda escaped unobserved and followed Abe. She gained on him and then darted forward and landed squarely on his back. Both fell to the ground. As they did so, Tilda struck the sharp edge of the axe blade with her foot, causing it to bleed profusely. Frantically, Abe tore pieces of cloth from his shirt and dressed her injury. Then he looked at her in blank astonishment. "Tilda, what will we tell Mother as to how this happened?" he asked. "I'll tell her I cut my foot on the axe," she sobbed. "That will be the truth, won't it?" Abe responded: "Yes, that's the truth, but it won't be all the truth, will it Tilda? Tell the whole truth, and trust your good mother for the rest." Tilda confessed to her mother, who merely scolded her, and warned her not to follow Abe again. This time, she obeyed.[14]

Dennis Hanks, meanwhile, developed a passionate interest in Abe's other stepsister, Sarah Elizabeth. When she was fifteen, they were married and set up a homestead about half a mile from the Lincoln farm. Sarah Elizabeth's marriage reduced the male work force on the farm to Thomas Lincoln, John Johnston, and Abe, with occasional help from John Hanks. By then Thomas had impaired vision and depended more on his farmhands. He appeared to have favored his stepson John over Abe, and Abe found himself with more work to do—farming, grubbing, hoeing, making fences, plowing, splitting rails, skinning coons, and butchering hogs. Thomas also leased Abe and his axe to work for other farmers—at twenty-five cents a day for hard labor—and then made Abe give him the money. By law Thomas was entitled to everything Abe earned until he became twenty-one, and Thomas took it. Abe would later describe the arrangement as "organized robbery" and remained outraged at the idea that someone could be forced to work in the hot sun all day, while someone else received all the profits.[15]

Abe's relationship with his father gradually worsened—possibly due in part to Abe doubting that Thomas Lincoln was really his

Abe cleared wood and split thousands of fence rails during his growing-up years in Indiana. "He was physically powerful," a neighbor said, but girls found his physical features repulsive and even made fun of him. AUTHOR'S COLLECTION.

father. Abe undoubtedly had heard the widespread gossip that mumps or an accidental castration had rendered Thomas impotent. Thomas sometimes whipped Abe when he found him reading instead of working. There was no "break time" in Thomas Lincoln's fields— at least not for Abe. Thomas tried hiding his son's books and some- times even threw them away—defying both his wife and his son. "Thomas never thought much of Abraham as a boy," A. H. Chapman, Abe's cousin, would later admit. They were opposites in temperament, values, abilities, motivations, and ambitions, and there appears to have been little rapport between them. Their sharpest exchange of words probably came over Abe's refusal to join the Little Pigeon Creek Baptist Church, where his parents wor- shipped. "Abe had no particular religion," his stepmother would later acknowledge. Perhaps to placate his father, Abe attended the church and served as a sexton—sweeping the floor and furnishing the candles—but he never became a member.[16]

In 1826 Abe's stepsister Tilda married Squire Hall. In the same year Abe's sister Sarah, then eighteen, left the family to marry Aaron Grigsby, who was from a leading family in nearby Gentryville. The two had met nine years earlier while fetching water from a spring, and their fondness for each other had blossomed over the years. Abe dearly loved his sister. The two had grown even closer after their mother's death. Sarah's marriage could have caused Abe to feel aban- doned again. Sarah was a cheerful, attractive girl with a bright mind, and Abe surely missed her.

A year and a half later, on January 20, 1828, Sarah Lincoln Grigsby went into hard labor, but Aaron was slow to realize she was having trouble. When he finally understood her life was in danger, he bolted out of their cabin and ran through the snow to his father's home. He and his father yoked a team of oxen to a sled and went back after Sarah. They wrapped her in deerskins, placed her on the sled, and took her to her father-in-law's home. A doctor was finally summoned, but he arrived drunk. A midwife was called, but she arrived too late to deal with the emergency. Sarah died in childbirth, and her baby was stillborn.

Distraught and frantic, Aaron ran to Abe's cabin and found him standing in the smokehouse doorway. Abe knew something was wrong and asked what had happened. "Sarah just died," Aaron announced. Abe sat down in the doorway of the smokehouse, buried his face in his hands, and wept. The sister he loved so dearly was gone at age twenty. With her stillborn baby cradled in her arms, Sarah was buried in the church cemetery.

Abe was engulfed in a depression at first, then his grief was replaced by anger. He blamed Sarah's death on Aaron's neglect. Aaron had let her "lay too long" before getting help, Abe believed, and he set out to "get even." With the help of friends, Abe planned a trick to embarrass Aaron and his family. It would occur after the double wedding of Grigsby's brothers—Charles and Reuben. When the two Grigsby brothers and their brides returned to the family home after the wedding, their father hosted an elaborate frontier-style reception with feasting, dancing, and the grand finale—"putting the bridal party to bed."[17]

At the appropriate time, the two brides were taken upstairs to separate bedrooms. The candles were then blown out, and the brothers were escorted to their brides. Through a friend at the celebration, Abe arranged for the bridegrooms to be led to the wrong rooms. The brothers' mother discovered the error at the last moment and sprang upstairs. "O Lord, Reuben, you are in bed with Charles's wife," she yelled. Alarmed, the brothers raced from their rooms in confusion and the party became an uproar. After the event Abe lampooned the men in a merciless satire he called "The Chronicles of Reuben." It was circulated in the community. The drama continued when the brothers' younger sibling, Billy Grigsby, challenged Abe to a fight. Abe refused, saying he was too big for a fair fight with Grigsby. Abe's stepbrother, John, accepted however, and the two young men engaged in what one witness called "a terrible fight." John got the worst of it and was bleeding and badly hurt. Abe stepped in, grabbed Grigsby, and hurled him several feet. That provoked a general fight among supporters—which became a brief but exciting frontier brawl.[18]

After the winter of 1829, which was marked by another outbreak of milk-sickness, the Lincolns heard glowing reports of rich lands available in Illinois on easy terms. Thomas had moved four times since his marriage but was still not much better off. After selling their

land, hogs, and corn in March 1830, the Lincolns loaded their meager household effects into two wagons—each pulled by a pair of
oxen—and began the arduous two-hundred-mile journey to Illinois.
Accompanied by the families of his two stepdaughters and their husbands—Dennis Hanks and Squire Hall—Thomas Lincoln's party
numbered thirteen. Abe drove one of the wagons.

They crossed the Wabash River at Vincennes and continued through
the village of Decatur to a tract of land on the north bank of the
Sangamon River, which Thomas Lincoln's cousin by marriage, John
Hanks, had staked out for them. Abraham Lincoln had come to
Illinois. All hands worked to prepare the new home, but the Illinois
weather was not welcoming. On Christmas Day, 1830, the snow
began to fall and did not stop until it reached depths up to twelve feet.
For nine weeks temperatures hovered ten to twenty degrees below
zero. The Lincolns were confined to their cabins all winter, surviving
on boiled corn and pounded meal. When spring arrived, the snow
melted, and the land soon flooded. Just a year after arriving in Illinois,
Abe was reminded of the harsh, unpredictable ways of farming.

Abe Lincoln was now twenty-two years old and ready to be on
his own.

The opportunity came from a person destined to shape Lincoln's
future—Denton Offutt, an adventurous, colorful speculator and
trader who trafficked goods up and down the Sangamon River. Offutt
had come downriver looking for reliable hands to deliver a boatload
of provisions to New Orleans. He first came to Lincoln's cousin John
Hanks. "I hunted up Abe," Hanks would later recall, "and I introduced him and John Johnston, his stepbrother, to Offutt. After some
talk we made an engagement with Offutt at fifty cents a day and sixty
dollars [for the trip]."[19]

Lincoln said good-bye to his family and left empty-handed, with no
land, no patron, and no profession. He would return home only a few
times in the future, and only for short visits. Whatever Lincoln's
future was to be, he was determined it would not be a repetition of
his father's difficult and unproductive life. He also vowed that if he
ever had children, he would give them unbounded liberty instead of
parental tyranny. Love was the chain to bind a child to parents,
Lincoln believed. It was a lesson he learned from his stepmother's

treatment of him. From his mother he held a vague but strong belief in fate and providence. So Abraham Lincoln left his family and his childhood behind and faced the future with the hard-won optimism typical of the frontier. Ahead lay countless experiences—and a girl named Ann.

3

"Teach Me, O Lord, to Think Well of Myself."

*A*nna Mayes Rutledge was born January 7, 1813, a few miles from the frontier village of Henderson, Kentucky, where forty houses dotted the landscape on high red bluffs above the Ohio River. The third child and second daughter of James and Mary Ann Rutledge, she would be known simply as Ann Rutledge.[1]

James, now thirty-one, had known Mary Ann Miller all her life, and they had been longtime sweethearts when he married her in Henderson five years earlier, on January 25, 1808. She was attractive, with reddish brown hair and dark eyes. They were married by their Presbyterian pastor, James McGready, and feted with a splendid wedding feast of roast venison prepared by James's three brothers and their sisters and cousins. After dinner the newlyweds rode horses to the new log home James had built for his bride. At bedtime family members and friends stood outside and for thirty minutes banged on pots and pans, rang cowbells, tooted whistles, and shouted raucously. It was a quaint custom called a "shivaree" and was intended to proclaim good tidings. Most couples accepted it good-naturedly.[2]

Buffalo roamed nearby, and in the summer flocks of geese settled gracefully into the Green River. All types of wild game were in gunshot of their cabin. Deer herds grazed peacefully until the first shot was fired and then fled in arching lopes.

James and Mary Ann farmed, planting corn and wheat, orchards of apples and peaches, and fields of strawberries. Their simple pleasures centered around the backwoods fiddler and his inspired renditions of "Polly, Put the Kettle On" and "Buffalo Gals."

Ann's grandparents were part of the great exodus of Scotch-Irish Presbyterians who migrated from Ireland to America in the eighteenth century.

John Rutledge was only eighteen when he left his parents and his work as a Dublin shoemaker around 1757 to seek religious freedom and better times in the new land. His family came from County Tyrone in Northern Ireland. Their ancestors, originally from Scotland, were lured to Northern Ireland by English inducements to acquire cheap farmland. Later, oppressive British rule over Ireland made their life intolerable. Brutal laws banned Presbyterian services, labeled as "fornicators" anyone married in their churches, and prohibited the Scotch-Irish from holding any position higher than that of postman.[3]

John's future wife, Jane "Jennie" Officer, migrated at age eight with her parents and grandparents, who were natives of County Antrim in Northern Ireland. Her father, Thomas, was a sheep farmer; her grandfather, James, a shoemaker. Their families also dated back to Scotland. The three-thousand-mile Atlantic crossing could be challenging for immigrants. Crammed into meager quarters, passengers slept on straw mattresses or hammocks. Rations were short, food was often vermin-ridden, and water tasted putrid. Many passengers died at sea. John Rutledge and the Officers survived the voyage and headed for Philadelphia, where established Presbyterian congregations would assist them. They looked forward to Pennsylvania's promised tolerance for all who acknowledged "one almighty God, the Creator, Upholder, and Ruler of the World."[4]

Although ten years older than Jennie Officer, John Rutledge was obviously charmed by the little girl and observed with more than passing interest her development into an attractive young woman. Around 1765, when he was twenty-six and she was sixteen, they married, probably in or near Philadelphia. Shortly thereafter, they migrated southward. Following the great Pennsylvania Wagon Road through Virginia and the Carolinas, they settled briefly in Charlestown, South Carolina, which was another colonial city noted for religious tolerance. Their first child was born there in 1768.[5]

It did not take long, however, for the Rutledges to dislike Charlestown. It was America's fourth largest and wealthiest city. Aristocratic merchants and planters ruled and reveled in a pleasure-oriented society where gambling and partying were daily occurrences. Tradesmen and other workingmen were expected to know their place. High rents, high prices, and competition from slave labor gave them much to be unhappy about.[6]

By 1770 the Rutledges had made their way westward to Winnsboro in what is now Fairfield County, South Carolina, taking a narrow, rough trail known as the "Charleston Path." Soon to link up with them were two other families—the John Millers of Ireland (Ann's future maternal grandparents) and the Thomas Camrons of Scotland. The Millers and Camrons crossed the ocean together from Ireland, landing in Charlestown. They all became close friends and remained in and around Winnsboro through the Revolutionary War. Their children grew up and played together, with six Rutledges and at least four Millers and four Camrons born in Fairfield County. Two of them—James Rutledge, born May 11, 1781, and Mary Ann Miller, born October 21, 1787—would later fall in love, marry, and produce a famous daughter.[7]

Winnsboro was a stylish town, influenced by Charlestonians who moved inland and built an academy and brick-and-frame churches, homes, and estates.

The Rutledge/Miller/Camron group worked as farmers and lived modestly in log homes. They worked to the rhythm of a song: housewives as they churned butter and rocked babies—"Hush, little baby, don't say a word, Mama's gonna buy you a mocking bird"; husbands as they planted corn—"One for the blackbird, One for the crow; One for the cutworm, And one to grow." Honoring their heritage in Scotland, while not forgetting their love for Ireland before English rule, they celebrated St. Andrews Day, the thirtieth of November. They sang Scottish ballads, such as bonny "Barbara Allen" and other songs "my mither sang." And they shared memories of full pipe bands and swinging kilts and of the land of the mountains and the mist.[8]

The men wore a nightshirt called an "ebenezer." At church, when they sang "Here I raise mine Ebenezer," young couples smiled at each other. Self-confident—a Scotch-Irish trait—they prayed, "Teach me, O

Lord, to think well of myself." On church-less Sundays it was common to see John Rutledge on a horse with a bed quilt or deer skin for a saddle and as many of his children as he could keep on the horse. Some rode in front and some behind him, with Jennie walking ahead, all going to spend the day with the Millers or Camrons, four or five miles away.[9]

These Scotch-Irish folks left Ireland because of English policies, and they were strong supporters of the Revolution. In 1781 Thomas Camron supplied the Continental army with "two beefes, two muttons, and six gallons of whiskey." His son-in-law, Robert McClary, was among the two thousand casualties at the 1780 Battle of Camden. Fought less than thirty miles from Winnsboro, it was a crushing defeat for the Americans. The war was all around the Rutledges. South Carolina recorded more battles than any other state.[10]

After the war the new American government offered free land in Georgia, and the Rutledge, Miller, and Camron families left Winnsboro to claim this favored earth. By the end of the 1790s, they had migrated a hundred miles west, ferrying the Savannah River to Augusta. They settled in the nearby counties of Elbert and Wilkes, a region of rolling hills and fertile bottom lands with rich, deep-loamed soil that was easy to cultivate. The area's good schools and Presbyterian congregations were added incentives for the newcomers from Winnsboro, as were the area's numerous fresh-water springs.[11]

John Rutledge set up a shoemaking shop and ran a farm. Thomas Camron Jr., who had married the oldest Miller daughter, established saw and grist mills in Elbert County. John Miller Camron was born in 1790 and eventually became close to his uncle James Rutledge, who was nine years older. In time they would form a partnership that would significantly change the life of Abraham Lincoln.[12]

James Rutledge benefited from growing up in the Winnsboro and Augusta areas, which were enriched by good schools and supportive kinfolk. The boy had a keen and thoughtful mind that would lead him to excel in debating, an interest that would take root and grow years later in a place called New Salem. His opinion of women's roles was surely affected by his firsthand observation of a professional female, Sarah Hillhouse, Georgia's first woman newspaper editor. She took over the Wilkes County paper, *The Monitor*, after her husband's death and built it into a successful enterprise. James was probably among the paper's avid readers.

With that background and his own intellectual development, enhanced by his growing book collection, James undoubtedly sensed the positive difference women could make in the community if unleashed from their dawn-to-night household chores and motivated by education and opportunity. Perhaps James resolved to provide such a foundation for any daughters he might have—a conclusion supported by his later actions.

Among other Scotch-Irish families attracted to the Georgia countryside were the Mayes, Hawthorns, Veatches, and Davidsons. From Georgia they followed or accompanied the Rutledges, Camrons, and Millers on their further migrations. They were intelligent and industrious, and most were devoutly religious. United by blood, marriage, and friendship, they would populate central and southern Illinois.[13]

Most members of these Scotch-Irish families were on the road again by the fall of 1807. They headed north to Henderson, Kentucky—which would become their home until 1813. In Henderson newlyweds James and Mary Ann Miller Rutledge visited often with James and Lucy Audubon in their log cabin and his general merchandise store. Both men were of similar age. Audubon, destined to become a famous ornithological illustrator, imitated bird calls on his flute, and his talented wife played the piano and violin. Associating with the Audubons made James and Mary Ann even more convinced of the importance of education for their children.[14]

James's brother Billy married Susannah Camron, John Miller Camron's sister, and on September 29, 1814, a son, McGrady, was born in Henderson County. McGrady and Ann Rutledge, a year and a half apart, would grow up to be close friends. Meanwhile, John Miller Camron met Polly Orendorff shortly after her family's wagon train arrived from Franklin County, Tennessee. Her great-great-grandmother was said to have been a Prussian princess who lived in a castle near the Rhine, and Camron bragged of eating cornbread made by the descendant of a princess. They were married on January 12, 1811.[15]

The Rutledge group might have remained in Henderson County had it not been for two developing nightmares: vengeful Indians who provoked frequent and bloody encounters and disputes among settlers over land titles and boundaries. In the spring of 1813, three months after the birth of Ann Rutledge, a visiting trader spoke of rich farmland soon to be opened to homesteaders in the Illinois Territory. Perhaps, Rutledge pondered, that was the promised land they sought. Neither Mary Ann Rutledge nor Polly Camron wanted to leave their beautiful setting in "God's country" for long, cold winters on the raw, wide prairie where, some said, grass was so tall a man on horseback could be lost in it. The women, however, were reconciled to follow their husbands.

That fall the seven related families were off to Illinois with some thirty children and a bevy of grandparents, including John and Jennie Rutledge. John Miller Camron's father, Thomas Jr., was captain of the wagon train, and his cart led the way. Close behind were James and Mary Ann Rutledge with Ann and her two older siblings. The train of oxcarts ferried the Ohio River near Shawneetown and then headed north along an old Indian trail. They all plodded along—the oxen pulling the carts, the men accompanied by their wives and their muskets. Some women, with babies in their arms, rode horseback; older family members and small children shared the carts. Boys in jeans and deerskin jackets and girls in sunbonnets and linsey-woolsey dresses led cows and coaxed pigs and sheep along the narrow path. The younger boys, dressed

Emigrants Crossing the Plains, by F.O.C. Darley, reflects the traveling conditions of the Rutledges as they migrated from South Carolina to Georgia and then to Kentucky and Illinois. LIBRARY OF CONGRESS.

only in long-tailed shirts, scampered about chasing stray sheep and helping their dads look for wild game.[16]

The carts' wooden wheels and axles creaked from their loads: farming implements, pots and kettles, feather beds, homespun blankets, young fruit trees, crates housing chickens and geese, and cuttings from roses and lilacs left behind in their Kentucky yards. A washtub turned upside down was the driver's seat.

For some thirty-five miles the trail took them through heavy forests of oak, maple, evergreen, and tall gum trees. Then, as they crested a hill, the pioneers saw an immense valley spread out before them. It was at least three miles wide and seven miles long, with a shaded stream—Seven Mile Creek—meandering through it.[17]

They agreed it was a good place to camp, and the whole cortege of men, women, children, cows, pigs, sheep, and horses rested and prepared to settle down for the night. According to White County historian Margaret Land, a descendant of several lines of these pioneers, the families cut evergreen branches for beds, fed the stock, roasted plump prairie chickens on sticks skewered over a fire of twigs and fallen limbs, and offered a prayer of thanksgiving. Guards kept fires burning to deter wild animals.[18]

The rays of the morning sun flowed through the crystal-clear air of the forest, adding splendor and richness to the wilderness, while awakening the settlers' latent energy and ingenuity. It was time to go to work and give birth to the Seven Mile Prairie community, forerunner of the town of Enfield in White County, Illinois.

Providing shelter and food were their first tasks, and the axe, the auger, the plow, the spade, and the hoe were soon put to work. Trees from their forested hill sites provided logs and fuel for their cabins and wood for fences and bridges. Underneath log floors, they dug out hiding places for women and children, lined them with beds of straw, and secured them with closely fitting trap doors. Cabin doors were made of boards split from logs, held together by wooden pins, and fastened with wooden hinges and latches. They made their chairs, tables, and beds and added other furnishings they brought with them—cornhusk mattresses, goose-feather pillows, spinning wheels, looms, corner cupboards, and Dutch ovens. Some made high beds with trundle beds underneath for children.

They planted the fruit trees they brought with them, as well as seeds for flax, corn, and other crops. It was a common sight to see a woman driving horses while a man maneuvered the plow. Corn was planted in rows about six feet apart, with peas, beans, and pumpkins in between. They enclosed fields and gardens with rail fences, but allowed their livestock to roam the woods. There, it cost almost nothing to raise them: they would feed themselves. Wild game supplied much of the food for the families. Prairie chickens were so numerous they could have had chicken pie every day of the year. The area also abounded in turkeys, deer, quail, and pigeons. One settler noted that wild pigeons flew overhead in such dense clouds that the sky grew dark and chickens went to roost. Smoked pork was a common meat. It was stored in large barrels. A family was considered to be "in a desperate way" when the mother could see the bottom of the pork barrel. As a housewife noted in James Fenimore Cooper's *The Chainbearer*: "Give me the children raised on good sound pork afore all the game in the country. Game's good as a relish and so's bread; but pork is the staff of life." Pigs grew quickly from eating acorns and roots, and after December's first cold spell, neighbors came together to butcher their porkers. They cooked in iron pots hung in the fireplace, and they ate from pewter plates, using pewter spoons, knives, and forks, and wooden cups.

Two years passed, and the settlement grew as more relatives came from Kentucky and Tennessee. James Rutledge's nephew, John Miller Camron, arrived in 1814 or 1815, accompanied by his wife, Polly, and their baby and toddler. Apple, peach, and pear trees bore fruit, providing their main beverages—cider and brandy. James Rutledge built the first grist mill. Powered by a pair of horses, the mill was said to grind so slowly that a hungry jaybird could peck up the meal almost as fast as it fell from the stones. Then came 1816—"the year without summer." A heavy snow fell on June 17, ruining many crops. Fall came, and there was no corn to grind at Rutledge's mill. Perhaps it was time to pack up and move farther west, Rutledge reportedly told fellow pioneers. As they argued options, their Kentucky pastor, James McGready, arrived at Seven Mile Prairie. He was well educated and noted for eloquence. He urged patience and faith; they listened, and he established in their community the first Presbyterian church in Illinois. It was housed in a small log structure. The first three ruling elders were James Rutledge, James

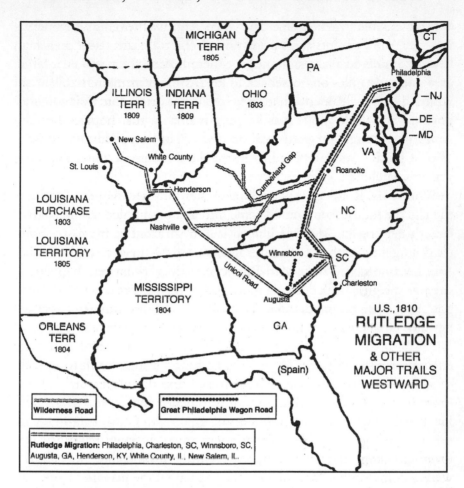

Mayes, and Peter Miller. Miller, who was Ann Rutledge's uncle, had a novel way of curing his wife's nervous seizures. He would draw a bucket of cold water from the well and dump it over her head.[19]

In that same "year without summer," the settlers received shocking news from Georgia. A milk-sickness epidemic had taken the lives of Ann's aunt, Susan Rutledge Mayes, and her husband, Edward. They left five children, ages two to thirteen. Uncles Tommy Mayes and Billy Rutledge loaded an oxcart with cornmeal and bacon and set out for Georgia to pick up the orphaned children. They were parceled out among the Rutledge, Mayes, and Miller families. The toddler, Minerva, was taken into Ann Rutledge's family. Ann, then three years old, had a new playmate.[20]

Ann and Minerva grew up together, played together, and occasionally got into trouble together. One day, when Ann was seven and Minerva was six, Ann's parents were preparing to entertain their new preacher. It was considered a special honor for them because he pastored a large area and rode miles on horseback to keep appointments. On this brisk winter day, Mrs. Rutledge had prepared a hot drink containing liberal portions of whiskey. She was keeping it hot on the fireplace hearth. Ann's parents seldom used "strong drink," but on a day like this, a "sip of toddy" was prepared to warm the Reverend's bones and prevent his catching a cold.

While Mrs. Rutledge was cooking dinner, Ann and Minerva decided to taste the toddy. Ann poured some into a cup, sampled it, and shared it with her cousin. Minerva gulped it and shrieked at the taste. Both tried it again and then took several sips until Minerva passed out and Ann became sick. When Mrs. Rutledge realized what had happened, she put the girls to bed, made more toddy for the preacher, and "forgot" to tell her husband about the incident. The next day Ann assured her mother she never wanted strong drink again.[21]

Ann's favorite male cousin, McGrady Rutledge, had his own encounter with whiskey. At age ten, he found a jug, drank too much of it, and became sick. His mother found him flat on his belly in the loom house. She pulled him out and drenched him with sweet milk. He too swore he would never drink again. McGrady's father had other ideas, however. He was confident that whiskey would prevent fever and chills, and tried to make McGrady drink some. The "chills" were a common health problem. Settlers called the disease "ague." It caused periodic shakes, fevers, weakness, and sweating, but was seldom fatal. When the child refused the whiskey, his father bristled! His mother understood, however, and intervened, and they argued over the benefits of whiskey. After McGrady pleaded, "I would rather be sick than drink it," his father finally gave in. McGrady turned out to be the healthiest one in the family.[22]

In 1818 Ann's uncle, Thomas Rutledge, started the county's first school. Tuition was twenty-five cents a week, and each child brought a candle for light. Thomas believed in strict and swift discipline. When a boy suggested that maybe some day men would fly through the air and talk across the ocean, Thomas thrashed him soundly, using a heavy whip toughened in hot embers. James Rutledge wanted his daughters to be educated, and Ann, being the smartest, may have been the first girl at the school. She enrolled in 1820, the same year her grandfather John Rutledge died at age eighty-one.[23]

These hardy pioneers tanned their own leather, made their own boots, and produced their own wool and linen. An acre of flax supplied enough linen to clothe a large family, with enough material left over for tablecloths and bedspreads. Making linen was an all-family project. The flax, after being thrashed, cleaned, and combed, was spun into linen thread, and the thread was then put into a hand loom. Out came linen cloth that was strong and durable, although a little rough by modern standards and nappy after worn awhile. For coloring they made dyes from sumac berries, indigo, and white-walnut bark. They also made linsey, combining wool and linen or wool and cotton. Five or six yards of linsey were enough for any dress.

For a while these pioneers tried raising cotton, but the climate was unfavorable. That was good news for the children who, in a frontier version of a sweat shop, had to lie before the fire at night and pick seeds from cotton bolls. The warmer the cotton, the better it picked. So everyone worked up a sweat.

One loom generally did the weaving for several families. Requiring space that could not be spared in a cabin, it was placed in a "lean-to," called a loom house. Ann Rutledge, by the age of ten, had learned to spin thread and work the loom. When she was older she became a superior seamstress, designing and making clothes for her siblings and parents. Like other young girls her age, she also learned to cook, churn butter, keep house, do chores, and care for younger brothers and sisters—duties that were essential for pioneer women.

Wool was highly prized but rare on the Illinois frontier due to scavenging packs of sheep-killing wolves. At night, the howling of a wolf pack could be terrifying. Sometimes they even chased men on horseback. To eliminate the thieving, troublesome pests, settlers hunted, trapped, and sometimes poisoned them. In traditional wolf hunts, a large number of settlers went into the wilderness and made a large circle. Shouting and whooping, they beat the bushes and tightened the circle until the wolves were trapped. Then they killed them with clubs. One settler who had lost sheep and had heard enough howling, vowed to "thin the wolf herd." He took his wagon-box about a mile out on the prairie, moistened a rope with a smelly solution that attracted wolves, and trailed the rope through the prairie from different points toward the wagon-box. About sunset he positioned himself under the box where he had cut portholes to shoot through. At it grew dark he heard one wolf howl, then another, and shortly, the howls came from all directions and became louder and louder. Soon the wolves surrounded the wagon-box and lunged toward him with vicious snarls. The settler fired again and again and killed several. But they kept coming, and he kept firing until his ammunition was gone. The wolves prowled, snapped their jaws, and kept him besieged all night. Finally, at daybreak, they departed. Panic-stricken, the settler skedaddled for home.[24]

Family dogs were prized possessions in early Illinois. A good coon dog was worth more than a horse, and some could not be bought at any price. Coonskins and whiskey were legal tender throughout southern Illinois and were traded for coffee, powder, and lead. With money scarce, and many people not knowing there was any, most business was by trade or barter. Coon hunting at night was not only profitable but was also considered to be great sport. When old Sounder treed a coon, he barked loudly, and everyone rushed to the scene. Sometimes the coon was shot, but often the tree was chopped down so the hunters could enjoy a dog and coon fight.[25]

Frontier fathers could be very particular about their daughters. A Rutledge neighbor, Tennessean William Davidson, promised his daughter a dowry of "a good, first-rate cow and a feather bed"—with which he hoped to attract a Presbyterian suitor. To his chagrin, his daughter eloped with an aspiring preacher of another denomination. The promised dowry was replaced by a small, spindly legged calf and a bonnet full of goose eggs. Advised the irate father: "If you want a first-rate cow, raise your own, and if you want a feather bed, make it!"[26]

In this environment Ann Rutledge spent the first twelve years of her life. Four siblings were born in White County: David in 1815; Robert in 1819; Nancy in 1821; and Margaret in 1823.

About 1817, however, families began to leave Seven Mile Prairie. They were sick of the chills and fevers that seemed to lurk behind every stump in White County, and they were lured by richer lands to the northwest. Ann's cousin, John Miller Camron, then twenty-seven, was among the first to seek greener pastures. He and his family followed a trail across the Illinois frontier to Looking Glass Prairie near St. Louis, where he staked out a farm twelve miles east of Belleville. Soon afterward, Camron and his wife, Polly, began attending the "camp meeting" that spread through the frontier during the Second Great Awakening. At one session Polly experienced a spiritual conversion and embraced Christianity; soon Camron was consecrated as a Cumberland Presbyterian elder. Later he became a minister.[27]

Camron's small farm eventually proved unprofitable. When a neighbor mentioned a "promising land" called Sangamon Valley— "the land where there is plenty to eat"—Camron listened. It was near Springfield, in central Illinois, about ninety miles northeast of Looking Glass Prairie. Soon the Camrons packed their goods and moved again. They first settled north of Springfield, then moved to Rock Creek on the west side of Sangamon County. Each time Camron moved he established a farm, set out an orchard, and hoped to prosper. The only thing that multiplied, however, was his family. By 1825 he had six daughters and one son with five more girls to come.[28]

A millwright by trade Camron decided his future was in saw and grist mills. Sangamon Valley, he thought, would be a perfect location for them. He rode down to Seven Mile Prairie to convince Ann's father, James Rutledge, to join him in a partnership. Rutledge thought highly of him even though their demeanors were quite different. Rutledge, of medium height, was quiet and dignified. Camron, who had great physical strength, was aggressive and outspoken—and persuasive.[29]

Intrigued by Camron's description of the distant valley, Ann's family hitched up the oxen and "headed right out" on the 160-mile trek to Sangamon County. The year was 1826. Others in the traveling party were Ann's uncle and aunt, Billy and Susa Rutledge, and their children—McGrady and his four brothers and sisters. At first James and Mary Ann seriously considered leaving Ann, then thirteen, with her grandmother. Finally they decided that Ann should go. Had she remained behind, Abraham Lincoln's life would have been affected dramatically.[30]

At Rock Creek, in Sangamon County, the Rutledges found a contented circle of friends, including Presbyterian minister John M. Berry and his brother Samuel. Samuel's son James was immediately attracted to Rutledge's oldest daughter, Jean, and would marry her two years later. Among the region's favorite pastimes was ice skating. One of Pastor Berry's sons taught Vian Camron and Ann Rutledge how to skate. Ann became a graceful skater, but Vian kept running into snowbanks. After warming themselves in the Rutledge cabin, James Rutledge suggested that the young people dramatize scenes from Shakespeare. They chose *A Midsummer Night's Dream*. Ann enjoyed Shakespeare and had read several of his plays and sonnets. Now she read aloud with the style and passion of an actress.[31]

On July 19, 1828, Camron and Rutledge selected a mill site about twenty miles northwest of Springfield. It was on the Sangamon River, a powerful winding stream bounded by high bluffs and broad plains. The site was at a point where the river was navigable and the water flowed steadily. The location seemed ideal. A road on the bluff connected Springfield and Havana and provided easy access for people in nearby settlements.[32]

Anticipating legislative approval to dam the river for water power, they moved in the fall of 1828 and built adjacent log homes on the high bluff above the Sangamon, in the midst of huge oak, maple, and walnut trees. Approval came in January. The construction was a massive undertaking, requiring a thousand loads of rock hauled in from nearby Green's Rocky Branch and Rocky Run. Then, on rock pillars, they built a fully enclosed grist mill, set well out in the river. On the shore they erected an opened-sided primitive saw mill.[33]

Settlers in the area who had been grinding their cornmeal by hand welcomed a neighborhood mill. From distances up to fifty miles, farmers began trading at the Camron and Rutledge mill. If a farmer had four sacks of grain, he would send four boys with a two-bushel sack on each horse. On some days as many as forty horses could be found hitched to nearby trees. The operation was profitable because there were no other mills in the area and cornmeal was the staple of the local diet. Babies ate corn bread crumbled in milk and a thick corn meal porridge called "mush." Adults ate corn bread, as well as corndodgers, which consisted of cornmeal and cold water patted into pones and baked in a greased skillet. The corndodgers sometimes came out so hard "they could split a board or fell a steer at forty feet," according

to one settler. They were usually served with honey and buttermilk. Another product was "ashcake," made of cornmeal and water, wrapped in green cornhusks or cabbage leaves, and cooked on the hearth in wood ash.

On October 20, 1829, shortly after the mills opened, Rutledge's wife gave birth to their tenth and last child, Sarah. She would live to be ninety-three. Pleased with the success of their mill, Camron and Rutledge employed a surveyor and on October 23, 1829, laid out a town on a wooded grove on the bluffs, one hundred feet above the river. They named the town New Salem and sold lots for about ten dollars. From eastern states, single men came to New Salem seeking adventure and wealth. From southern states, especially Kentucky, families came to "break prairie" or create a business. One- and two-room log houses were constructed with split-rail fences enclosing grazing areas for horses and cattle. Attracted by the mill's growing business, bachelors Sam Hill and John McNeil came from back East and opened the first general store. They sold groceries, whiskey, and dry goods.[34]

An industrial center of sorts developed. Kentuckian Henry Onstot, in his mid-twenties, built a cooper shop. He fashioned buckets and tubs for domestic use and barrels for produce and whiskey. He was vital to the community since almost all produce was shipped in barrels—wet ones for whiskey or meat products, dry ones for flour. He sold flour barrels for forty cents and wash tubs for $1.50. Joshua Miller, a short, heavyset man, erected a blacksmith shop, forging shoes for oxen and horses and iron parts for wagons and farm implements. It was one of the town's busiest and noisiest places. The clanging of the anvil could be heard throughout the village from early morning until night. Miller and his brother-in-law, Jack Kelso, built a double residence for their two families. Kelso, childless and with little incentive to accumulate property for descendants, observed the habits of fish and wild animals and became an expert hunter and fisherman. He was also adept at robbing a bee tree of its honey. Soon a tinner, a wheelwright, a weaver, a shoemaker, and a hatter were in business. The wheelwright, Robert Johnson, a devout Presbyterian, made spinning wheels, looms, and furniture. The shoemaker, Peter Lukins, was a devoted drinker and one morning, after a night of drunken debauchery, was found dead in bed. The hatter, Martin Waddel, made caps of felt, rabbit fur, and coonskins, the last type being the most expensive at two dollars each. Later Sam Hill erected a storage building for wool and added a wool-carding treadmill. It was propelled by an ox walking endlessly on a circular inclined plane.[35]

Just above the dam, off the main street and around a bend in the road, Tennessean Bill Clary started a saloon, with liquor costing from twelve to twenty-five cents for a half-pint. Clary's saloon became the hangout of a gang of ingenious and reckless rowdies from Clary's Grove, a settlement southwest of New Salem. Night after night, the Clary's Grove Boys raced down the half-mile main street, raised a ruckus, and made all good citizens shake their heads. Always up to mischief, they trimmed horses' tails and put stones under saddles to cause horses to throw their riders.

Near Clary's saloon, foot races and horse races began and ended, and men bet money, coonskins, ginseng, and other items. Gander pullings were regular attractions. An old male goose was swung head down from a tree limb, with his neck greased. Riders paid ten cents to compete. They rode fullspeed, and the one who grabbed the neck and pulled off the head got the bird. On Saturdays, men from New Salem and nearby settlements competed in wrestlin' and shootin' matches and carried feisty roosters under their arms to fight in the cockpit, a spectacle that generated deafening shouts and raucous laughter. North of Clary's saloon, an outcropping of stone was turned into a quarry, providing material for foundations and fireplaces. Bill Clary also initiated a ferry service to improve access from the east. He charged fifty cents for a team and wagon to cross.

More stores opened, and a young spiritually minded physician, Dr. John Allen, arrived from Vermont. He constructed a three-room log home and office across the street from the Hill-McNeil store. Allen reportedly had tuberculosis of the lungs and had come west for his health. Crippled from youth, he walked with a slight limp. A post office was established on December 25, 1829, with Samuel Hill as postmaster. Previously, settlers rode twenty miles to Springfield to get their mail.[36]

New Salem became a flourishing trading place for the surrounding area—a place where farmers could get their corn ground and walk up the hill and buy supplies, have a few drinks, and play card games such as euchre and seven-up. As the town prospered James Rutledge converted his log home into a small tavern where travelers could enjoy a meal and a bed for 37 1/2¢ per day. Between Chicago (which had a population of 150) and New Salem, inns were scarce and primitive, and few villages of any size existed. A traveler between the two towns reported stopping at a one-room inn crowded with twenty-seven lodgers. Rutledge Tavern was luxurious by comparison.

On January 7, 1830, Ann Rutledge quietly observed her seventeenth birthday. Ann had had several beaux but had not found one who had a mind to match hers. From her father's library she had read the works of Robert Burns, Thomas Paine, and Constantine de Volney. Not many men on the frontier wanted a woman who read and recited Shakespeare, could talk about the great philosophers, and had not yet joined a church—even though her parents were deeply religious. On the other hand, she was an excellent seamstress and dedicated to her duties, whatever they were. But would she be satisfied as a merchant or farmer's wife whose main goals in life were to keep house and rear a bunch of children, with no one to share her intellectual interests? She was looking for someone special. Soon she would have four interesting choices.

This anonymous young woman is "the very picture of Ann Rutledge," said Ann's close friend, cousin, and confidant, McGrady Rutledge. Ann's hair was not dark, however. AUTHOR'S COLLECTION.

This idealized portrait of Ann was based on the picture at left. With lightened hair and a cheerful countenance, this portrait by Dan McGregor may be a better likeness. Ann died before photography existed. AUTHOR'S COLLECTION.

4

"There's More in Abe's Head than Wit and Fun."

1830–31

The girls of New Salem chose their future mates at an early age—thirteen or fourteen—and were usually "hitched" by fifteen or sixteen. Most girls on the prairie planned to be homemakers, and there was no reason to delay marriage. Once married, few of them continued whatever schooling they may have begun. They were too busy fixin' meals, keepin' house, and raisin' kids.

So when Mentor Graham started a school about a half-mile southwest of town, only a few older girls were among the thirty to forty learners from ages six to eighteen in the small log church building loaned by the Baptists for school use. This subscription school wasn't cheap, especially for large families—thirty to eighty-five cents a month per child, based on age. With money scarce most paid their tuition with commodities, such as corn, pork, chickens, butter, eggs, and whiskey. Corn was worth only twenty cents a bushel; hogs, $1.25 per hundred pounds, dressed; butter, five to eight cents a pound; and eggs, three to five cents a dozen. Thus, a full school meant a full stomach for Mentor Graham and his family. A teetotaler, Graham accepted whiskey but traded it for sugar and coffee or a bright new calico fabric for his wife, Sarah.[1]

Graham, age thirty, was an antislavery Kentuckian of Scotch-Irish

43

Schoolmaster Mentor Graham was Ann Rutledge's teacher at New Salem. Later he was Lincoln's mentor for grammar, mathematics, and surveying. AUTHOR'S COLLECTION.

origin. Tall, lithe, and strong muscled, he walked with a swift, determined gait. A stylish dresser, he usually wore a black, velvet vest, cutaway coat, and stovepipe hat. His curly red hair and freckled face were matched by his rough, red hands, calloused from cutting brush to feed his livestock and from making bricks for the fireplaces and chimneys of "stuck-up folks' houses."[2]

Graham's proposed contract with parents called for reading, writing, arithmetic, geography, and grammar, but many parents objected to the last two. "Nobody needs no grammar," some said. Nevertheless, Graham taught grammar to every child; he just did not refer to it by name. He taught them to think and to say what they thought—audibly, clearly, and well.[3]

His students were a mixture of youngsters just starting school and older students in various stages of literacy or, as one put it, "jest ketchin' up a bit." Some were sincere learners; others were there because they preferred school to farm work. Graham's endless energy, powerful voice, and forceful gestures commanded their attention. Strict and stern, he kept large hickory switches beside his desk and, as some of the boys remembered, was "apt to whip mighty hard" or to "thump y' on the gourd." Graham taught by the "blab" method. Students recited their lessons aloud, over and over, and Graham listened through the din for errors. But when a student had mastered a lesson, he or she had to stand before the others and recite. Then, all became quiet.[4]

Ann Rutledge was one of the best students in Graham's school. She had attended since the age of fourteen with strong support from her parents. Graham admired her "quick mind" and her scholarship "in all the common branches, including grammar." Billy Greene, himself

Rutledge Tavern, twenty by forty feet, was erected by James Rutledge in 1828 for his family. When New Salem began to prosper, he converted it into an inn where travelers could enjoy a meal and a bed. AUTHOR'S COLLECTION

bright and college-bound, noted her "sharp intellect." Ann's younger brother Robert acknowledged she had "the brightest mind of the family," and was "devoted to her duties of whatever character."[5]

Ann and her brothers walked to the one-room school from Rutledge Tavern, their parent's home and boardinghouse. They took a wooded path down a bluff, crossed Green's Rocky Branch, and climbed another bluff to reach the school. From time to time Ann shopped for her family at the Hill-McNeil Store, across the street from Rutledge Tavern. It carried groceries and dry goods, ranging from coffee, sugar, salt, and whiskey to blue calico, brown muslin, homemade jeans, and ladies' bonnets. Ann often traded butter for a few yards of calico. On her rounds and in the Rutledge Tavern, Ann could not go unnoticed, whether alone or in a crowd, even while attired in her plain green calico dress, sturdy calfskin shoes, and straw sunbonnet. At eighteen she had blossomed like a lily-of-the-valley, bringing beauty and color to the New Salem landscape.

She was slender, pretty, and graceful, with a pink rosebud complexion, a good figure, large blue eyes, and cherry-red lips. Her long curly hair was described by some as light sandy and others as reddish blond. Her mouth was "well-made, beautiful," with good teeth. She stood about five-foot-four and weighed around 125 pounds. Everyone knew her to be vivacious, yet gentle and tenderhearted. She was amiable and loving. She was not sophisticated in the traditional sense, as one could not expect her to be, given her circumstances, but she stood out as "cultured" in contrast to those around her. Billy Greene said she was "full of love, kindness, and sympathy" and that her character was "positively noted throughout the county." Ann's cousin McGrady Rutledge said he never knew her to complain. "She's always cheerful," he observed, "and a good conversationalist."[6]

William F. (Bill) Berry, son of the Presbyterian minister at Rock Creek, was the first New Salem bachelor to seek Ann's affection. They had known each other since Ann was thirteen and had skated together on Rock Creek. In December Bill Berry and Ann were invited to a goose dinner celebrating Vian Camron's sixteenth birthday. Her father, John Miller Camron, being a Presbyterian minister, took down the Bible after dinner and asked each guest to read a favorite passage. Ann chose the opening of the Twenty-fourth Psalm: "The earth is the Lord's and the fullness thereof . . . . Who shall stand in his holy place? He that hath clean hands and a pure heart; who hath not lifted up his soul unto vanity, nor sworn deceitfully." As the party drew to a close, Ann reached for her cape. Bill helped her put it on and offered to accompany her home. She consented.[7]

Soon, however, Bill developed a taste for whiskey, and

Sam Hill, a wealthy New Salem businessman, was a key figure in the lives of Lincoln and Ann Rutledge. AUTHOR'S COLLECTION.

the taste turned into an addiction, which more than a little irritated his father, who preached total abstinence. Ann was a teetotaler, and when Bill called on her one evening and was visibly groggy from too much whiskey, she broke off the relationship. Clearly, Bill had neither "clean hands nor a pure heart," as the Scriptures advised.

Next came Samuel Hill, co-owner of the successful Hill-McNeil Store. He had migrated from his native New Jersey to Cincinnati, Ohio, at age twenty and to New Salem at age twenty-eight. A shrewd businessman, he cultivated the drinking crowd, and his store profited greatly as a result. Hill was New Salem's Ebenezer Scrooge—hot-tempered, irritable, rash, and thrifty to the point of stinginess. He disliked "loud-mouth yellin' preachers" and let them know it.[8]

Methodist circuitrider Peter Cartwright fit that description in Hill's opinion. Of gigantic build and not easily intimidated, Cartwright was both a preacher and a politician. The Hill-McNeil store was the gathering place for the gossips, gabbers, and loafers. Cartwright hoped to convert them, so he would sit on Hill's porch, wearing his broad-rimmed white hat, and entertain them with his keen wit and spunky conversation. At one point Cartwright ridiculed Hill in front of his own store, exclaiming: "I always thought that Hill had no soul until he put a quarter to his lips and his soul 'came up to get it.'" A slender man of average height, Hill often got even with his enemies by hiring ruffians to beat them up, but Cartwright was a match for most frontier bullies, and none wanted to fight him. Hill had to find another way to retaliate.[9]

Women seldom saw Hill's explosive side. To them he was polite and attentive. So when he asked Ann out, she accepted, and they courted. Believing he had captured Ann's heart, Hill requested her hand in marriage. To his surprise, she said no. Ann had become interested in Hill's handsome, urbane partner, New Yorker John McNeil. McNeil eventually began courting Ann—an action destined to detonate Hill's explosive temper.

The winter of 1830-31 was known in New Salem as "the winter of the deep snow." Under the top surface of four feet of snow was a layer of ice from freezing rain that came between blizzards. David Rutledge, fifteen, and Tom Camron, sixteen, worked long hours in below-zero temperatures to keep paths open between their homes.

Ann Rutledge and other villagers gathered on the river bank to watch four
strangers, including Abe Lincoln, struggle with a stranded flatboat.

COURTESY OF LLOYD OSTENDORF

For days, they skated from one house to the other. With drifts up to
twelve feet, families had to cut trees high off the ground to get wood
for the fireplace. They melted ice to make coffee. They heated bricks
to warm the sheets. Chest colds were common. Constant applications
of bear oil helped them survive.

The deep snow starved the deer, turkeys, and prairie chickens.
Some animals froze to death and were eaten by wolves. McGrady
Rutledge said two deer came to his father's feed lot "and were fed
with the cattle and sheep."

Finally, the spring of 1831 brought welcome relief.

On April 19, 1831, the residents of New Salem, including Ann
Rutledge, were drawn to the river bluff to witness a bizarre sight. A
large flatboat—eighty feet long and eighteen feet wide—had come
around the bend of the river, and was stuck on the milldam. Loaded
with live hogs and barrels of bacon, wheat, and corn, the boat could
not negotiate the receding river. Its bow hung over the dam, and its
down-tilting stern was taking on water at a perilous rate.[10]

Four men were aboard. One of them, noticeably taller than the others, was taking charge. He directed them to transfer cargo from the stern to a ferry boat just below them. They then rolled the remaining barrels forward toward the bow. Next, the tall stranger waded ashore and inquired about a cooper shop. He needed an auger. He was directed to Henry Onstot's shop about a quarter mile down the road.

Onstot thought the boatman strange-looking. He had a "rather singular grotesque appearance," Onstot would later write, with a long, scraggy neck and a narrow, thin chest that appeared to have been stretched by his towering six-foot-four body. His head, with long, hollow cheeks, seemed much too small for his stature, while his nose and ears seemed much too large for his head. Feeling sorry for him, Onstot loaned him an auger. Lincoln thanked him, and while returning to the boat, he cut a limb and fashioned a plug the diameter of the auger bit.[11]

Back on the riverbank the villagers awaited his next move. He did not disappoint them as he worked in the water, with his "boots off, hat, coat, and vest off; pants rolled up to his knees and shirt wet with sweat and combing his fuzzy hair with his fingers as he pounded away on the boat." With the auger he bored a hole in the bow to release the accumulated water. Next, he called for volunteers to stand in the bow to weigh it down. The stern lifted, the water drained, Lincoln plugged the hole, and the boat floated over the dam. The villagers cheered.[12]

Ann Rutledge undoubtedly shared Onstot's analysis of the stranger. To this "lily of the valley," Lincoln must have looked like "the ragweed of the prairie." It certainly was not love at first sight, at least not on her part. But while she was not charmed by his appearance, she was surely intrigued by his ingenuity.

Meanwhile, the crew reloaded the boat and passed on down the river. Villagers learned that the other voyagers were Lincoln's cousin and stepbrother, John Hanks and John Johnston respectively, and their employer, Denton Offutt. They were headed for New Orleans, a thousand-mile river trip, with stops along the way to deliver produce to Southern markets. From New Salem the crew piloted the boat northward to the Illinois River and then south to the Mississippi. They glided past Alton, St. Louis, and Cairo in rapid succession, tied up for a day at Memphis, and made brief stops at Vicksburg and Natchez. Early in May they reached New Orleans, where they disposed of their cargo and lingered a month.

In New Orleans, Lincoln beheld the true horrors of human slavery. He saw "Negroes chained—maltreated—whipped and scourged," John Hanks later told Herndon. At a slave auction, Lincoln observed "a vigorous and comely mulatto girl" being sold, Herndon would later write. "She underwent a thorough examination at the hands of the bidders; they pinched her flesh and made her trot up and down the room like a horse [so] that the bidders might satisfy themselves whether [she] was sound or not." Lincoln moved away from the scene "with a deep feeling of unconquerable hate." Herndon said the information was furnished to him by John Hanks and that he also "heard Mr. Lincoln refer to it himself." Having had enough of New Orleans, Lincoln and his colleagues boarded a steamboat for the return trip. They disembarked in St. Louis.[13]

Offutt was profoundly impressed with Lincoln's abilities and with New Salem's potential boomtown profits. So he decided to establish a store there and employed Lincoln to operate it. Offutt remained in St. Louis to secure merchandise, and Lincoln visited his parents in their new home in Coles County. He then walked to New Salem, arriving in late July. This time his unrolled pants attracted even more attention because they were several inches too short. William Butler, a Kentuckian who later became Lincoln's friend, described him "as ruff a specimen of humanity as could be found."[14]

The bad impressions soon changed, however, when villagers found him to be articulate and intelligent. "He's no green horn," one said. Waiting for Offutt to return, Lincoln loafed about, spinning out Indiana yarns such as this one:

An itinerant preacher stepped into the pulpit and announced as his text, "I am the Christ, whom I shall represent today." Just as he started his sermon, a green lizard crept up his baggy pant leg. With one hand, he gestured the strong points of his sermon; with the other he tried to stop the upward advance of the lizard. Finally, he opened the button of his pantaloons and, with one sweep and a kick, he freed himself of his jeans while continuing his sermon without missing a word. However, the lizard was now making its way up his back, and the preacher unfastened the button holding his shirt and divested himself of that garment too, with the flow of his eloquence uninterruptedly marching on. The congregation was stunned, and one elderly woman rose, pointed an accusing finger at the preacher, and shouted: "If you represent Jesus Christ, then I am done with the Bible."[15]

When Denton Offutt returned to New Salem with supplies, Lincoln helped him build the small log store he would manage. It opened for business in early September 1831. Offutt's store was adjacent to Clary's saloon, just above the mill dam and across from the cockpit. In that location Offutt anticipated the patronage of those bringing grist to the mill from both sides of the river. It was also convenient for loading flatboats with products he accepted in exchange for goods he sold. The location put Lincoln side-by-side with the rowdies. The challenge he would soon be forced to meet was how to walk untouched by their excesses and meanness and yet win their admiration and respect. To their disappointment he refused to join them in their drinking bouts and carousals. He reportedly abstained from intoxicating liquors and never smoked or chewed tobacco. Lincoln said he used to drink some, but it had threatened his self-control. He said he could not allow that to happen.[16]

Offutt expanded his enterprise by renting the mill from Camron and Rutledge, and Lincoln ran from the store to the mill, where he unloaded, measured, and settled for sacks of grains brought in by farmers. To assist Lincoln at the store, Offutt hired Charles Maltby as his chief assistant and Billy Greene as the credit-checker. Greene knew the financial standing of people in the community and could tell Lincoln whose credit was good. Most settlers bought on credit and paid with produce. Greene had an exceptionally keen mind, especially in financial matters. Some called him "Slicky Bill." He lived with his father, a drinking and illiterate man, on a farm two miles from town, but he often stayed overnight at the store, sharing a bed with Lincoln. They developed a lifelong friendship.[17]

Lincoln paid village cofounder John Miller Camron one dollar a week to dine with his large family of eight girls and one boy, with another girl on the way. Lincoln's main love at the Camrons turned out to be Polly's pies, although he was fascinated by the girls. Solena and Sorena, four-year-old twins, were especially amused by the tall stranger who told them stories. Mary, 11, Martha, 9, and Sarah, 7, teased him about his long legs, long arms, and horsy "ways," and he admitted he was not much "to look at." Nancy, 13, ignored him. Vian, 16, made fun of his appearance: "He's as thin as a beanpole and as ugly as a scarecrow!" Vian piqued Lincoln's interest with her coal-black hair, flashing brown eyes, keen wit, and frisky, frolicsome ways. "You're full of spice and vinegar," he said to her. "I'll call you 'Quinine.'" Her beau was William Prosise, a prosperous farmer. "I'd not bother with him," Lincoln teased her. "A lawyer's who you want." Later, she would remember thinking, "How dare he talk to me like that!"[18]

The oldest daughter, Betsy, age eighteen, was a dark-haired beauty, well poised and courteous, with a regal manner like that of her mother. Lincoln called her "Queen Isabella." Camron told her not to get too interested in Mr. Lincoln, declaring that "he's poor and won't amount to much."

On one occasion when Lincoln was visiting the Camrons, he saw one of Betsy's suitors, Billy Greene—whom she did not like—coming toward the house. Roguishly, Lincoln told Betsy that her favorite beau was headed their way. Not wanting anything to do with "Slicky Bill," she slipped into a rocking chair on the far side of the room. Greene came in, and then Lincoln saw Betsy's true love, Baxter Berry, approaching on the path. As Berry knocked at the door, Lincoln pushed Greene onto Betsy's lap, and Greene tried to kiss her as Berry entered the room. Betsy reacted with a strong uppercut to Greene's head, knocking him off the chair. She then rose with a vengeance and slapped Lincoln, who was laughing hysterically. Berry sized up the situation. He took Betsy's arm and led her outside. A year later Betsy married Berry, with Lincoln acting as best man. When he delivered his gift—matching berry bowls decorated with roses—Vian met him at the door. "These are for Queen Isabella to dine with in fine style," he reportedly said.[19]

Twice a day, after meals, Camron conducted devotions. Some of the girls would read from the Psalms or the Epistles, and then he would pray for fifteen to twenty minutes or longer. Abe, during his first day of dining with the Camrons, was not aware of the ritual and had stretched out by the fire after supper. Camron quickly advised him to kneel for Bible readings and prayer. Lincoln apologized as he assumed the proper position. After Camron closed his eyes and began praying, Lincoln procured a pillow from Vian for his knees. Then, as the prayer ended, he pushed it away. He repeated the procedure daily.[20]

Offutt's grocery store offered varied goods, including calico prints from Massachusetts, teas from China, coffee from Brazil, stoneware from Pennsylvania, and gloves and mittens made by New Salem women from tanned deerskins. Lincoln showed a pair of dogskin gloves to a customer one day. "I ain't never heard of dogskin gloves," said the farmer dryly. "How do you know that's what they are?" "Well," said Lincoln, "I reckon I can recollect how that came 'bout. Jack Clary's dog killed Tom Watkin's sheep. Then, Tom Watkin's boy killed the dog, and old John Mounts tanned the dogskin, and Sally Spears made the gloves. That's how I know." The man bought them for seventy-five cents.[21]

In making change for another customer, Lincoln accidentally took out six-and-a-quarter cents too much. He discovered the error at closing time and reportedly walked six miles to return the money. In New Salem, he became known as "Honest Abe."[22]

Lincoln's respect for New Salem women was demonstrated by his reaction when Charlie Reavis cursed around women shoppers. Lincoln demanded that Reavis desist, saying he would not tolerate such language in his store when ladies were present. When Reavis continued the vulgarity, Lincoln admonished him: "I have spoken to you a number of times about swearing in the presence of ladies, and you have not heeded. Now I am going to rub the lesson into you so that you will not forget again." Thereupon he seized Reavis by the arm and led him out of the store to the side of the street where there was a patch of smartweed. Throwing Reavis on his back and putting his foot on his chest, Lincoln grabbed a handful of the stinging weeds and rubbed Reavis's face, mouth, and eyes with them until he yelled for mercy. Reavis begged Lincoln to stop and swore he would never again swear around ladies if Lincoln would let him up. But Lincoln told him that was not sufficient; he would have to quit

THE WOMEN IN LINCOLN'S LIFE

This statue at New Salem State Historical Site represents Abraham Lincoln, holding a book and an axe, as he looked during his years in the frontier village. It was presented to the State of Illinois by the National Society of Utah pioneers. PHOTOGRAPHED BY WARD W. MOORE, FROM *ABRAHAM LINCOLN IN PRINT AND PHOTOGRAPH*, DOVER PUBLICATIONS: MINEOHA, NY 1997.

swearing altogether. Having little choice, Reavis agreed.[23]

Frequently, Lincoln would stop at the homes of widows and ask if they needed any wood chopped. If so, he would chop it at no charge. When Lincoln saw a barefooted boy chopping wood one cold, winter day, he asked what he would get paid for the job and what he would do with the money. The boy replied, "one dollar" and pointing to his naked feet, said, "a pair of shoes." Lincoln sent him inside to get warm and said he would chop for a while. Lincoln finished the job and told the boy to collect his pay and buy the shoes.

If a traveler got stuck in the mud in New Salem's main street, Lincoln was always the first to help pull out the wheel. "Abe will do anything to help anyone," a merchant said. Lincoln's spontaneous, unobtrusive helpfulness endeared him to everybody and inspired them to help him when he needed it. "All loved him," said Mentor Graham, because he was one of "the most companionable persons you will ever see in this world." He would even stop reading to play marbles with children.[24]

Once, when a merchant was wrongly informed that Lincoln had spoken unkindly of his wife, he tore into Lincoln with foul and abusive language. Lincoln kept his temper and denied the accusation.

"In fact," said Lincoln, "I have a very high opinion of her, and the only thing I know against her is the fact of her being your wife!" The merchant laughed and apologized.[25]

In Lincoln's day New Salem was a man's world. For an hour at the close of most days Lincoln sought out athletic activities—wrestling, jumping, and lifting heavy weights. He would lift heavy timbers and pile one upon another, and he would take a barrel of whiskey and hoist it up to his head, a difficult feat he accomplished easily. He once wrestled the town bully, Jack Armstrong, and was about to win when Armstrong made an unfair move, grabbing Lincoln by the thigh. Reacting, Lincoln seized him by the throat and thrust him at arm's length from him. "If you want to 'wrastle' fair, I am ready," Lincoln said calmly, "but if you want to fight, I will try that." Armstrong preferred to call it a draw. "Boys," said Armstrong, "Abe Lincoln is the best fellow that ever broke into this settlement. He shall be one of us."[26]

Armstrong was the leader of a gang of ingenious and reckless rowdies from Clary's Grove. Night after night they raised a ruckus, always up to mischief. Despite the gang's rowdy ways, Lincoln's fair play and his good-natured attitude in the wrestling match won the gang's admiration. From that time on the Clary's Grove Boys were Lincoln supporters.

After the wrestling match Lincoln was often called upon to judge contests because he was regarded as the most impartial man in town. He once refereed a cockfight between Babb McNabb's bird and a fighting veteran. McNabb had bragged incessantly about his bird's abilities. Bets ran high. When the two birds were thrown into the pit, McNabb's rooster "turned tail and ran." At a safe distance he mounted a fence, spread his feathers, and crowed. Babb paid his wager and addressed his bird: "Yes, you little cuss, you're great on dress parade, but not worth a damn in a fight." Years later, during the Civil War, Lincoln would remember the incident when forced to deal with Gen. George B. McClellan. Lincoln compared General McClellan to McNabb's rooster. McClellan would exhaust Lincoln's patience by endlessly drilling and reviewing the Army of the Potomac while persistently refusing to fight.[27]

Adding further diversity to New Salem events, a temperance society was organized in December 1831. The group hoped to reform its hard-drinking neighbors but had little success. T. G. Onstot, the cooper's son, complained that the worst opponents of temperance were "the church members, most of whom had barrels of whiskey at home."[28]

When Mentor Graham joined the society and signed a temperance pledge, the local Hardshell Baptists threw him out. At the same time another member was expelled for getting drunk. These activities prompted still another member to ask: "I should like to have some-one tell me just how much whiskey a man has to drink to be in full fellowship and good standing in this church." No one responded. However, some predestinarian Baptists rationalized that temperance societies were bad because they tried to alter matters predestined by God. That would explain why the Baptists readmitted Graham after the temperance society expelled him for breaking his pledge.[29]

Lincoln enjoyed male company, and he entertained them and him-self. He swapped stories and opinions with the blacksmith, the saloonkeeper, the cobbler, and others. Lincoln's knack for story-telling attracted the fun-loving men of New Salem, while his range of knowledge caught the attention of more prominent citizens, such as Mentor Graham and James Rutledge. Lincoln knew their intellectual and literary resources, and he drew upon them. He borrowed books from Graham, Rutledge, Bennett Abell, John McNeil, and folks in Springfield, walking there or riding on farmers' wagons. He read everything he could find. And he wrote down everything he wanted to remember. History held a special fascination. Lincoln read and re-read William Grimshaw's *History of the United States*. Denouncing slavery and stressing the significance of the American Revolution, it exhorted readers: "Let us not only declare by words, but demonstrate by our actions, that 'all men are created equal.'"

Lincoln borrowed Shakespeare's works from an unlikely source, Jack Kelso, a lazy fisherman and jack-of-all-trades who had the gifts of a poet. When others got drunk, they fought, but when Kelso got drunk he astonished the rustic community with lengthy, memorized quotations from Robert Burns and William Shakespeare. Although Lincoln hated fishing, he loitered away whole days talking with Kelso along the banks of quiet streams where Kelso expounded on "our divine William" and "Scotia's Bard" in his intervals of fixing bait and dropping line. From Kelso, Lincoln learned to appreciate the finer sentiments of poetic expression. Some folks said Lincoln seemed to read more than he worked, and they wondered if he were shiftless. "My father considered me lazy," Lincoln told Billy Greene. "When he caught me reading when he thought I should have been doing chores, he gave me a good thrashing. . . . He taught me to work, but he never taught me to love it." Lincoln readily admitted he didn't like physical labor and thought there were better ways to make a living.[30]

While intellectual pursuits were not commonplace on the Illinois prairie, New Salem was by contrast an intellectual center. Debating societies were the vehicle, and Ann Rutledge's father was the primary mover. In 1831 he organized what was probably the first debating society. Lincoln's first speech in the region was at Rutledge's debating club. Dr. John Allen said he delivered a strong argument "pretty well." Lincoln spoke in the high-pitched voice that became his trademark, but he did not know what to do with his hands. After waving them about he finally placed them in his pockets. Another debating club was started by Thomas J. Nance, a well-educated Kentuckian and future legislator. Lincoln walked six miles to participate. Topics included: Should females be educated and have the right to vote? Should people join temperance societies? Should a wife promise to obey her husband? David Rutledge, who wanted to be a lawyer, debated and argued questions with Lincoln. So did Mentor Graham. James Rutledge, who owned a library of thirty books, was impressed with Lincoln's debating skills. He remarked to his wife, "There's more in Abe's head than wit and fun. All he lacks is culture." Rutledge took a deeper interest in Lincoln and urged him to announce himself as a candidate for the legislature. "In time it will do you good," Rutledge advised. Rutledge's daughter Ann had read many of her father's books and was especially fond of Shakespeare and Burns. Her literary interests were similar to those of Lincoln. Through such intellectual activity Lincoln built up a following. Eventually he was viewed by his New Salem neighbors as everybody's friend. He had won his own way—with his fists and his wits.[31]

During his years in New Salem, Lincoln never had his own home. He slept anywhere and everywhere there was a vacant bed. Since everyone liked him, he never had any trouble finding a place to stay. Almost any villager could have posted a sign, "Abe Lincoln slept here." Lincoln frequently visited Armstrong's home where Jack's wife, Hannah, "took a likin'" to him, washed and patched his clothes, and made shirts for him. Although she was about the same age as Lincoln, he called her Aunt Hannah. She often chopped her own stove wood, but when Lincoln visited, he chopped it for her. "Abe would come out to our house," she would later recall, "drink milk, eat mush, cornbread and butter, bring the children candy, chop wood, and rock the cradles of our twin sons, Duff and Boger, while I got him something to eat." One of Lincoln's favorite snacks was bread with honey.[32]

Lincoln related well to the young married women of New Salem, and Aunt Hannah and others became like surrogate mothers or sisters to him. While he was shy and bashful around available single women, he was completely at ease around women who were not potential mates. Lincoln was such good company that the Armstrongs wanted him to visit. If Jack or Aunt Hannah needed help or learned that Lincoln was idle, they would send for him. "Do stay to supper, Abe," they would implore, "stay all night, might as well." He usually did. Some twenty years later Aunt Hannah needed Lincoln's help twice, and she got it. Her son Duff was charged with murder in a late-night drunken brawl with James Metzger in 1857. Jack had died, and Hannah offered Lincoln her farm to defend him. Lincoln refused any payment and took the case. The prosecutor's star witness said he clearly saw Duff strike Metzger because a full moon was shining directly overhead. Lincoln opened a copy of the 1857 almanac and read a page to the jury. At the time of the incident, the moon was not directly overhead. It was low in the sky. Duff was acquitted. Then during the Civil War, President Lincoln received another request from Hannah—to discharge Duff from the Union Army because he was needed to run the farm. Lincoln honored the request.[33]

In addition to the uncultured Armstrongs, Lincoln developed a close relationship with a couple at the opposite end of the cultural spectrum: Elizabeth and Bennett Abell. Well-to-do Kentuckians, they owned one of the area's finest farms about two miles north of the village. Elizabeth, in her late twenties, was smart and cultivated. She was attracted to Lincoln, and he to her. She washed clothes for him; they had many long talks; and she urged him to seek a "higher plane of life." Lincoln lived luxuriously with the Bennetts for several months and dined on such scrumptious delicacies as roast duck and gooseberry pie. Row Herndon, a village resident, noted that young married women "all liked Lincoln and he liked them as well." Herndon then added a shocker that gave his statement new meaning: "Elizabeth Abell has a daughter that is thought to be Lincoln's child. They favor very much." "Lincoln did live with the Abells in a sort of home intimacy," acknowledged William Butler, another Kentuckian and close friend of Lincoln. Elizabeth later described Lincoln admiringly: "He was very sensitive . . . [never rash], and . . . the best-natured man I ever got acquainted with. . . . He was always doing good."[34]

Lincoln also enjoyed the company of Mentor Graham's wife, Sarah, who was in her early twenties. He often sought her advice about boy-girl relationships, love, and other personal matters. While he liked being around married folks, Lincoln found young single women to be as antagonistic toward him as they were in his Indiana neighborhood. They made fun of him, but on occasion he used his sharp wit to retaliate. Taking odd jobs to earn money, he once served food at a party where, as one guest recalled, "a girl there who thought herself pretty smart" protested when he filled her plate with an exceptionally generous portion. She said sharply, "Well, Mr. Lincoln, I didn't want a cartload." A little later when she asked for more food, he announced in a voice loud enough for all to hear, "All right Miss Liddy, back up your cart and I'll fill it again." Everyone laughed except for Miss Liddy, who "went off by herself and cried the whole evening."[35]

Sexual gossip spiced up conversations around New Salem, and some of it centered on Lincoln. Nancy Burner was an attractive woman with strong passions, weak will, little sense, and a "strong desire to please and gratify friends." When she became pregnant, the gossips said it was Lincoln's or Dr. Jason Duncan's child. "Yes, Lincoln knew the girl," Billy Greene said, "but never touched her." Billy's younger brother, Gaines, however, suggested otherwise: "I really don't know who the father is. . . . Billy and Lincoln do as they please." John McNeil later pointed a finger at Billy. Once, McNeil said, when a group of New Salem young people were walking home from an outing, Billy was "trudging along in silence" because Dr. Duncan had taken Nancy away from him. "Then, Billy came alongside Nancy, who was with Dr. Duncan, and pleaded his lost cause with her. The girls in the rear moved up to hear. After many arguments . . . Billy finally put in a clincher: 'You know, we have done things we ought not if we are going to separate.' The girls wilted and fell back." According to both of the Greene brothers, Billy Greene and Lincoln persuaded Dr. Duncan to marry Nancy and move away. Before leaving, Dr. Duncan gave Lincoln a copy of the poem, "Mortality," by Scotsman William Knox. Lincoln later memorized it—all fourteen quatrains—and recited it often. The first stanza: "Oh, why should the spirit of mortal be proud / Like a swift-flying meteor, a fast-fleeting cloud / A flash of the lightning, a break of the wave / He passeth from life to his rest in the grave."[36]

That fall of 1831 Scotsman John McNeil initiated a courtship with Ann Rutledge. McNeil had boarded briefly at Rutledge Tavern, where he first noticed her. He was cultured, erudite, and debonair. Ann's father was less than enthusiastic, however, because McNeil was twelve years older than Ann and seemed cold and unfriendly. McNeil had come west from New York and had formed a partnership with Sam Hill. Plucky and industrious, McNeil made high-interest loans and purchased low-cost land from distressed farmers. He acquired considerable property and was believed to be worth about twelve thousand dollars. His wealth and standing placed him at the top of the social ladder. Ann's brother Robert regarded him as "high-toned, honest, and moral." McNeil supposedly fell in love with the "gentle, amiable maiden with the bonny blue eyes." Ann doesn't have "any of the airs of the city belles," he told a New Salem friend, "and I like that."[37]

5

"He Has Dumped Her—
Ho, Ho, Ho."

1832–33

$\mathcal{A}$s Lincoln measured calico prints for fewer and fewer customers, he surely suspected that Offutt's store was about to collapse. Ann Rutledge came in occasionally when she could not find what she wanted at the Hill-McNeil Store. Lincoln always enjoyed seeing her, but it was good to see anyone at the store. Offutt was near bankruptcy, and soon, in Lincoln's words, his enterprises "petered out." Pondering his future Lincoln decided to follow James Rutledge's advice and run for the state legislature. On March 9, 1832, the twenty-three-year-old merchant announced his candidacy in a statement published in the *Sangamo Journal* in Springfield. He had asked the lettered John McNeil to correct the grammar. McNeil, who was courting Ann Rutledge, was an avid reader and had an extensive library for that time and place.[1]

Lincoln's decision to seek political office was an adventurous step for a young man who just a year earlier was, in his own words, a "friendless, uneducated, penniless boy, working on a flatboat—at ten dollars per month." His credentials for public office were nonexistent. He "had nothing only plenty of friends," as one contemporary phrased it.[2]

Lincoln's campaign was interrupted in mid-April. As redbuds and dandelions colored the landscape, a rider on a muddy, sweating horse stopped in New Salem and distributed handbills conveying terrible news: Indians were on the war-path in northwestern Illinois, and the governor urgently sought volunteers to help federal troops repel them. By early May some two thousand men had volunteered for one month's service and were off to become heroes and make extra money. Lincoln signed up in New Salem, as did his fellow store clerk Billy Greene, the

Major John T. Suart, the well-educated son of a college professor and preacher, met Lincoln during the Black Hawk War. Stuart later helped Lincoln to become socially and politically polished. AUTHOR'S COLLECTION.

Clary's Grove Boys, and two of Ann Rutledge's brothers, John and David. Lincoln reenlisted twice, serving a total of three months—time spent fighting mosquitoes and trying to survive in the sweltering heat and swampy wilderness.

At Beardstown, where several companies bivouacked, Lincoln met Major John T. Stuart of Springfield. A well-connected Kentuckian, Stuart was a young, college-educated attorney and the son of a college professor and Presbyterian minister. Like Lincoln, he was a Whig candidate for a seat in the Illinois legislature. The two men became close friends. Stuart, a worldly man with a reputation for pursuing and seducing women, apparently coaxed Lincoln to accompany him to a house of prostitution in Galena, Illinois. "We went purely for fun and devilment, nothing else," said Stuart, without elaborating on what those words meant.[3]

Lincoln returned to New Salem two weeks before the election. He campaigned by horseback from house to house and farm to farm. As he talked to farmers in the fields, he helped them pitch hay, feed hogs, or shuck corn. In one speech, he said: "Fellow citizens, I presume you all know who I am—I am humble Abraham Lincoln. I have been solicited by many friends to become a candidate for the legislature. My politics are short and sweet, like the old woman's dance. I am in favor of a national bank. I am in favor of the internal improvement system and a high protective tariff. These are my sentiments and political principles. If elected I shall be thankful; if not, it will be all the same."

He was not elected. However, where he was best known, in his own precinct, he received 277 of the 300 votes cast. Stuart, who was elected in his district, noted that even though Lincoln lost, he gained a reputation for candor, honesty, and effective speech-making. "He made friends everywhere he went," Stuart would later recall, "and thereby acquired the respect and confidence of everybody." After the election, Lincoln debated what to do next. His resources totaled $124—his compensation for military service. He wanted to stay in New Salem, however, because—he would later admit—he "was anxious to remain with his friends who had treated him with so much generosity, especially as he had nothing elsewhere to go to."[4]

While Lincoln was running for the legislature and serving in the war, John McNeil was courting Ann Rutledge. They went to barbecues, cornhuskings, dances, house-raisings, and just about anywhere it was proper for a young couple to be seen together. At square dances, she danced every set and never appeared tired. Finally, he asked her to marry him, and she agreed. In money and looks, McNeil was considered "a good catch."

The engagement broke up the Hill-McNeil partnership. Hill, jealous and distraught over McNeil's success with the village belle, wrote McNeil an angry, abusive letter demanding, "you either buy me out or sell out to me at the inventory price." McNeil agreed to sell.[5]

Around late June, McNeil revealed a long-held secret to his betrothed. Telling her he desired to keep nothing from her, he declared that the name McNeil was an assumed one; that his real name was McNamar. "I left behind me in New York," he said, "my parents and brothers and sisters. They are poor, and were in more or

63

less need when I left them in 1829. I vowed that I would come West, make a fortune, and go back to help them. I am going to start now and intend, if I can, to bring them back with me on my return to Illinois and place them on my farm." He changed his name, he said, because he feared that if the family in New York had known where he was, they "would have settled down on him, and before he could have accumulated any property would have sunk him beyond recovery." Now he believed he was in a position to help them. He told Ann he would return to New Salem as soon as possible and then they "could consummate the great event to which they looked forward with undisguised joy and unbounded hope."[6]

Ann believed his story because she loved him. "She would have believed it all the same if it had been ten times as incredible," wrote Ward Hill Lamon years later. Whether he really loved her is a matter for speculation. McNamar's decision to return to New York came after he had learned that Ann's father desperately needed money. McNamar capitalized on Rutledge's problem by purchasing one-half of his eighty-acre farm in Sandridge for the meager sum of fifty dollars. Rutledge perhaps settled for the small amount as a favor to his anticipated son-in-law. (Rutledge sold the remaining half of his farm to John Jones for three hundred dollars.) The acreage McNamar bought was adjacent to his own farm, which he had acquired earlier from John Miller Camron.[7]

After extensive research in the 1920s, author William E. Barton concluded that Rutledge and Camron sold their farms because they were "on the brink of a financial precipice." They had staked everything they had on the New Salem venture, and they were losing money. Even the Rutledge Tavern was a financial failure. Barton speculated that McNamar left New Salem sensing that Rutledge was close to bankruptcy and realizing that Ann was no longer "the prospective heiress of the great fortunes of one of the founders of New Salem."[8]

In August, shortly after Lincoln's return from the Black Hawk War, McNamar began his trip to New York. It was only after he was gone that Ann told his story to her family. They were skeptical. They raised questions: Why would anyone desert his family in order to save it? Did he change his name because he had a lurid past? Was he really jilting Ann? "I never really trusted the man," said Ann's cousin Mary Mayes Miller. "I don't know why, but I always thought he wasn't all he was cracked up to be." They kept their concerns to themselves, not wanting to cause Ann public embarrassment. Spurned women were objects of scorn.[9]

Buying and selling real estate in New Salem hit rampage proportions in the summer and fall of 1832. Camron and Rutledge sold their mills to entrepreneur Jacob Bale. Camron then unloaded his other properties and moved north to the Spoon River country, where his father had settled. Lincoln would miss his "fun and games" with the Camron girls.

In late November Lincoln moved into Rutledge Tavern and stayed about four months. The tavern was New Salem's biggest home. It had two large rooms on the ground floor—a kitchen-dining-living area and a sleeping-sitting room with several beds. An upstairs loft accommodated twelve boarders on hay mattresses. Guests and family ate and talked around a long table. Afterward, they sat by the fireplace, told

In front of this fireplace in Rutledge Tavern, Lincoln stretched out his long legs from a rocking chair and kept everyone in an uproar with his amazing tales.
AUTHOR'S COLLECTION.

stories, and related the day's gossip. Stools, baskets, and wooden boxes lined the walls, and jugs, crocks, and platters covered the mantle. A heavy walnut china cupboard was filled with delicately patterned blue and white dishes. Kettles over the flames in the fireplace released savory whiffs of delicious country cooking. Filled with people, furniture, and utensils, the home radiated a homey and lively ambiance.

Earlier, Lincoln had boarded with the Rutledges while sleeping elsewhere. He also "dropped in," as was the custom with other villagers, sometimes bringing a watermelon and placing it in a tub of cold water, ready for the next meal or afternoon snack. He retrieved potatoes, beans, and turnips from the root cellar where they were stored for the winter. While he was being neighborly, he was also satisfying his desire to be near Ann Rutledge.

Ann's parents were serious and pious, forthright and down-to-earth. They called a spade a spade. As Cumberland Presbyterians they took the Bible seriously. In contrast to her quiet, reserved parents, Ann was vivacious and cheerful. When Lincoln came to live at the Tavern, there were eight Rutledge children at home. The oldest, Jean, had married James Berry in 1828. Ann, now nineteen, helped her mother run the inn. Ann was surrounded by protective brothers close to her age— John, 21; David, 17; and Robert, 13. Then there was Nancy, 11; Margaret, 9; William, 6; and Sarah, 3. The older ones shared household duties: preparing and serving food, churning butter, making soap and candles, and scrubbing utensils and floors. Ann was the family's seamstress, perhaps the best in the village. It was said that she performed magic with her spinning wheel. Her styles were notable for tiny buttons of contrasting colors produced from bits of cloth.[10]

Strangers popped in and out for stays ranging from overnight to a few days. On one occasion the visitors included a lady from Virginia with three stylish teenage daughters, and they stayed for about two weeks. Lincoln, who was often tongue-tied and awkward around teenage girls, refused to eat at the same table with them throughout their visit. He had been mocked so often by attractive, eligible girls that he ignored them when possible. But just as Lincoln was comfortable around married women, he also was at ease around "spoken-for" women. He felt he could be himself, with no need to put on "airs" to attract their interest. Consequently, after Ann Rutledge became engaged to John McNamar, Lincoln developed a rapport with her. She treated him with kindness and respect, and he admired her lively and inquisitive spirit, which was akin to his. Although she was four years younger than he, she was a mature woman by prairie standards. Ann had also become comfortable with him, and enjoyed their conversations—which she considered intellectually stimulating. He was someone whose mind she enjoyed probing. It was therefore easy for the couple to have a warm and tender friendship.[11]

Among their common interests was a love for animals and a hatred for those who mistreated them. Lincoln's attitude dated back to childhood days in Indiana. Abe's father was a good hunter, and he taught his son to shoot to kill. Game meant food and skins, and skins meant clothes and a trading commodity. When a flock of wild turkeys approached their cabin one day, seven-year-old Abe picked up a gun, shot through a crack between the logs, and killed one. But Abe's momentary joy quickly turned to grief as he watched the turkey squirm, bleed, and die. The sight made him sick, and he vowed he would never kill another animal. He would not be a hunter or a fisherman. Just as Lincoln respected all life, so did Ann Rutledge. She cared for lame dogs and birds with broken wings and other critters in need of help. John McNamar thought she was wasting her time. He could see no financial profit in it. Ann also raised pigs and chickens. Her father gave her a pig from each litter; any profits she made were set aside to go toward her education. When Lincoln found three baby rabbits whose mother had been killed, he put them into his pockets and took them to Rutledge Tavern. He asked Ann if she would like to take care of them, and she happily agreed.[12]

Ann's homework in grammar also caught Lincoln's attention. One morning while having a breakfast of flapjacks with Mentor and Sarah Graham, he mentioned a desire for a grammar textbook. Graham responded, "If you expect to be before the public in any capacity, I think it is the best thing you can do." Lincoln agreed. "If I had a grammar, I would commence now," he vowed. Graham said there was none in the village, but he knew of a grammar at the Vances, about six miles from New Salem, which he thought Lincoln could get. When Lincoln had finished eating, he walked to the Vances and got the book. It was *Kirkham's Grammar*, which Graham described as "the hardest grammar

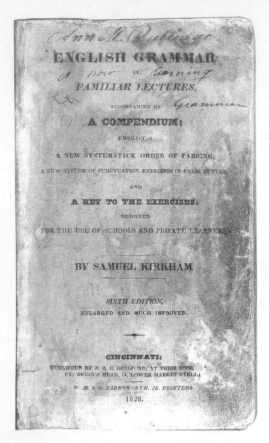

ENGLISH GRAMMAR,

Ann M. Rutledge

A now in learning

FAMILIAR LECTURES,

ACCOMPANIED BY Grammar

A COMPENDIUM;

EMBRACING

A NEW SYSTEMATICK ORDER OF PARSING,

A NEW SYSTEM OF PUNCTUATION, EXERCISES IN FALSE SYNTAX

AND

A KEY TO THE EXERCISES;

DESIGNED

FOR THE USE OF SCHOOLS AND PRIVATE LEARNERS.

BY SAMUEL KIRKHAM.

SIXTH EDITION,

ENLARGED AND MUCH IMPROVED.

CINCINNATI:

PUBLISHED BY N. & G. GUILFORD, AT THEIR BOOK
STORE, FRANKLIN'S HEAD, 14, LOWER MARKET STREET.

W. M. & O. FARNSWORTH, JR. PRINTERS.

1828.

Lincoln and Ann Rutledge studied Kirkham's *English Grammar* together. LIBRARY OF CONGRESS.

I think anybody ever studied." Lincoln gave the book his full attention, however, and in Graham's words, "mastered it in an astonishing manner."[13]

Back at Rutledge Tavern Lincoln came and went as one of the family. One evening, while seemingly engrossed in study, he picked up Ann's youngest brother, six-year-old William, tucked him under an arm, and with Kirkham's *English Grammar* in the other hand, he walked along with William yelling and kicking. Then Lincoln pretended he had just discovered he was toting a boy and released him. Lincoln was like that around all children, and most seemed to enjoy his pranks and never-failing humor. Lincoln watched as Ann gave her youngest sister, three-year-old Sarah, her first sewing lesson. Sarah sat on a low stool beside Ann; Ann stopped her work, threaded a needle for Sarah, and taught her to make a stitch. Later, Sarah tried pulling Lincoln's "big ears and mouth," and he laughed. "He's so good-natured everybody loves him," Nancy, age eleven, told her friends.[14]

Lincoln and Ann studied grammar together. He laughed when she had difficulties with the lesson, and one day, in a spirit of fun, he wrote below her name on the title page, "is now learning grammar." Lincoln gave her the book, and from her it was passed to her siblings.[15]

In relaxing moments at Rutledge Tavern, Lincoln would stretch out his long legs from a chair by the fireplace and tell funny stories to the children. Once, when Nancy was sitting alone by the fire, Lincoln came in, sat down beside her, looked at her teasingly, and sang softly: "When in death I shall calmly recline, / Oh hear my heart to my mistress dear / Tell her it lived on smiles and wine / Of brightest hue while it lingered here / Bid her not to shed one tear of sorrow / To sully a heart so brilliant and light, / But balmy drops of the red grape borrow / To bathe the relict from morn till night." Nancy did not understand the intent of his action and failed to realize it was a prank. His look and manner so distressed her that she left the room.[16]

On January 7, 1833, Ann turned twenty. A few days later, a neighborhood tragedy occurred. On the night of January 17, Lincoln and Ann's older brother John had gotten into a friendly "romp and scuffle" and had broken a bed-board. The next morning Ann started to repair it, and Abe told her he "must" help her. Needing a wrench, they sent Ann's sister Nancy to Row Herndon's cabin, their nearest neighbor, to borrow one. When Nancy arrived, Herndon was loading his gun, and suddenly it discharged. His wife, who was talking to Nancy, was shot through the neck and was mortally wounded. Nancy saw blood spurt out of each side of the woman's neck. Frightened, Nancy hurried home and told Ann and Lincoln what had happened. "I can never forget how sad and shocked they looked after having been so merry just a moment before," she later recalled. The loss of this well-liked woman, who was Mentor Graham's sister, was mourned throughout the region. Soon afterwards, her husband left New Salem.[17]

Business opportunity came Lincoln's way when Row and James Herndon decided to sell their general store. Lincoln signed a note for a half-interest, and William F. Berry bought the remaining interest. Berry, who was Ann's first suitor, had been a corporal in Lincoln's company during the Black Hawk War. This first Berry-Lincoln store was soon replaced with one more centrally located—across the street from Rutledge Tavern. Lincoln and Berry acquired it from Billy Greene, who had gotten it from Reuben Radford after the Clary's Grove Boys trashed it. This newer store was the town's only frame structure. It had a covered porch, with a bench along the front wall. Under a nearby maple tree Lincoln often stretched out with his books in the cool, inviting shade with his feet up against the tree. Directly across the street, when Ann sat at her spinning wheel by the window, he could call out to her and run across and visit. He did that many times.[18]

With their new store Berry and Lincoln had assumed a major debt. Unfortunately for both the store did not prosper. It was said they weren't "gee-hawing" well together. Berry loved liquor as much as Lincoln loved books. Now, more and more, Berry devoted himself to consuming the store's whiskey while Lincoln talked, joked, and read. It was not a recipe for success. Stores were permitted to sell liquor without a license if they sold it only in quantities greater than a quart and for consumption off premises. Unknown to Lincoln, Berry secured a license in April 1833 to sell liquor by the drink. Lincoln was so upset that he withdrew as an active participant in the store. Soon, in Lincoln's words, the store "winked out."[19]

On May 7, 1833, Lincoln was unexpectedly appointed postmaster at a salary of fifty dollars a year. His predecessor, Sam Hill, had operated the post office from his store, which had done a brisk trade in liquor sales. It was customary for women to pick up the family mail, and they were often compelled to wait while Hill was selling whiskey. In protest, the women successfully petitioned the government for his removal. As postmaster Lincoln became aware of letters exchanged between Ann Rutledge and John McNamar. Ann told close friends that McNamar's first letter was loving and kind, but succeeding ones grew less ardent and more formal. He wrote that there was sickness in the family and he could not return as quickly as he had hoped. Then there were other postponements—all due to circumstances beyond his control. But he did not elaborate. After a few months the correspondence ceased altogether. Twice each week Ann checked with Lincoln for mail from McNamar. But there was none. The absence of letters cast a shadow across her happiness.[20]

Ann's friend Parthena Nance later wrote that "some of the girls lorded it over Ann who sat at home alone while we other young people walked and visited." They whispered in her ear that McNamar had deceived her and deserted her, and that she had a rival in her affections. These girls were jealous and resentful of Ann's engagement to the town's most eligible bachelor. Now they talked about her behind her back, saying such things as, "He has dumped her—ho, ho, ho."

Ann was, in effect, socially ostracized. Her heart was broken, and more than that, she was humiliated. Her mind was tortured by suspense and disappointment. She doubted he had ever loved her.[21]

Lincoln sensed the situation and felt sorry for her. First, he asked her to walk with him in the evenings, and she consented to do so. Then they started hiking over the hills. They sometimes sat on the bluff above the river and read to each other. Both enjoyed Shakespeare and took turns reading or reciting sonnets or passages from *Macbeth* and *King Lear*.[22]

Lincoln reportedly asked Ann if she wanted him to help find McNamar. "No," she replied, "he knows where I am, and if he doesn't care enough to write to me, I'm sure I don't care enough about him to try to find him." By revealing to Lincoln her fast-ebbing feelings for McNamar, she was motivating Lincoln to pursue his long-repressed passion for her. He got the message and acted upon it.[23]

At every opportunity Lincoln sought to be with her—on her way to and from Sunday school, in frequent strolls along the winding paths of the village, and in cold and wet weather in nightly gatherings around the fireplace in Rutledge Tavern. Ann loved horseback riding, and the couple sometimes rode through the fields around New Salem, occasionally stopping for a picnic beside a shady brook or on a hillside overlooking the river. They picked bucketfuls of crab-apples, grapes, and persimmons, and gathered walnuts, pecans, and hazelnuts. For the first time in his life, Abraham Lincoln was deeply in love.[24]

The postmaster's pay was low, so Lincoln did odd jobs, from making rails to harvesting hay and grain. Then he experienced another windfall. Friends learned that John Calhoun, county surveyor, needed an assistant. They advised Calhoun of Lincoln's intelligence, honesty, and trustworthiness. "Let him lay out the roads and towns and farms," one said, "and they will be done right." Calhoun offered the job to Lincoln. It surprised him: Calhoun was a Democrat and a "Jackson man," while Lincoln was a Whig and a "Clay man." "If I can be perfectly free in my political action I will take the office," Lincoln remarked, "but if my sentiments or even expression of them is to be abridged in any way I would not have it or any other office." Calhoun assured him that he would not be expected to compromise his principles. "That being the case, I accept," replied Lincoln.

Lincoln had studied surveying while clerking at Offutt's store in 1831, and Mentor Graham had advised him. Now Lincoln borrowed more books on surveying and in six weeks mastered the subject.[25]

Needing money, James Rutledge sold his tavern in May 1833. Mrs. Rutledge moved to the farm of her relative James Short to keep house for him until he married on September 10. Ann Rutledge took over management of the tavern in an arrangement allowing her father and siblings to remain there until mid-summer. Ann also assisted her mother at Short's home. Then, at the urging of Dr. Allen, the Rutledges moved to McNamar's farm, eight miles from town, down a dusty road bordered by tall prairie grass.

In the fall of 1833, the men of New Salem noticed an unusual female visitor. "She wore the finest trimmings I ever saw," one said. Talk in town changed from politics to Mary Owens, who was in town for a four-week visit with her sister, Elizabeth Abell. Mary Owens was the cultured, well-spoken daughter of a wealthy Kentucky landowner. Her silk dresses, leghorn hat, and kid shoes and gloves contrasted sharply with the simple sunbonnets and homespun attire of local women. Pleasingly plump and refined, she was described by one New Salem resident as "fair as the moon, clear as the sun, and terrible as an army with banners." She was sharp, shrewd, and intellectual, "decidedly the most intellectual woman I ever knew," said Gaines Greene. Mary was twenty-five—an old maid by prairie standards—and Elizabeth thought it was time for her to marry. She and other young married women of the village also agreed that Abe Lincoln needed a wife. So, being the good matchmaker that she was, Elizabeth made sure that Mary and Lincoln met. During Mary's four-week visit, Lincoln saw her several times. He described her as "intelligent and agreeable," and he found her to be jovial and responsive to his wit and humor. However, she was no Ann Rutledge.[26]

6

"My Comfort by Day, and My Song in the Night."

1834

*W*hile Ann turned yarn into clothes for the family, Lincoln surveyed the territory around New Salem, laying out roads, school sections, and town sites. He earned three dollars a day—good pay for the times, with board and lodging costing only one dollar a week. His travels and work also enabled him to extend his acquaintances and to sound out public opinion. One assignment was to survey the hills between New Salem and Petersburg—frontier land full of brush, briars, and snakes. He was often an overnight guest with his close friends, Bennett and Elizabeth Abell, whose home was midway between the two villages. It was not unusual for Lincoln to come in at night, Elizabeth would later recall, "all ragged and scratched up with the briars." He laughed about it and said that was "a poor man's lot." Elizabeth advised him to "get a buckskin" and she would fix his pants so that "the briars would not scratch [him]." He got the buckskin, and she sewed it on the trousers legs. It made his work much less painful, and he was grateful.[1]

Surveying enabled Lincoln to exercise his passion for precision, but occasionally, his heart overruled compass and chain. In his tale, "Mitch Miller," Edgar Lee Masters described a surveying incident involving Lincoln:

Look at this house partly in the street and look at the street how it jigs. Well, Linkern [Lincoln] did that. You see he surveyed this whole town of Petersburg. . . . It was after the Black Hawk War . . . and when Linkern came here to survey, he found that Jemina Elmore, which was a widow of Linkern's friend in the war, had a piece of land, and had built a house on it and was livin' here with her children. And Linkern saw if the street run straight north and south, a part of her house would be in the street. So to save Jemina's house, he set his compass to make the line run a little furder south. And so this is how the line got skewed. . . . This is what I call makin' a mistake that is all right, bein' good and bad at the same time.[2]

Lincoln was still postmaster, and when he went surveying, he often delivered the mail too—carrying letters in his hat. When his surveying took him several miles from the Abells, he lodged with other families. In the two-room houses common on the frontier, family members of all sexes, along with any strangers, often slept in the same room. Undergarments were never removed, and no one seemed concerned about the arrangement. Lincoln spent one night with the Cottenbarger family, whose bedsteads were arranged so that the foot of one bed was against the head of the other. During the night, the feet of the family's teenage daughter somehow ended up on Lincoln's pillow. Lincoln reached up and tickled the girl's leg. The girl awoke and went to her mother's bed to tell what had happened. "For God's sake," her mother said "say no more and go to bed, the man means nothing. If your father hears of this, the deuce will be to pay." Lincoln was reportedly mortified at what he or "the devil in him" had done. Early in the morning, when Cottenbarger went to the woods, his wife hustled Lincoln off as quickly as she could. Lincoln sometimes spun a different version of the story:

Once, when surveying, I was put to bed in the same room with two girls, the head of my bed being next to the foot of the girls' bed. In the night I commenced tickling the feet of one of the girls with my fingers. As she seemed to enjoy it as much as I did, I then tickled a little higher up; and as I would tickle higher the girl would shove down lower and the higher I tickled the lower she moved.

He never told how his version of the story ended.[3]

Lincoln's surveying territory included Sandridge, where his friend "Uncle Jimmy" Short and the Rutledges lived a half-mile apart. Lincoln visited the Shorts at least four times a week, usually overnight, and then rode over to the Rutledges to be with Ann, whom he affectionately referred to as "Annie." While not secretive about their love, they seldom showed it in public, preferring to be discreet until there was closure on the McNamar problem. The Rutledge farm was near the Sangamon River, and Lincoln and Annie found a special place on a high, flat rock with a wide view of the river and valley below. They would ride their horses across the meadow and into the woodlands, where they dismounted, tied their horses to a tree, and climbed the rock to their majestic spot. These private moments of chatting and laughing refreshed their souls and deepened their love for each other. Often, they talked about the future and what it might hold. Annie, picking up where her father had left off, encouraged Lincoln to run again for the legislature. One day she told him that if women could vote, he would win in a landslide. How he responded is unknown, but two years later, on June 13, 1836, he endorsed women's suffrage in a letter to the editor of the *Sangamo Journal*.[4]

Annie, who had attended weekend "singing schools" taught by itinerant singing masters, often sang for Lincoln's benefit. The two sang together from a hymnal, *The Missouri Harmony*, which contained such songs as "We're Marching to Zion" and "While Shepherds Watched Their Flocks by Night." The song Lincoln had sung earlier for Annie's sister Nancy came from this book. The hymnal also offered advice: "Let us live so in youth that we blush not in age. . . . All kinds of spirituous liquors . . . are destructive to the voice." A good voice may be "much injured by singing too loud." Browsing through the book, Lincoln and Annie found a hymn titled, "New Salem": "O Thou in whose presence my soul takes delight / On whom in affliction I call / My comfort by day, and my song in the night / My hope, my salvation, my all."[5]

The song reflected their feelings for each other. She would sing it to him flirtatiously, and he is believed to have whispered it in her ear in public settings, which often made her blush. Although Lincoln had many talents, singing was not one of them. When Short was asked if Lincoln could sing, he replied, "Can a pig whistle?"[6]

Lincoln escorted Ann Rutledge to and from quilting bees, where women turned scraps of cloth into magnificent quilts. COURTESY OF ABBY ALDRICH ROCKEFELLER FOLK ART CENTER, WILLIAMSBURG, VA.

Lincoln escorted Annie to and from quilting bees, where a dozen or so thimbled hands stitched patterns from scraps of leftover cloth, producing magnificent quilts. They did not name the patterns, but referred to them as copies of "Grandma Brown's quilt" or "my neighbor Mrs. Owen's quilt." They lined them with goose-down or layers of homespun. Bees lasted about six hours, starting before breakfast and ending around two o'clock. When Lincoln took Annie to Fanny Bale's bee, he even went inside, where men were considered out of place, and sat by Annie's side as she worked on a quilt. Fanny, who was fond of Lincoln, had her eye on him, and he had his eye on Annie. To make Annie more attentive, he winked at Fanny, and Fanny stuck a needle in her finger. Lincoln pulled it out. Moments later Lincoln supposedly whispered to Annie, "You are my comfort by day and my song in the night, my hope, my salvation, my all." Her stitches suddenly became irregular and uneven. The other women noticed it. Years later, the quilt's owner proudly pointed out the bad stitches and told their history. These hand-made quilts were part of the proud dowry of many frontier brides and were passed down as family treasures. Women also valued their quilt patches and were quick to tell visiting friends where every piece came from: "This one is from grandmother's dress; this is from my aunt in Kentucky; this came from my first dress."[7]

The Fourth of July was the single most important holiday in New Salem. Patriotism was second only to God. It was not a day for fireworks, loud parties, or noisy parades. It was primarily a day for solitude and for reflection, inspiration, and renewal—a day to remember the men who signed the Declaration of Independence and pledged a willingness to risk "our lives, our fortunes, and our sacred honor."

It was more like a memorial day, with quiet flag-waving, chest-pounding, and pulse-beating oratory on the greatness of the founding fathers and the blessings of this noble land. Although no record exists of Lincoln's involvement in the festivities, no rising politician—especially one whose political guide and inspiration was the Declaration of Independence—would have avoided the celebration. The Rutledges would probably have participated also and may even have helped plan the activities. Annie's father was born just five years after the Declaration was signed and had grown up in battle-torn South Carolina during and after the Revolutionary War. In all likelihood, Lincoln and Annie joined the New Salem residents for the observance.

Englishman William Oliver, who toured the United States in the early 1840s, recorded an account of Independence Day "at a small town in Illinois" in his book, *Eight Months in Illinois*. His description was probably typical of events in New Salem. About noon, he said, a crowd assembled in the street. Soon three men with fiddles and a flute appeared, playing "Hail! Columbia," and were followed by ladies marching in pairs. After the ladies had passed, the gentlemen followed in similar style.

"All was done with the most profound gravity," Oliver observed. "There was no hurrying, no laughing nor talking, nor indeed any sounds save those proceeding from two very bad fiddles and a flute, and the [chirping of birds] overhead. It would have been considered the very height of indecorum had one of the beaus offered his arm to any of the ladies. . . . [This] demeanor prevails at all public meetings of the sexes and is a national trait."

The procession left the town and entered the forest, where "among the tall stems, stood a wagon, onto which mounted the orator and another gentlemen who introduced him. The oration consisted of . . . reminiscences of previous and similar occasions and was delivered in a hesitating, unanimated style, which contrasted strangely with the [fine-sounding] language.

"The audience sat or lay at full length on the ground, the ladies on one side of the wagon, and the gentlemen on the other, whilst some boys . . . were overlooking the whole from bushy trees. There was no drunkenness or riot consequent on this occasion; indeed, the first example of drunkenness I saw in this neighborhood was in a grocery to which I was attracted by the sound of a fiddle, where, on entering, I found the barkeeper playing 'Old Coon' to a tipsy man who was dancing."[8]

New Salem's gander-pullings and wrestling matches were no competition for one of the great events of the early nineteenth century—religious camp meetings. The Rutledge family regularly attended the meetings at Concord Creek. They wanted their children to find salvation. If Annie were there, then Lincoln must have

Camp meetings were old-fashioned revivals that featured evangelistic preachers and emotionally charged worshippers. Lincoln and Ann Rutledge attended out of curiosity. While both were deeply religious, neither ever joined a church. LIBRARY OF CONGRESS.

been also—not only to be with Annie but also to further his political career. Methodist Peter Cartwright conducted camp meetings each summer; Baptists and Presbyterians did so following the harvest. At Concord, under a large shed in a grove of walnut trees, evangelists preached electrifying two-hour sermons. They had to contend with ornery boys who set fire-rings in the woods and made ghost-shrieks to rattle worshippers.[9]

"At the close of one meeting," Cartwright wrote, "we had many seekers who had not obtained comfort. Twelve got into a two-horse wagon, and myself with them. We had to go about fifteen miles, but before we reached our home every one of them got powerfully converted, and we sung and shouted aloud along the road, to the very astonishment of those who lived along the way." Annie's little sister Nancy was converted at the Concord Camp Meeting; her oldest brother John was converted on the road home from Round Prairie Camp Meeting.[10]

Lincoln and Annie were apparently never converted; neither of them ever joined a church. Yet Annie was a devoted worker in her parents' church, and both Lincoln and Annie believed in God and were kind, compassionate, and moral. Both shared a common inquisitiveness about religion and a common belief in universal salvation. Lincoln believed in the "Doctrine of Necessity"—that the human mind is impelled to action by some power over which the mind itself has no control. "What is to be will be," he once declared, "and no cares of ours can arrest nor reverse the decree." He would come to see himself as "the means" for certain results—as an "instrument foreordained by God to aid in accomplishing great works" and as one "deeply sensitive of the need for Divine assistance." Quoting Hamlet, he once said: "There's a divinity that shapes our ends, rough-hew them how we will."[11]

Lincoln, and perhaps Annie, were greatly influenced by Scotland's national poet, Robert Burns. Burns had reportedly rebelled against his family's religion, and Lincoln found in him "a like thinker and feeler." Billy Greene told friends that Lincoln "knew all of Burns by heart" and could quote him with a Scottish accent. Burns's "Holy Willie's Prayer" was a Lincoln favorite. It was about a hypocritical church elder who was held up to scorn. Row Herndon related one of Lincoln's practical pranks inspired by Burns's poem, *Tam o'Shanter*:

There was a man who used to come to New Salem, and [got drunk], and stayed until dark. He was afraid of ghosts and someone had to go home with him. Well, Lincoln persuaded a fellow to take a sheet and go in the road and [pretend to be a] ghost. The ghost made his appearance, and the man became much frightened. Lincoln also had sent another ghost. [When he] made his appearance he frightened the first ghost half to death. That broke the fellow from staying until dark anymore.[12]

Over the years, Annie's well-educated father and teachers had given her a broad knowledge of literature and philosophy. She had read many of the books in her father's library, and she was evolving her own philosophy of life. She may have explored Burns's unorthodox views, as well as his use of verse to express emotions of love, friendship, or amusement at his ironical contemplation of the social scene. Did she discuss these matters with Lincoln? Besides her beloved brother, David, and her friend, Parthena Nance, he was just about the only other person with whom she could have comfortably pondered such controversial issues. Two other books that may have influenced Lincoln and Ann Rutledge were *The Age of Reason* by Thomas Paine and *Ruins* by Constantin de Volney, which were passed among New Salem's freethinkers. They became part of Lincoln's self-education and motivated his lifelong intellectual inquiry.[13]

Years later when asked why he had not joined a church, Lincoln responded by paraphrasing Jesus in Mark 12:30–31. Lincoln said he would join one only if it had for its creed, "Thou shalt love the Lord, thy God, with all thy heart, with all thy strength, and with all thy mind, and thy neighbor as thyself." Ann Rutledge might have given the same response. Put simply, they both believed in the Fatherhood of God and the brotherhood of man.[14]

Lincoln and Annie's religious positions ran counter to those of the rigidly orthodox frontier community of New Salem, a place where arguments about religion were as common as whiskey and corn bread. Lincoln joined in frequent discussions on store porches and around potbellied stoves. As if begging to be persecuted, Lincoln wrote an essay suggesting that certain parts of the Bible did not represent divine revelation. In his essay he even questioned the virgin birth, the divinity of Christ, and the immortality of the soul. He showed it to Sam Hill and said he planned to publish it. Hill read it, advised Lincoln it would ruin him politically, and threw it into the fire. Annie's friend Parthena Nance once asked Lincoln: "Do you really believe there isn't any future state?" "I'm afraid there isn't," he replied. "It isn't a pleasant thing to think that when we die that is the last of us." A few years later, while lingering in the office of the clerk of the court in Springfield, Lincoln picked up a Bible, read a passage, made a critical comment, then ridiculed the Scripture. He shocked many people, including his friend John T. Stuart, who said, "Lincoln went further against Christian beliefs, doctrines, and principles than any man I ever heard."[15]

Lincoln later modified his position, either from religious growth or political expediency, or both. In a campaign handbill, he wrote: "I have never denied the truth of the Scriptures; and I have never spoken with intentional disrespect of religion in general, or of any denomination of Christians in particular." Describing himself as a "religious seeker," Lincoln was always questioning, always demanding proof—not just about the Bible but about everything he encountered.

Some thirty years later, shaped perhaps by the burden of leadership in the Civil War, his position had changed to a point where he told a friend: "Take all of the Bible upon reason that you can, and the balance on faith, and you'll live and die a happier and better man."[16]

Lincoln's belief in a Creator who possessed all power and wisdom was due in no small part to his belief in the "order and harmony of all nature." "It would have been more miraculous for this order and harmony to have come about by chance than to have been created and arranged by some great thinking power," he told friends. Looking up at the starlit sky one night, he said: "I never behold the stars that I do not feel that I am looking in the face of God. I can see how it might be possible for a man to look down upon the earth and be an atheist, but I cannot conceive how he could look up into the heavens and say there is no God."[17]

Annie and Lincoln's friend from the Black Hawk War, John Stuart, persisted in encouraging him to study law and to run for the legislature again. Now he committed himself to it. Lincoln finally agreed with them that law could be his passport out of poverty and into national politics. Stuart, a legislative "veteran" with one term behind him, became Lincoln's political mentor. A symbol of urbanity in the boondocks, Stuart helped the uncultivated Lincoln to become more socially and politically polished. Both men were about the same age, and both were Whigs.

Lincoln gained support from the Whigs and the Democrats, thanks to Stuart and Bowling Green, a powerful Democrat who was New Salem's justice of the peace. Green urged his party's faithful to back Lincoln. Since Democrats were in the majority, Green's support was significant. Green's wife, Nancy, was among the more mature women of New Salem who were, in effect, Lincoln's surrogate mothers. Nancy was fully aware of Lincoln's courtship of Ann Rutledge and acknowledged it after Lincoln's death. In his court, Green observed Lincoln as an amateur lawyer. The two became friends, and Lincoln thought of him as a second father. Lincoln later said he "owed more to Mr. Green for his advancement than any other man." The two enjoyed each other's wit and humor. When they were together, they looked like strange opposites—Green with his "peaches and cream" complexion, Lincoln with leathery, weather-beaten skin. Lincoln was tall and thin; Green, of average height, weighed 250 pounds. He was nicknamed "Pot" for his protruding belly, which, like St. Nick's, "shook when he laughed, like a bowl full of jelly." His bulging trousers were held up by one linen suspender.[18]

Lincoln stumped the countryside, talked to farmers while on surveying trips, solicited votes as he delivered the mail, and attended numerous barbecues where each candidate spoke. He campaigned at horseshoe pits, cockfights, and wolf hunts. His popularity was enhanced by his advocacy of a forty-mile canal from the Sangamon River below Petersburg to Beardstown, on the Illinois River. The canal would expedite the shipment of farm produce. During the campaign, Lincoln frequently stopped at the Shorts' farm for overnight lodging and visits with Annie, who lived a half-mile down the road. Lincoln won handily. He was twenty-five.

On a cold November morning, supporters gathered at dawn to see him off for the state capital. "Do right by us, Abe. Good luck, Abe," they yelled. "Our prayers go with you." He thanked them and stepped into the Yellow Bank stagecoach for the ninety-five-mile, two-day ride to Vandalia.

Lincoln gained a reputation as one whose vote could not be bought. He grew in his understanding of the political process and of the importance of legal knowledge. His style was to avoid any posturing, but instead to know the issues, understand the system, and study matters carefully before putting himself forward. The Assembly did focus on one of Lincoln's major concerns—internal improvements—and provided for clearing and deepening rivers and building canals and railroads. The Assembly also granted charters for private undertakings such as toll bridges. Lincoln introduced a bill for one of these bridges—Musick's bridge across Salt Creek—to replace a ferry. It would be long remembered by Illinois travelers.[19]

During his nearly three months away from New Salem, he and Annie undoubtedly wrote often to each other although no letters now exist. The session ended February 13, 1835, the day after his birthday, and Lincoln returned to New Salem in sub-zero temperatures with his legislative earnings of $258. He was more ambitious than ever, but not without problems. On January 10 his store partner, William Berry, had died from chronic alcoholism. His death left Lincoln saddled with the store's notes and debts totaling eleven hundred dollars, a huge obligation for a person earning only a few dollars a month. Lincoln referred to it as his "national debt." He assumed the liability and paid on it for at least fifteen years before finally clearing it.

Pursuing his ambition, while continuing as a surveyor and postmaster, he borrowed law books from Stuart, bought others at auctions in Springfield, and studied so intensely that people became concerned about his health. "He became wholly engrossed [in the study of law]," noted Robert Rutledge. It wasn't unusual to see Lincoln studying barefooted while sitting on the ground in the shade of a tree.

Russell Godbey saw him on a woodpile absorbed in a hefty book. "What on earth are you reading, Abe?" he asked. "I'm not reading," Lincoln replied, "I'm studying law." "Law!" Godbey exclaimed, "Good God Almighty!"[20]

7

"Annie's Whole Soul Seemed Wrapped Up in Lincoln."

1835

*L*aw and love dominated Abe Lincoln's life in the spring and summer of 1835. For nearly two years, he had loved Ann Rutledge, but he did not know if her ties with John McNamar had been permanently severed. Finally, that spring the scrupulous Lincoln concluded that the "insurmountable barrier" had been removed, and he decided to act. While the exact scenario is unknown, it is likely that after one of his frequent overnight stays with "Uncle Jimmy" Short, he rode to the Rutledge farm. Constant rain showers had produced a kaleidoscope of spring colors on nearby fields and hills—red clover, Virginia bluebells, sunshine roses, purple nettle, and golden buttercups. Somewhere in that setting or a similar one, he apparently found the courage to propose to Ann Rutledge. She responded positively, according to at least fifteen sources. "There is no kind of doubt as to the existence of this engagement," wrote Robert Rutledge years later. "Annie's whole soul seemed wrapped up in Lincoln," said her sister Jean.[1]

But both Lincoln and Annie were concerned about propriety. Before announcing marriage plans, Annie wanted to contact McNamar, inform him "of the change in her feelings," and "seek an honorable release." She wrote the letter and mailed it. Several months passed, and there was no response. Annie's brother David, in whom she often confided, urged her to marry Lincoln immediately, without regard to anything but her own happiness. She had no obligation to the long-silent McNamar, he insisted. But some of the Rutledges thought Lincoln was undeserving of Annie. Her cousin Mary Mayes Miller said a few family members were concerned that Annie would pass up prosperous suitors for one plagued with poverty and riddled with debt. It bothered them that her "Prince Charming" was, if not an ugly duckling, a peculiar specimen of humanity.[2]

Annie, however, was not swayed by their attitudes. She loved Abe Lincoln. That was all that mattered. She knew that no one else could match his remarkable qualities—his probing mind and kind heart, his good-natured and openhanded style, his wit and intelligence, his rock-solid character, his unselfish nature, and his enjoyment of life. He was fun to be with. She did not focus on his homely face and lanky physique. She knew him as a man of purpose, a man with powerful potential. Thus, with no word from McNamar, Annie and Lincoln apparently proceeded with wedding plans. She was twenty-two. He was twenty-six. They reportedly set a date for the fall of 1836—one year away. "Both wished to better equip themselves for the positions they would eventually occupy," Nancy Rutledge would say later. That view was confirmed by both Annie's brother Robert and her cousin McGrady Rutledge. McGrady, who was in her confidence, said, "Ann gave me to understand, that as soon

Ann Rutledge and Abe Lincoln share a few moments near Rutledge Tavern. COURTESY OF LLOYD OSTENDORF.

as certain studies were completed, she and Lincoln would be married."[3]

By the next fall, Lincoln expected to complete his law studies and gain admission to the bar. He would then be able to support a family. Annie would attend the Jacksonville Female Academy for a year. It was about thirty-five miles southwest of New Salem. "I must prepare myself to be the wife of a senator or governor," she told her family. They encouraged her. The importance of knowledge and education was deeply instilled in the Rutledge clan. To bolster her preparation, Annie was being tutored by Arminda Rogers Rankin in rhetoric, grammar, and elementary studies. Her tutor was from a well-educated family in Athens, seven miles east of New Salem. Lincoln had borrowed books and newspapers from Arminda's father, Colonel Matthew Rogers.[4]

Arminda had observed Annie "passing out of and above the depression and anxiety she had shown over McNamar's absence and neglect" and was fully aware of the "new love" in her life. Annie "manifested no regret or wavering in the choice she had made," Arminda said. "On the contrary, there was a decided spirit of offended maidenly dignity manifested in all the references she made to McNamar, such as could be expected of a well-bred Southern girl under circumstances showing such unaccountable neglect."[5]

Lincoln and Annie also shared their plans with Mentor Graham, Billy Greene, other close friends, and members of the Rutledge family. Annie was reportedly buoyant and happy. As she worked, she often sang one of Lincoln's favorite songs. While the words were not exactly cheerful, they had a playful meaning: "Vain man thy fond pursuits forbear; / Repent, thy end is nigh; / Death at the farthest can't be far; / Oh, think before thou die." In the evenings, when Lincoln came by, they joyfully imagined the wonders ahead. "The earth was their footstool," Carl Sandburg would later write. "The sky was a sheaf of blue dreams."[6]

Annie's education at Jacksonville Female Academy would have been comparable to her brother David's at Illinois College in the same community. Illinois College was founded by a Presbyterian minister and a group of Congregational students at Yale University in 1829 as a frontier "seminary of learning" connected with the intellectual life of New England. The college's president, Edward Beecher, gave up his church on Boston Common to train youth in the new state of Illinois.

Beecher was the brother of Harriet Beecher Stowe, the abolitionist author of *Uncle Tom's Cabin*, and of Henry Ward Beecher, the liberal Congregational minister who was one of the most influential Protestant clergymen of his time.

On July 27, 1835, David wrote to Annie from Jacksonville: "I am glad to hear that you have a notion of coming to school, and I earnestly recommend to you that you would spare no time from improving your education and mind. Remember that Time is worth more than all gold, therefore throw away none of your golden moments."[7]

In late July, another letter came for Annie. This one was from John McNamar—the first letter from him in over a year. He either had not received her letter of withdrawal from the engagement, or he pretended ignorance of it in order to try to re-win her affections. He told her to "be ready" to marry him soon. He was on the way back to New Salem. He would buy furniture for them in Cincinnati. He wanted to get married as soon as he got to New Salem and set up housekeeping. He never explained his delay to her nor why he had not written.[8]

Years later McNamar said it was the illness and death of his father that caused his continued absence. But in a letter to William H. Herndon, he explained that other hardships and tragedies were involved: "One of those long interminable fevers . . . came into my father's family and prostrated every member, that is except myself, and continued for months, making victims of three of them, one of whom was my father." Medical records of the attending physician, Dr. Timothy Bancroft of Colesville, New York, indicate he treated the McNamar family for nearly three months at the start of 1833, making eighty-one house calls. Two of McNamar's brothers died in March and April, and his father died on April 10. Settling family matters could have taken a few months. But McNamar waited another two years before returning to New Salem. Perhaps his mother did not want to leave New York, or perhaps McNamar had second thoughts about marrying a frontier woman.[9]

Regardless, he was now returning to marry Ann Rutledge, and her worst nightmare had become real. She had no way to communicate with McNamar until his arrival, and she feared his reaction. What would she say to him? How would he handle it? In her conflicts of

Dr. John Allen was Ann Rutledge's doctor. He organized the village's first Sunday School and a temperance society. COURTESY OF DAN McGREGOR.

honor, duty, love, and promises, she struggled through sleepless nights. Lincoln was surveying, and Annie could not reach him immediately to discuss the pending crisis. She did share the letter with Parthena Nance Hill. Parthena had just married Annie's former suitor, Sam Hill, on July 28. Annie and Parthena were so close they even wore duplicate riding habits made from bottle-green flannel. Parthena read the letter, shook her head in dismay, and suggested that Annie would have to tell McNamar that their relationship was over. Critical events intervened, however, before Annie had to confront McNamar.[10]

The weather in Illinois that spring and summer was consistently bad. From the first of March to the middle of July, it rained almost every day, and the whole country was literally covered with water. Then the rain ceased, a tornado whipped through the area, and the weather became excessively hot and dry from late July through much of August. There were endless swarms of horseflies "as big as bats" and "skeeters as fat as birds." Crops suffered. Wheat was ruined. In early August, people began falling ill. Soon many began dying. In Springfield, which had a population of fifteen hundred, twelve practicing physicians were almost continually engaged day and night. Lincoln suffered with chills and aching bones. Some of his acquaintances died, and he made their coffins.[11]

Early in August Annie felt ill. At first she had no pain, just fatigue. She tried to continue her household duties, but one morning she was unable to get out of bed. That day her fever shot up, and one of her brothers rode to New Salem for Dr. Allen, a Dartmouth-educated physician. He said she had "brain fever." It apparently was typhoid fever, caused when the heavy rains and floods had contaminated the Rutledges' well. She "burned" all over, she said, except for her feet. They were so cold they had to be warmed with hot stones.[12]

While no record exists of her medical treatments, Dr. Allen and other doctors relied on a system of medical knowledge that dated back to the Dark Ages. Sickness meant bad elements were in the body, and to get well a person had to be purged of these elements. So doctors prescribed grains of calomel (a toxic powder used as a strong laxative); they raised blisters to draw out the poison; and they practiced bloodletting, frequently puncturing the jugular vein behind the ear to collect a few ounces of blood. Some or all of these practices were probably used on Annie, and any of them would have weakened her and contributed to her death. But Dr. Allen did what he was taught to do at medical school. He ordered "absolute quiet," with no visitors.[13]

Many times Lincoln sought to visit her but was turned away. Days dragged by, the fever stayed high, she was unable to eat, and her situation deteriorated to the point where she could not even raise her hands. Some said her stress over McNamar's pending return had sapped her energy and weakened her resistance, making recovery difficult, if not unlikely. When Annie realized she would not get well, she pleaded that she be allowed to see Lincoln and her brother David, who was in college at Jacksonville. At first her parents refused, following her doctor's orders. Annie kept asking for Lincoln and David, prayed for them to come, and then demanded to see them. Finally, Lincoln's friend Bowling Green was asked to notify Lincoln, who was surveying in an adjoining county, and McGrady Rutledge was sent to Jacksonville to get David.[14]

Lincoln got word late in the day. He immediately jumped on his horse and was racing back when a menacing electrical storm developed. Great lightning flashes pierced the darkness, booming thunder roared across the heavens, and strong winds uprooted trees and plants. Seeking a safe haven until the storm passed, Lincoln stopped at the home of the Reverend John Berry at Rock Creek. As the candlelight shone on Lincoln's face, Berry saw that he was distraught and insisted that he spend the night with them. Lincoln agreed to stay but was restless. Berry read from the Scriptures, and both men knelt as the pastor prayed for Ann's recovery. Unable to sleep, Lincoln walked the floor all night. Very early in the morning the storm subsided, and he struck out for Sandridge and Annie.[15]

John Miller Camron co-founded New Salem with James Rutledge. Lincoln boarded with the family a short time. Camron preached at Ann Rutledge's funeral service. AUTHOR'S COLLECTION.

Her sickbed was in the Rutledges' living room. Several family members were there when Lincoln arrived. John Miller Camron had come down from Fulton County and was leading long, fervent prayers. Lincoln went to Annie, and the others left the room and closed the door. He was alone with her for about an hour. No one knows what they said to each other. It was their private moment, and it would remain private forever. William H. Herndon, Lincoln's biographer, described it in his lecture on Ann Rutledge in 1866: "The meeting was quite as much as either could bear and more than Lincoln, with all his coolness and philosophy, could endure. The voice, the face, the features of her; the love, sympathy, and talk fastened themselves on his heart and soul forever." As he left the room Lincoln "stopped at the door and looked back. Both of them were crying." Annie's fifteen-year-old sister Nancy was sitting on the porch when he came out. His head was bowed as the tears streamed down his cheeks. He passed her without a word. "I can never forget how broken-hearted he looked," Nancy said later. Lincoln confided to a friend: "Annie told me always to live an honest and upright life."[16]

Dr. Allen, who was attending Ann, became so concerned about Lincoln's emotional state that he took him to his home for the night. A few days afterward Ann became unconscious and remained so until her death on the twenty-fifth day of August, 1835. She was twenty-two.

Ironically, her death occurred in the house owned by her first fiancé, who had purchased it from her cousin, John Miller Camron, co-founder of New Salem with her father. Lincoln had lost the third major woman in his life—first his mother, then his beloved sister, and now his future bride whom he had loved with a passion he had never known before and, many assert, would never know again.[17]

Ann's funeral service was simple. It was beside her grave at Concord Cemetery, a country burying-ground about seven miles northwest of New Salem on the west bank of Berry's Creek. About an acre in size, it was a peaceful place bordered by an extensive prairie, by a field where sheep and cattle grazed, and by forests to the north and south. John Miller Camron gave the eulogy. Everyone in New Salem was there, with Lincoln's tall figure dominating the crowd. At the end of the service, Camron took Lincoln's hand and quietly suggested, "Come up and see us any time you care to. Maybe Aunt Polly can help you." In the days ahead Camron prayed that "the humor and faith that mean so much to his friends, . . . might be restored to Lincoln's bleeding soul."[18]

Lincoln somehow kept his deep, hidden emotions under control for about a week, but then a heavy rain saturated the area, and he became unnerved and plunged into a black hole of despair. He told the Abells, "I cannot bear the idea of it raining on her grave." From then on rains and storms precipitated a steady drizzle of incidents of despondency. The death of the first woman he truly loved marked the tragic end of the most beautiful hopes Lincoln had entertained for his personal life. His whole life was affected by the blow. The shadow of her death would always hang over him.[19]

Almost daily, he walked seven miles to visit her grave, sitting beside the grassy mound for hours. Many times he was found at the cemetery with one arm across her grave as if trying to communicate with her in spirit. McGrady Rutledge became worried about him and on several occasions went to the cemetery to bring him home. Some thought he became suicidal. Billy Greene said Lincoln was watched with special vigilance "during storms, fogs, and damp, gloomy weather for fear of an accident." Dark hollows appeared beneath his deep-set eyes. He was no longer talkative and cheerful, no longer fun to be around. Henry McHenry, a Sandridge neighbor of the

A recently placed granite headstone marks the site of Ann Rutledge's original grave (1835–1890) at Old Concord Burial Ground hidden behind corn fields about six miles northwest of New Salem. AUTHOR'S COLLECTION.

Rutledges, said Lincoln seemed "wrapped in profound thought, indifferent to transpiring events, had but little to say, but would . . . wander off in the woods by himself, away from the association of even those most esteemed."[20]

In town he was often heard repeating the sad lines from the William Knox poem that began, "Oh! Why should the spirit of mortal be proud? / Like a swift-flying meteor, a fast-fleeting cloud, / A flash of the lightning, a break of the wave, / He passeth from life to his rest in the grave." Hannah Armstrong saw him "weep like a baby," and her husband, Jack, feared he "would go crazy." He hummed sad songs and wrote them with chalk on fences and barns. On a visit to the Rutledge home, he stood by the window of the room in which Annie died, and sobbed. Mrs. Rutledge went to him and put her arms around his shoulder. "Don't let your grief destroy you or spoil your life," she said. "Go on and fulfill the high promise the future has in store for you."[21]

Squire Bowling Green, afraid that Lincoln might commit suicide, brought him to his home, about a mile from New Salem. It was a quiet and secluded place with a tree-covered bluff rising behind the house and a flat land in front stretching down to a creek. Dr. Allen visited Lincoln there and ministered to his sick soul and his weak body. "Give him something to occupy his mind," he advised the Greens.[22]

Lincoln was tortured by memories from his childhood when he heard preachers exclaim that God sometimes took the lives of children to punish their parents for their sins or that the Lord had taken away the loved one because "it was for the best." God made no mistakes, they said. Pondering such ideas, Lincoln seemed to grow bitter and to question God's justice and mercy. The devout Dr. Allen helped Lincoln understand that God hadn't picked him out for punishment. Such ideas were "preposterous," Dr. Allen assured him. Lincoln sat silently by the fireside one night watching the flames dance as a driving windstorm whistled through the trees and stirred up dust and leaves. He went to the door, looked out into the black horizon, and came back, clenching his hands and mumbling, "I can't stand to think of her out there alone."[23]

For several days Lincoln rested. The Greens, who were "salt-of-the-earth" people, nursed him as if he had been their son. Then they had him doing chores—cutting wood, digging potatoes, picking apples, and milking cows. Neighborly kindness showed up everywhere. Friends visited daily. They brought cakes and pies, and they lingered to talk and share stories, jokes, and witticisms. Their compassion helped to soften his grief. Within two weeks, he was much improved, and he went back to New Salem. His joyous feeling for life was gone, however, replaced by fits of melancholy and moody silence that would haunt him the rest of his life. Those who knew them both said her death taught him compassion and gave him the strength to endure all the sorrow he would later face. Others said he became obsessed with death and the meaning of his life and with related questions to which his reasoning mind could find no final answers.[24]

After Ann's death Lincoln erected an emotional barrier between himself and others, especially women. More than ever he avoided intimacy and became abstracted and cool. Having loved deeply and passionately, and having been traumatized by his tragic loss, he was unable to allow himself to love another woman the same way he had loved Ann. He erected a defensive wall of passivity around himself— a wall that would antagonize other women who sought to be close to him. The word "love" all but vanished from his vocabulary. He no longer wanted to be called "Abe." "It seems too familiar," he said, "and familiarity breeds contempt."

For a few weeks he even became careless in his work. Young Matthew Marsh, eagerly awaiting money from home, dropped by the post office to check his mail. But Lincoln, the postmaster, was not there. Marsh glanced at the mail cabinet; it was open, the letters exposed. He fingered through them and found the one he expected, but twenty-five-cents was due. Needing the money order that accompanied it, he took it and left a note for Lincoln. Marsh returned the next day to pay the postage. This time Lincoln was there, but he marked the bulky letter "Free." That was not the normal character of "Honest Abe." Months after Ann's death, Billy Greene remembered Lincoln's continuing grief: "Abe and I would be alone . . . and Abe would sit there, his face in his hands, the tears dripping through his fingers."[25]

Looking for solace in his heartbreak, Lincoln made a rare visit to his parents in their poor, desolate log cabin near Charleston in Coles County, Illinois. He especially wanted to see his stepmother, who loved him and could sympathize with him. Her sensibilities always "seemed to run together" with his, she once said. In a small Charleston hotel, Lincoln met Usher Linder, who would become his longtime political friend. Among other things they talked about familiar acquaintances, such as Lincoln's Uncle Mordecai, Thomas's brother who had prospered. Uncle Mordecai was "wonderfully humorous," Linder said, and Lincoln noted that he had "run off with all the talents" of the family. To Linder, Lincoln seemed "modest and retiring," totally unlike what Linder had heard about his high spirits and homey charm, a man supposedly "out of the ordinary." But to Linder, he seemed very ordinary. "He told me no stories and perpetrated no jokes. . . . He had the appearance of an unambitious man." Linder was not aware of Ann Rutledge's death or of Lincoln's love for her. Thus, he was seeing a man in mourning, not the person he had anticipated.[26]

Downcast, Lincoln later moaned to a friend that "he had done nothing to make any human being remember that he had lived." Time and time again, Ann had urged him to pursue a higher calling, to achieve distinction, and to fulfill his noble destiny. Now he resolved to respond to her supplications. Nothing mattered more to him than to please her and to reach these goals. He was a changed man: quieter, more determined, and decidedly more serious in manner and intellect. In six years at New Salem, he had developed from a self-admitted "aimless piece of driftwood" to a merchant, surveyor, militia captain, postmaster, and first-time legislator. In this small frontier village, he had mastered mathematics and studied grammar and the works of Shakespeare and the poetry of Burns. He had made friendships and fallen in love. In a very real sense, New Salem was the turning point in his life. Somehow the place and its people, especially Ann Rutledge, changed Lincoln and the course of history.

8

"I Want in All Cases to Do Right."

1836–43

After Ann Rutledge, Lincoln seemed unable to love any woman the way he had loved her. He tried, however—at least four times. Two were named Mary, the others, Matilda and Sarah. Three were introduced to Lincoln by their sisters. Two were also aggressively pursued by Lincoln's best friend. All had Kentucky roots in well-to-do families. The two Marys expected Lincoln to marry them. With both, he wavered and wept, and while he did so, they surprised him by gaining weight. Not feeling the genuine, mutual love he had known with Ann Rutledge and not certain he could make either Mary happy, he had second thoughts about each and tried to walk away. But after he did, he felt his actions were dishonorable. Finally, one Mary aggressively cornered him, perhaps through unbridled passion, and they suddenly rushed into marriage. "It was the honorable thing to do," he said. The first woman was Mary Owens; the others, Matilda Edwards, Sarah Rickard, and Mary Todd.

Lincoln first met Kentuckian Mary Owens in 1833 when she visited her sister and brother-in-law, Elizabeth and Bennett Abell. He remembered she was witty, jovial, and noble-looking, but a little stout and a bit flirtatious and outspoken. About a year after Ann Rutledge's death, in the autumn of 1836, Elizabeth mentioned to Lincoln she was going to Kentucky and would bring back Mary if he would marry her. Surprisingly, Lincoln accepted the offer. As he later wrote, he was

Mary Owens rejected Lincoln's marriage proposal, remarking later that he "was deficient in those little links which make up the great chain of woman's happiness." AUTHOR'S COLLECTION.

"most confoundedly well pleased with the project" and "saw no good objection to plodding life through hand in hand with her."[1]

When Mary Owens returned to New Salem, Lincoln was astonished and chagrined. He regretted his promise. He felt "that her coming so readily showed that she was a trifle too willing." Among other things, he was concerned about her appearance. She had put on some weight. "I knew she was over-size," he wrote, "but she now appeared a fair match for Falstaff" and had such a "weather-beaten appearance" that she looked ten years older than her age of twenty-eight—an age approaching "old maid" status at that time. However, Lincoln wrote that he "had told her sister that [he] would take her for better or worse." "I made a point of honor and conscience in all things," he said, "to stick to my word, especially if others had been induced to act on it, which in this case, I doubted not they had, for I was now fairly convinced that no other man on earth would have her, and hence the conclusion that they were bent on holding me to my bargain." He said he planned "how I might procrastinate the evil day for a time, which I really dreaded as much—perhaps more—than an Irishman does the halter."[2]

Nevertheless, Lincoln had made up his mind to make the best of it and to focus on her good qualities—she was witty, wealthy, and polished in her manners. "I also tried to convince myself that the mind was much more to be valued than the person; and, in this, she was not inferior . . . to any with whom I had been acquainted." So he courted her for several months. It was strained, overly formal, and about as passionate as his father's expression of love for him. New Salem observers took notice, for Ann had been in her grave just a few months and Miss Owens "dressed much finer than any lady" in the area. She even had a fashionable silk dress, a striking contrast to the calico dresses Ann had worn.[3]

Mary admired Lincoln but realized "his training had been different from mine, hence there was not that congeniality which would otherwise have existed." To her, he seemed deficient in the nicer attentions she felt to be due from the man she pictured as an ideal husband. He seldom spoke and said nothing funny or romantic. Further, Mary was troubled by his lack of manners. She wondered why he failed to show her the common courtesies he demonstrated at New Salem. For example, when she and Lincoln and other young couples crossed a deep stream on horses, he went ahead without assisting her. Mary recalled: "The other gentlemen were very officious in seeing that their partners got over safely, [but he never looked back] to see how I got along. When I rode up beside him, I remarked . . . 'I suppose you did not care whether my neck was broken or not.' He laughingly replied (I suppose by way of compliment) that he knew I was plenty smart to take care of myself."[4]

Mary decided to test Lincoln's love. He had arranged to visit her at her sister's home. He arrived on schedule and asked for Mary. Elizabeth replied that she had gone to Mentor Graham's residence. Puzzled, Lincoln asked if she did not realize he was coming to see her. Elizabeth said "no," but one of the children blurted out, "Yes, Ma, she did, for I heard her tell someone." He sat for a short time and then returned to his boardinghouse without going to the Grahams' cabin. He had failed the test. Lincoln assumed Mary regarded herself as his superior and was trying to put him in his place. Mary in later life told her cousin Gaines Greene she "regretted her course" and should have played her cards differently. Still, they continued to see each other, and when Lincoln left for the legislature in Vandalia in December 1836, they agreed to write. Vandalia was so cold, wet, and windy that Lincoln was ill and he wrote to Mary he would "rather be any place in the world than here. . . .Write back as soon as you get this, and if possible say something that will please me, for really I have not [been] pleased since I left you."[5]

To reenergize himself, Lincoln plunged into Whig politics; helped enact an internal improvements bill appropriating ten million dollars for railroads, canals, and turnpikes; and pushed through legislation transferring the capital from Vandalia to more centrally located Springfield. On March 1, 1837, as the legislature neared adjournment, Lincoln attained a long-time goal—he was now officially an attorney, and he accepted an invitation from John Todd Stuart to join his Springfield law firm. At twenty-eight, Lincoln had lived half his life.

In New Salem, on April 15, 1837, Lincoln borrowed a horse from Bowling Green, placed all his personal possessions in the saddlebags, and rode twenty miles to Springfield, his new home. It was soon to be the new state capital. He had seven dollars in his pocket. A growing frontier town, Springfield had fifteen hundred inhabitants, nineteen dry-goods stores, four hotels, two politically opposite newspapers, and six retail groceries. A dozen eggs cost six cents; beef was three cents a pound. On rainy days, pigs wallowed freely in the town's muddy streets and rooted out garbage.

A month after his arrival, Lincoln wrote a carefully crafted letter to Mary Owens. It was one of many attempts to get out of the liaison without hurting her feelings or betraying his honor. His goal was to diplomatically persuade her to be the one to break it off. He began this letter as he would all others, "Friend Mary," with no mention of "love." The gist of the letter was that she would probably never be happy as his wife in Springfield—she would have to live in unaccustomed poverty while others lived more luxuriously. He asked her to think about that because he wanted her to be happy. "Whatever woman may cast her lot with mine, should any ever do so," he wrote, "it is my intention to do all in my power to make her happy and contented; and there is nothing I can imagine, that would make me more unhappy than to fail in the effort. . . . My opinion is that you had better not [marry me]. You have not been accustomed to hardship, and it may be more severe than you now imagine. I know you are capable of thinking correctly on any subject; and if you deliberate maturely upon this, before you decide, then I am willing to abide your decision."[6]

Three months later, Mary visited Springfield. Nothing had been resolved, however, and she left confused. Preferring letters to face-to-face discussion, and attempting to force a decision, Lincoln wrote to her again:

I want in all cases to do right, and most particularly so, in all cases with women. I want, at this particular time, more than any thing else, to do right with you, and if I knew it would be doing right, as I rather suspect it would, to let you alone, I would do it. And for the purpose of making the matter as plain as possible, I now say, that you can now drop the subject, dismiss your thoughts (if you ever had any) from me forever, and leave this letter unanswered, without calling forth one accusing murmur from me. And I will even go further, and say, that if it will add any thing to your comfort, or peace of mind, to do so, it is my sincere wish that you should.

Do not understand by this, that I wish to cut your acquaintance. I mean no such thing. What I do wish is, that our further acquaintance shall depend upon yourself. If such further acquaintance would contribute nothing to your happiness, I am sure it would not to mine. If you feel yourself in any degree bound to me, I am now willing to release you, provided you wish it; while, on the other hand, I am willing, and even anxious to bind you faster, if I can be convinced that it will, in any considerable degree, add to your happiness. This, indeed, is the whole question with me. Nothing would make me more miserable than to believe you miserable—nothing more happy, than to know you are.[7]

Offended, Mary Owens finally terminated their relationship. A year later Lincoln admitted he had "made a fool of himself," but he would try "to outlive it." "I have now come to the conclusion never again to think of marrying," he wrote, "and for this reason: I can never be satisfied with any one who would be blockhead enough to have me."[8]

Mary Owens did not court anyone else for several years. She returned to Kentucky in early 1838 and eventually married Jesse Vineyard of Weston, Missouri. Two of their sons served in the Confederate army. In 1839, when Mary's sister Elizabeth Abell planned to visit her, Lincoln asked Elizabeth to tell Mary "that I think she was a great fool because she did not stay here and marry me." That was "characteristic of the man," Mary wrote to William H. Herndon in later life.[9]

A Springfield woman who also regarded Lincoln as tactless was

Rosanna Schmink. She consented to go to a "wool picking" with him, but he failed to provide her with a horse. She had to ride on the same horse with Lincoln—something that proud Southern girls did not do. It was the last time she went anyplace with Lincoln.[10]

The closest friend Lincoln ever had was Joshua Speed, a well-educated, wealthy Kentuckian with dark curly hair and an air of elegance. Five years younger than Lincoln, he was a handsome man who was well liked by Springfield ladies. They first met when Lincoln walked into Speed's general store shortly after arriving in Springfield. Lincoln said he wanted to buy furniture, mattresses, sheets, and blankets for a single bed. Speed calculated the cost at seventeen dollars. Lincoln said that was perhaps cheap enough, but small as the sum was, he was unable to pay it. "But," Lincoln said, "if you will credit me until Christmas and my experiment here as a lawyer is a success, I will pay you then. If I fail in that, I will probably never pay you at all."[11]

Speed recalled that "the tone of his voice was so melancholy that I felt for him. I looked up at him and I thought then, as I think now, that I never saw so gloomy and melancholy a face in my life. I said to him, 'So small a debt seems to affect you so deeply, I think I can suggest a plan by which you will be able to attain your end without incurring any debt. I have a very large room and a very large double bed in it, which you are perfectly welcome to share with me if you choose.'" "Where is the room?" Lincoln asked. "Upstairs," said Speed, pointing to the stairs leading from the store to the room. Without saying a word Lincoln took his saddlebags on his arm, went upstairs, set them down on

Joshua Speed was Lincoln's most intimate male friend. They counseled each other on matters of the heart and competed with each other for the love of Matilda Edwards. AUTHOR'S COLLECTION.

the floor, came down again, and with a face beaming with pleasure and smiles, exclaimed, "Well, Speed, I'm moved." For the next four years they shared the bed—it was customary for two or three men to sleep in the same bed—and they also shared their innermost thoughts. Lincoln apparently was not charged any rent.[12]

They organized a private literary society of young men of Springfield. It met around the fireplace in their room, where they read spicy poems and amusing papers they had written. One of Lincoln's creations reflected his sense of injustice about seduction and the double standard applied to extramarital sex—considered immoral for both sexes, but doubly shameful for women. Lincoln wrote: "Whatever Spiteful fools may say / Each jealous, ranting yelper / No woman ever went astray / Without a man to help her."[13]

"Lincoln and Speed were quite familiar with the women," wrote Lincoln's law partner William H. Herndon. "I cannot tell you what I know, especially in ink. Speed was a lady's man in a good and true sense. Lincoln only went to see a few women of the first class, women of sense. Fools ridiculed him; he was on this point tender footed. Lincoln was unsure of himself in his encounters with young, fashionable women of the class he aspired to," Herndon said. Consequently, "Lincoln wasn't much for society," one Springfield woman noticed. "I don't think he [was] bashful. He was never embarrassed, and he seemed to enjoy the ladies' company. But he didn't go out much, as some young men did." He knew that women saw him as homely, simple, peculiar, and para-doxical—as a man who drifted from funny street-corner stories to a granite-like calm. They did not realize his long-silent reveries stemmed from the tragic loss of one he dearly loved, a loss that made it all the more difficult for him to ever love again because he associated deep love with untimely death and personal grief.[14]

Not having a way with women of society but reportedly endowed with a strong sexual appetite, Lincoln apparently sought other out-lets. In the fall of 1839, he learned that Speed was "keeping a pretty woman" in Springfield. "Speed, do you know where I can get [some-one like her]?" Lincoln inquired. "Yes, I do," replied Speed, "I will send you to the place with a note. You cannot see her without a note or by my appearance." Speed wrote the note, and Lincoln took it and went to see the woman. Before anything happened Lincoln asked how much she charged. "Five dollars," she replied. "I only have three dollars," he said regretfully. She said she would trust him for the two dollars. Lincoln thought a moment and said, "I do not wish to go on credit. I'm poor, and I don't know where my next dollar will come from, and I cannot afford to cheat you." After some words of encouragement from the girl, Lincoln got out of bed, buttoned up his pants, and offered the girl three dollars for her time, but she would not take it. She said: "Mr. Lincoln, you are the most conscientious man I ever saw." Lincoln bid the girl good-bye. Speed asked him no questions about the evening, but she later told Speed what was said and done.[15]

In an escapade back in 1835 or 1836, several months after Ann's death, Lincoln reportedly feared he had contracted syphilis from a woman, presumably a prostitute, "during a devilish passion" in Beardstown, Illinois. Lincoln was in Beardstown to help a fellow Whig promote the Beardstown canal and gain a charter for the developer. Lincoln invested in it himself. Lincoln may not actually have had syphilis, but he was concerned about the possibility. The disease—and the fear of having it—was widespread in Illinois in the 1830s, partly because of the army's presence and the easily found houses of prostitution.[16]

Four years later, in December 1840 or January 1841, Lincoln wrote to one of the nation's most distinguished physicians, Dr. Daniel Drake of Cincinnati. Lincoln read most of the letter to Joshua Speed. It dealt with Lincoln's hypochondria. But Speed said that "there was a part of the letter he would not read." It could have been about the syphilis question. Speed said he remembered Dr. Drake's reply, "which was that he would not undertake to prescribe for him without a personal interview."[17]

Dr. Anson Henry of Springfield probably referred Lincoln to Dr. Drake. Dr. Henry later said Lincoln told him things he said he had never discussed with anyone else. Whatever those things were, they would remain confidential forever. Dr. Henry drowned in a shipwreck off the California coast in 1865.[18]

Wearing his black stovepipe hat, a "boiled" shirt, baggy trousers, and a wrinkled black satin waistcoat, Lincoln knocked on the front door of one of Springfield's most luxurious mansions—the hilltop home of Ninian and Elizabeth Todd Edwards. Ninian, a state legislator, was the son of Illinois's first territorial governor. He was famous as "a fashion plate in black broadcloth, with a gold-headed cane" and known as an aristocrat who "hated democracy . . . as the devil is said to hate holy water." His stunning young wife was the queen of the social elite, arranging outings, teas, games, and dances for Springfield society—a roster of the brightest young men that any state could produce, men whose names hold a prominent place in history, as well as a galaxy of beautiful, intelligent young women.[19]

Lincoln, then thirty, was invited to the Edwards's exclusive soirees because he was the undisputed leader of the Whigs in the Illinois General Assembly, having been reelected in 1836 and 1838 and chosen as a presidential elector at the Whig convention in October 1839. He was also an up-and-coming Springfield lawyer. This gathering in December 1839 celebrated the first session of the state legislature to be held in Springfield, the capital having been moved from Vandalia through Lincoln's leadership.

Another regular guest was Elizabeth Edwards's youngest sister, Mary Todd, twenty-one, who had moved into their home in the fall of 1839. "Come out and make our home your home," Elizabeth had written to Mary, whose constant quarrels with her stepmother in Lexington, Kentucky, necessitated a change. In Springfield Mary enchanted everyone with her engaging personality, graceful demeanor, and cultivated chatter. She was "capable of making herself quite attractive to young gentlemen," a friend remembered.[20]

Lincoln took off his hat as Elizabeth opened the front

Mary Todd, at age twenty, was painted by her niece Katharine Helm. AUTHOR'S COLLECTION.

door. She had grown accustomed to his appearance and welcomed him warmly. Escorting him into the parlor, where other guests were assembled, she introduced him to Mary Todd. Wearing a pink organdy and lace gown cut low at the neck, with the skirt fluffed out in a slightly balloonish hoop, Mary was about thirteen inches shorter than Lincoln and almost ten years younger. Her vivid blue eyes sparkled from underneath a mass of soft brown hair. Her complexion—always lovely—contrasted vividly with Lincoln's weather-beaten face.[21]

Soon the guests were dancing, and Lincoln, shy and nervous, allegedly said to Mary: "Miss Todd, I want to dance with you the worst way." She accepted and later joked about his lack of dancing skills. "Worst, indeed," she later commented—he could not dance a lick. Later, as Ninian Edwards watched his sister-in-law mimic Lincoln dancing the Virginia Reel, he whispered, "Mary could make a bishop forget his prayers."

Mary had mastered ballroom dances in private boarding schools, where students conversed only in French. Her hometown of Lexington was called the "Athens of America" and celebrated for its culture and refinement. There, she was pampered by her parents and their slaves. Yet this belle of the aristocracy seemed charmed by her new acquaintance of log-cabin origin. So when Lincoln asked if he might call on her the following evening, she responded affirmatively.

On that occasion they sat on a horsehair couch in the Edwards's parlor and talked about politics and poetry—two common interests of two otherwise opposite persons from very different social, financial, and educational planes. Both had lost mothers at an early age, Mary's mother having died when Mary was six. Her father was an eminent Whig banker who had served in both houses of the Kentucky legislature. He remarried and had nine more children. While Lincoln loved his stepmother, Mary hated hers. Growing up Mary felt lost in the crowd of children, and when she could not cope, she threw temper tantrums and wept uncontrollably. Once, Mary put salt in her stepmother's coffee, and her stepmother called her "a limb of Satan."

Now, in Springfield, she was the picture of culture and refinement, and she smiled and talked to the tall politician seated beside her. In fact Mary dominated their conversations. Lincoln listened and gazed at her, intrigued by her turned-up nose and dazzled by her wit and intelligence and her outspoken views on almost any topic. To him, she was "a very creature of excitement."[22]

Mary thought Lincoln had "the most congenial mind she had ever met." Both were fans of Robert Burns; both were Whigs; and both were fond of reciting poetry. Mary could recite "page after page of classic poetry, and liked nothing better." Further, Mary had known Lincoln's ideal statesman, Henry Clay, from childhood and as a family friend. "He was the handsomest man in Lexington," she said. Mary's acquaintance with Clay impressed Lincoln, as did Mary's relationship to other Whig leaders—first cousin and U.S. Congressman John T. Stuart, also Lincoln's law partner; cousin Stephen T. Logan, an elected circuit judge; and still another cousin, Jacksonville legislator John J. Hardin.[23]

Mary was politically astute and would take an active role in the presidential campaign of 1840—the rowdiest, noisiest one in the nation's history up to that time. It was between the incumbent Democrat Martin Van Buren, who allegedly was an aristocrat who ate his meals from gold plates, and his Whig opponent and eventual winner Old Tippecanoe, William Henry Harrison—the poor man's friend, the farmer's champion, and the hard-cider candidate, although in reality he was born in a plantation mansion to a signer of the Declaration of Independence. Women across the nation supported Harrison. They rode on floats, distributed pamphlets, and stood on balconies, waving handkerchiefs and banners and exhibiting flags and garlands. Vice President Richard Johnson claimed to be shocked to see ladies "wearing ribbons across their breasts with two names printed on them." Johnson, who reportedly lived "in sin" with a black woman, admonished ministers of the gospel for showing up at Harrison rallies sponsored by women.[24]

Politics was very much on Lincoln's mind too. He was the Whig floor leader in the state legislature; he was running for re-election; he had accepted new responsibilities for organizing Whigs across the state; and he was a leader of the Young Whigs, who held running debates with the Young Democrats, led by Stephen A. Douglas. Lincoln was also on the legal circuit, attending to legal duties in the Illinois Supreme Court and the Sangamon Circuit Court, where he had more than fifty cases. So while Lincoln and Mary were attracted to each other, they could not have actively courted over the course of a year—contrary to the standard account of their relationship. Their schedules kept them apart, and no record exists of a courtship in progress during the next seven or eight months. In fact from the first of April until the November election, Lincoln was out of town at least half the time, including two weeks in April and nearly all of May.[25]

Mary Todd left Springfield in early June to visit relatives in Missouri. She did not return until mid-September. Her correspondence with her closest friends offered no evidence of a romance-in-progress. On August 18, Lincoln went on an extended speaking trip. He stumped all the middle and lower part of the state, traveling from the Wabash to the Mississippi. He was not back in Springfield until late September. A few days later he was off again—for six weeks, until November 2—to represent his legal clients on the circuit. Thus, Mary and Lincoln could not have seen each other from sometime in June until he returned in September and, then, just briefly.[26]

Further, in late November Mary was entertaining the attentions of Joseph Gillespie, the traveling companion of an Illinois legislator. Surely she would not have done so had she been romantically attached to Lincoln. Joshua Speed later reported that during the latter part of Lincoln's August-September trip, he did, indeed, make romantic overtures to Mary by mail, and she is said to have responded eagerly. As the mail heated up, it sparked a love affair—one with no face-to-face encounters. Apparently, they reached an "understanding" by mail. She regarded it as a commitment. But an engagement was never announced, and only Mary and her family referred to it as such. No one else was aware of it.[27]

Upon his return, Lincoln had only a couple of days before leaving for his legal travels. He did see Mary briefly then, but he saw a person physically different from the person he had met the previous winter. In Missouri Mary had gained considerable weight. A friend wrote in jest: "Verily, I believe the further West a young lady goes the better her health becomes. If she comes here she is sure to grow—if she visits Missouri she will soon grow out of our recollection and if she should visit the Rocky Mountains I know not what would become of her." It must have reminded Lincoln of Mary Owens's similar weight problem.[28]

While away through October until early November, Lincoln apparently developed second thoughts about his relationship with Mary Todd. Had he moved too quickly in expressing his love for her? Had he been tricked? Within days of Lincoln's return to Springfield in November, he realized he had made a mistake. It hit him around November 15, as legislators began arriving for the special session. Among them was a prominent Whig politician, Cyrus Edwards of Alton. With him was his strikingly beautiful eighteen-year-old daughter, Matilda, a poised and polished student of the fashionable Monticello Female Seminary near Alton. She would lodge for the winter with her cousins, Ninian and Elizabeth Todd Edwards—the same place Mary Todd stayed. They were probably bedmates. Ready for the social season, they had filled their closets with new dresses and "many party frocks."[29]

At a party in honor of legislators, Lincoln met the tall, blond newcomer and was instantly "in love" or, at least, totally infatuated with her. He said if he had it in his power, he would not alter any feature in her face. "She is perfect!" His moments with Matilda confirmed his ever-present doubts: he did not love Mary Todd! And even more startling, he loved Matilda! Now he wondered how he could get out of the relationship with Mary. He asked his roommate, Joshua Speed, for help. Having started the affair with Mary by mail, Lincoln resolved to end it the same way. He handed Speed a letter he planned to send to Mary. In it he stated his feelings, telling her he had thought the matter over with great deliberation and felt he did not love her sufficiently to warrant her marrying him. "Speed, I want you to deliver this letter." Speed read it and shook his head. "No, let's think about it," Speed warned. "It would give her an advantage. Words are forgotten in a private conversation, but once put in writing they stand as an eternal monument against you." "Speed, I always knew you were obstinate," Lincoln said icily. "If you won't deliver it, I'll get someone else to do it." Speed frowned, threw the letter in the fire, and then admonished Lincoln: "Now if you have the courage of manhood, go see Mary yourself; tell her, if you do not love her, the facts, and that you will not marry her. Be careful not to say too much, and then leave at your earliest opportunity."[30]

Lincoln bristled, buttoned his coat, and walked to the Edwards's mansion. After a few pleasantries, Lincoln became startlingly blunt. He told Mary he did not love her and wanted to be released from his "commit-ment." She gasped and burst into tears while wringing her hands as if in agony. "The deceiver [has been] deceived, woe is me," she cried, alluding to the man she had been attentive to in recent weeks to make Lincoln jealous. The scene was too much for

Political enemies Stephen A. Douglas and Abraham Lincoln were rivals for the affection of Mary Todd. COURTESY OF LLOYD OSTENDORF.

Lincoln, and tears trickled down his own cheeks. He held her in his arms, kissed her, and then parted, doubtful that his mission had been accomplished.[31]

Lincoln reported the meeting to Speed. "And that's how you broke the engagement," sneered Speed. "You kissed her! That was 'a bad lick.' You not only acted the fool, but your conduct was tantamount to a renewal of the engagement, and in decency you cannot back down now." "Well," drawled Lincoln, "if I am in again, so be it."[32]

With the social season at its height, Lincoln persisted in being seen with Matilda Edwards. A well-placed observer said Lincoln "couldn't bear to leave Miss Edwards' side." "He was deeply in love with her," said Mrs. Benjamin S. Edwards, Ninian's sister-in-law. Some of Lincoln's friends thought he was acting wrongly and imprudently and told him so.[33]

Not to be outdone, Mary cavorted and danced with other "mar-riageable gentlemen," especially Stephen A. Douglas, the state's leading Democrat, with whom she was flirting boldly and conspicuously, some-times looking over her shoulder to see Lincoln's reaction. But he was not looking at her. He was talking to Matilda. Mary's companion, Stephen

Douglas—barely five-foot-four—was called the "Little Giant" because his power belied his size. He promenaded the streets arm-in-arm with Mary—frequently passing Lincoln—and in every way made plain his intention to become Lincoln's rival. It apparently was Mary's courtship strategy to play one suitor against another. "She was the most ambitious woman I ever knew," her sister said later, and "Mary often contended that she was destined to be the wife of some future president. . . . She loved pomp and power."[34]

Just before the close of the special legislative session, December 5, Lincoln forced a second encounter with Mary. He expressed, in no uncertain terms, his concern about her flagrant attentions to other suitors, and he again asserted that he did not love her and that he wanted out of the relationship. With her world reeling, Mary attacked him for his interest in Matilda and for "behaving dishonorably." "I know you love her," she scathingly remarked. "[But] you are honor-bound to marry me . . . honor-bound!" Her angry charge cut Lincoln like a Damascus blade. He left. Fifteen months would pass before he would call on her again. The breakup was now official. But it and other stresses in Lincoln's life plummeted him into a brief but painful breakdown. He had endured a solid year of hard campaigning; he had traveled dirt roads on horseback in all kinds of weather; and he had given stump speeches almost daily, sometimes to hostile crowds.[35]

Despite all his efforts, the year of 1840 was politically painful for him. Democrats maintained control of the Illinois legislature, and in Sangamon County he barely won reelection for a fourth term, placing last of five Whigs sent to the House. It was his worst political showing since his first race in 1832. Further, in July he had received the first public chastisement of his career. In a speech on July 20, a well-connected young lawyer and politician, Jesse B. Thomas Jr., called Lincoln and his associates to task for a political dirty trick—attributing a letter to him that they had written themselves. Lincoln replied with a relentless assault.

"He imitated Thomas in gesture and voice," Herndon later reported, "at times caricaturing his walk and the very motion of his body. Thomas, like everybody else, had some peculiarities of expression and gesture, and these Lincoln succeeded in rendering more prominent than ever. The crowd yelled and cheered as he continued. Encouraged by these demonstrations, the ludicrous features of the speaker's perform-ance gave way to intense and scathing ridicule." Thomas, a former cir-cuit judge, broke down, cried, and fled the platform. Lincoln's assault became known as "the skinning of Thomas." It surprised even Lincoln's closest friends. While he had made fun of antagonists in writ-ten material, it was totally unlike him to personally abuse them on the platform. The *Illinois State Register* criticized him editorially for his "game of buffoonery" and "an assumed clownishness in his manner that does not become him, and which does not truly belong to him. . . . We seriously advise Mr. Lincoln to correct his clownish fault before it grows on him." Lincoln, too, realized he had gone too far, and he hunted up Thomas and apologized to him.[36]

The final political blow of the year came during the special legisla-tive session in December to deal with the skyrocketing state debt—a debt built by internal improvements bills Lincoln and his fellow Whigs had put through in 1837. The public works program was halted, and unfinished projects such as railroads were canceled. Lincoln was devastated. Finally, on the session's last day, December 5, the Whigs sought, unsuccessfully, to block an anti-bank measure by staying away to prevent a quorum. Only a handful of Whigs showed up. To their surprise, a quorum was achieved, and then the doors were barred to keep anyone from leaving. Lincoln and two other Whigs quickly raised a window and jumped out. It was to no avail. The state bank was dissolved.[37]

Lincoln's nerves were frazzled. Enough was enough. He rested several days, returned for the legislature's general session, and continued to see Matilda, who showed no mercy to Mary. She declared that if Mary could not keep her lover, she need not expect any help from other girls. So Mary found an older man. On December 15, Mary wrote to her best friend and closest confidante, Mercy Levering, without mentioning Lincoln. She referred to her "present companion, a congenial spirit." Later in the letter she identified him: "Mr. [Edwin B.] Webb, a widower of modest merit, is [my] principal lion, dancing [with me frequently]." Webb was twenty years older than Mary and had two children Mary referred to as those "two sweet little objections." Mary's letter to Mercy continued: "You would be pleased with Matilda Edwards, a lovelier girl I never saw. Mr. Speed's ever-changing heart . . . is offering [his] young affections at her shrine, with some others." The "others," according to various informants and witnesses, included Lincoln. Mary also referred to a prospective late-December outing: "We have a pleasant jaunt, in contemplation, to Jacksonville next week, there to spend a day or two. Mr. Hardin & Mr. Browning [married men] are our leaders [chaperones], the van brought up by Miss Edwards, my humble self, Webb, Lincoln, and two or three others whom you know not."[38]

Since Webb's attention would obviously be directed toward Mary, she apparently assumes the prospective pairing of Lincoln and Matilda. The letter, however, named Speed as a contender for Matilda's love—Speed was the most prosperous young bachelor in Springfield. Thus Lincoln had a double predicament. He was desperately trying to free himself from Mary Todd so that he could profess his love to Matilda Edwards. But his best friend, Joshua Speed, was observed offering his own affections to Matilda. Lincoln's knowledge of it in December 1840 undoubtedly sidetracked him and kept him from addressing Matilda romantically. What a revolting development this must have been for Lincoln. His best friend was his rival for the girl he loved.[39]

Speed's "ever-changing" heart was also flirting with sixteen-year-old Sarah Rickard. But on January 1, 1841, he apparently does an "unknown something" that infuriates Sarah and ends their relationship. Perhaps they had a repeat performance of the Lincoln-Todd encounter, with Speed declaring his love for Matilda. The situation was so explosive that in later years, Speed had all references to Sarah erased from letters he forwarded to historian William H. Herndon. Showing an obvious concern about Sarah's unhappiness, Speed wrote to her brother-in-law, William Butler, that "[I am] much happier than I deserve to be." With Sarah out of the picture, Speed professed his love to Matilda and asked her to marry him. She turned him down. Possibly, both events occurred on the same date—January 1, 1841.[40]

Lincoln, meanwhile, apparently had a quiet New Year's Day, contrary to views shared by many historians that he was supposed to have been married on that date, but didn't show up. That opinion was based on comments made by Elizabeth Edwards at age 75, five years before her death. She told interviewer Jesse W. Weik that wedding arrangements had been made, "but Lincoln failed to appear" and "Mary was greatly mortified." Ninian Edwards, however, disagreed with his wife's recollection. "No such thing had ever taken place," he told Judge Broadwell, who shared the comment with Mrs. John T. Stuart, who, in turn, told journalist Ida M. Tarbell. Mrs. Benjamin S. Edwards, a member of the family circle, agreed. Further, after extensive study historian Douglas L. Wilson found "no signs of anything unusual" in Lincoln's life on January 1, 1841. He said there was evidence to suggest that Mary Todd was not even in Springfield on that date. However, something on that date prompted Lincoln to refer to it as "that fatal first of January" in his correspondence with Speed. If the aborted wedding ceremony never occurred, as now appears to be the case—based on the known sequence of events in the Lincoln-Todd relationship—then that fateful "something" probably related not to Lincoln's life but to developments in Speed's life—possibly Speed's rejection by Sarah Rickard and/or Matilda Edwards.[41]

Whatever happened, Speed disposed of his business interests on the very same day—January 1, 1841. He would return to his family home in Louisville that spring. "I endeavor to persuade myself there is more pleasure in pursuit of an object than there is in its possession," Speed wrote to his younger sister. "This rule I wish now to most particularly apply to women. I have been most anxiously in pursuit of one—and from all present appearances . . . I may have as much of the anticipation and pursuit as I please, but the possession I can hardly ever hope to realize."[42]

By terminating his partnership in James Bell and Company, Speed was also ending his long-time living arrangement with Lincoln in the large room over the store—a room where they and their friends had gathered by the fireplace on winter nights to tell stories and anecdotes. Lincoln would sorely miss these associations while surely having mixed feelings about Speed as a rival for Matilda.

Just when Lincoln thought he had Matilda to himself, he proposed to her, and she rejected him, according to Orville H. Browning, a well-educated Whig legislator and friend of Lincoln. Matilda, as it turned out, was not seriously interested in any Springfield beaux. She was having fun playing the field. A pious woman, she is said to have rejected Stephen A. Douglas because of "bad morals" (something Mary Todd never complained about in her relationship with him). Matilda did not really dislike Lincoln. He was just a little fling.[43]

Lincoln was crushed. He had loved and lost and was discarded abruptly like an old rag. He collapsed. One acquaintance said he had thrown "two cat fits and a duck fit." It was January 13, 1841, and he went into seclusion for a week at the home of Mr. and Mrs. William Butler, where he boarded. He lay there, shrouded in gloom, unable to sleep, tossing and turning every night as winter storms pelted the window with snow and freezing rain. He ventured out only to vote once in the legislature and to see his physician, Dr. Anson Henry. Hypochondria was the doctor's diagnosis, brought on by extreme anxiety, overwork, and exhaustion.[44]

Dr. Henry, concerned about Lincoln's debilitating condition, encouraged Mary to write him an official letter of release, thinking she might be partly responsible. She finally did so, but added: "I have not changed my mind, but feel as always." Mrs. Butler, who helped care for Lincoln, went into his room on January 17, closed the door, and walking over to his bed, said: "Now, Abraham, what is the matter? Tell me all about it." He did. Mrs. Butler's sister Sarah Rickard (Speed's former girlfriend) later told a reporter: "Suffering under the thought that he had treated Mary badly, knowing that she loved him and that he did not love her, Mr. Lincoln was wearing his very life away in an agony of remorse. He made no excuse for breaking with Mary, but said, sadly, to my sister: 'Mrs. Butler, it would just kill me to marry Mary Todd.'"[45]

Aside from his feelings toward Mary, he resented the Edwards's perception of him as a gangly, quirky country bumpkin no longer welcome in their home, a person no longer suitable for a lady from the proud and educated Todd family. Commenting on the two *d*s in the Todd name, Lincoln said, "One *d* is enough for God, but the Todds need two." On January 23 Lincoln wrote to his law partner, John Todd Stuart: "I am now the most miserable man living. If what I feel were equally distributed to the whole human family, there would not be one cheerful face on the earth. Whether I shall ever be better I can not tell; I awfully forebode I shall not. To remain as I am is impossible; I must die or be better, it appears to me."[46]

Lincoln's friend Orville H. Browning lodged at the Butlers. He had spoken often to Mary. He made this judgment: "I think that Mr. Lincoln's aberration of mind resulted entirely from the situation he thus got himself into—he was engaged to Miss Todd, and in love with Miss Edwards, and his conscience troubled him dreadfully for the supposed injustice he had done, and the supposed violation of his word which he had committed." Mary's good friend Mercy Levering, who was kept well-informed, wrote to her future spouse, James Conkling, on January 24: "Poor Lincoln! How are the mighty fallen! He was confined about a week, but though he now appears again he is reduced and emaciated in appearance and seems scarcely to possess enough strength to speak above a whisper. His case is truly deplorable. . . . He can declare 'That loving is a painful thrill, and not to love more painful still' [referring to his breakup with Mary Todd]. . . . He has experienced 'That surely 'tis the worst of pain to love and not to be loved again' [an obvious reference to his romance with Matilda]. . . . And Joshua [Speed] too is about to leave."[47]

Three days later another letter shared similar sentiments. This one was from Jane Bell, who was related by marriage to Speed's business partner, James Bell. Part of the Springfield "in crowd," she wrote to Ann Bell of Danville, Kentucky: "Miss Todd is flourishing largely. She has a great many beaus. You ask me how she and Mr. Lincoln are getting along. Poor fellow, he is in a bad way. . . . He is on the mend now. . . . The doctors say he came within an inch of being a perfect lunatic for life. . . . It seems he had addressed Mary Todd and she accepted him and they had been engaged some time when a Miss Edwards of Alton came here, and he fell desperately in love with her and found he was not so much attracted to Mary as he thought."[48]

Mrs. Ninian Edwards, furious with Lincoln for hurting her sister's feelings, said he was grieving over making Mary unhappy. But Mr. Edwards had a different theory: Lincoln loved Matilda, he said, and his conflicts of love and honor made him "crazy as a loon." For several months, Lincoln moped and coped, dropping out of social circles while attending legislative proceedings in Springfield and venturing into a new law partnership with the town's most knowledgeable practitioner, Stephen T. Logan. If Mary was upset, she did not show it. She socialized gaily and flirted and accepted the attentions of other men. The correspondence between lovers Mercy Levering and James Conkling continued with the following note from James to Mercy on

March 7, 1841: "The Legislature has dispersed. . . . Miss Todd and her cousin Miss [Matilda] Edwards seemed to form the grand center of attraction. Swarms of strangers . . . hovered around them, to catch a passing smile. By the way, I do not think they were received, with even ordinary attention, if they did not obtain a broad grin or an obstreperous laugh. And Lincoln, poor hapless simple swain who loved most true but was not loved again—I suppose he will now endeavor to drown his cares among the intricacies and perplexities of the law."[49]

In Springfield eligible bachelors outnumbered marriageable young ladies by ten to one. Mary and Matilda were obviously making the rounds, and Mary, who previously "had very bitter feelings toward her rival," now seemed less resentful. As Lincoln sulked and Mary seethed privately, Matilda ended her one-year social swirl in Springfield in the autumn of 1841. It was said that she broke more hearts, male and female, than any other girl in Springfield's history. "Well," she reportedly said, "if the young men liked me, it is of no fault of mine!"[50]

Waiting for her in Alton was handsome, straight-laced Newton Strong, a Connecticut Yankee and Phi Beta Kappa graduate of Yale University. He had come to the bustling town on the banks of the Mississippi in 1839 to begin his professional career as a law partner to his college roommate Junius Hall. Strong, who met Matilda just before her departure to Springfield, was overjoyed when she returned to Alton unattached. He had learned of her flirtations from Springfield attorneys, including Lincoln himself. Strong and Lincoln argued various cases before the Illinois Supreme Court, sometimes on opposite sides, at other times jointly representing a client. Good friends, Strong even nominated Lincoln for governor in 1841. Both were Whigs and of the same age. Matilda, however, was not easy to win over. It took Strong three years to convince her to marry him. When asked why she married such "an old Buck" (he was thirty-four, she was twenty-two), she said, "he has lots of horses and gold."[51]

Meanwhile, back in Springfield in 1841, the legislature's adjournment marked the end of Lincoln's legislative career. He was not renominated, but he did not seem to care. He preferred to practice law. In early August Lincoln accepted Speed's invitation to visit him for several weeks at his stately family mansion, Farmington, near Louisville.

Their common failure to gain Matilda's love appeared to strengthen their own relationship. In Kentucky Lincoln experienced a life of leisure and luxury he had never known. He occupied an elegant room and was assigned his own servant from among the plantation's slaves. Speed's mother, whose family had been Thomas Jefferson's neighbors in Virginia, gave him an Oxford Bible and scrumptious dishes of peaches and cream to accelerate his emotional convalescence.[52]

Long walks with Speed and romps with his half-sister, Mary, regenerated Lincoln's mind and soul. He playfully locked Mary in a room to keep her "from committing assault and battery on me!" He later wrote her a long, gracious letter saying they were "something of cronies" at Farmington and that he was "subsisting on savory memories." Lincoln improved gradually, day by day gaining strength and confidence in himself until at last the black cloud had lifted and passed away.[53]

Lincoln and Speed both possessed poetic tenderness and keen minds. Both also supported and were sympathetic to the other's anxieties and decision-making hurdles. They shared their innermost thoughts. During Lincoln's visit Speed courted and proposed to beautiful, vivacious Fanny Henning, who lived on a nearby farm. Fanny accepted. Lincoln was partly responsible. He distracted Fanny's guardian-uncle so Speed could pop the question. Then Speed, like Lincoln, was consumed with self-doubt. Their roles reversed, and Lincoln counseled Speed on matters of the heart.[54]

Speed accompanied Lincoln back to Springfield and then returned to Kentucky in January 1842. He and Lincoln exchanged personal letters. Lincoln asked: "Are you afraid you don't love her enough? What nonsense! Remember . . . that you love her as ardently as you are capable of loving." Everybody worries about marriage, Lincoln said, but "you are naturally of a nervous temperament." In time, that feeling will go away, he counseled, if you "avoid bad weather," which "my experience clearly proves to be very severe on defective nerves. . . . In two or three months . . . you will be the happiest of men." Speed finally relented and married Fanny on February 15, 1842. Upon hearing the news, Lincoln wrote Speed: "I have no way of telling you how much happiness I wish you both. I feel somewhat jealous of you both now." Then Speed notified Lincoln that he was "far happier than I ever expected to be." Lincoln responded in a letter dated March 27: "It now thrills me with joy [to learn of your happiness]. . . . Your last letter gave me more pleasure than the total sum of all I have enjoyed since that fatal first of January, '41."[55]

Lincoln noted he had seen Sarah Rickard "and am fully convinced she is far happier now than she has been for the last fifteen months past" (which would date her unhappiness back to early January 1841). Lincoln said he "should [be] entirely happy, but for the never-absent idea, that there is one still unhappy whom I have contributed to make so. That still kills my soul. I can not but reproach myself, for even wishing to be happy while she is otherwise." He, of course, was referring to Mary Todd. Speed, again advising Lincoln, pleaded with him to either wed Mary or forget her. Lincoln agreed. "But before I resolve to do one thing or the other, I must regain my confidence in my own ability to keep my resolves when they are made. . . . I have not regained it; and until I do, I can not trust myself in any matter of much importance." Reasserting that destiny was controlled by a Higher Power, Lincoln wrote: "I believe God made me one of the instruments of bringing Fanny and you together, which union I have no doubt he had foreordained. Whatever he designs he will do for me yet. 'Stand still and see the salvation of the Lord' is my text just now."[56]

Meanwhile, politics monopolized Lincoln's mind in that summer and early fall of 1842. State Auditor James Shields, a Democrat, announced and enforced an unpopular order prohibiting the use of State Bank currency to pay state taxes. The currency was depressed because the bank was near collapse. The action was a political windfall for the Whigs, and a nightmare for Shields and the Democrats. A fictitious farm woman named Rebecca, from the "Lost Townships," entered the fray with a series of scurrilous letters in the *Sangamo Journal*. The first, published on August 19, was a relatively mild attempt at political humor. It was probably written by the editor. But the second letter was nasty enough to gag a buzzard. It attacked James Shields and the Democrats with a vengeance. Full of satire, political insults, and racy metaphors about married women in tight clothing, it lampooned the vain Irish bachelor and called him "a conceity dunce" and "a liar as well as a fool." Lincoln wrote the letter, but signed it "Rebecca."[57]

In one passage Lincoln drew upon Shields's reputation as a handsome man who fancied himself irresistible to women. The letter spoke of Shields "floatin' about on the air, without heft or earthly substance, just like a lock of cat fur where cats had been fightin'" and of the "sweet distress" he seemed to be in because he could not marry all the girls around him. "Too well I know how much you suffer," Shields exclaims in the parody, "but do, do remember it is not my fault that I am so handsome and so interesting."

More letters from Rebecca appeared in September, leaving Lincoln baffled. Someone else had written them. By now Shields was madder than a rained-on rooster. "I am the victim of slander, vituperation, and personal abuse," he complained. "Tell me the writer's name," he demanded of Editor Simeon Francis. Francis sought Lincoln's advice. Covering for the other writers, Lincoln replied, "Oh, just tell Shields I am responsible."[58]

As Lincoln later learned, three of the letters were from the pen of Mary Todd and her friend Julia Jayne, the daughter of a Springfield physician. Shields had squeezed Julia's hand, much to her dislike, at a party at the Edwards's mansion, and she and Mary took revenge by writing the letters. Unaware of their involvement, Shields blamed Lincoln and demanded "a full, positive, and absolute retraction of all offensive allusions" or suffer "consequences which no one will regret more than myself." When negotiations failed to resolve the conflict, Shields, an expert marksman, challenged Lincoln to a duel. As the man who was challenged, Lincoln could name the weapons and he chose "cavalry broadswords of the largest size"—weapons advantageous to him as a tall man with long arms. Shields was only five-foot-nine. "I did not want to kill Shields," Lincoln later told his friend Usher Linder. "[I] felt sure I could disarm him, having had about a month to learn the broadsword exercise; and furthermore, I did not want the darned fellow to kill me, which I rather think he would have done if I had selected pistols."[59]

On September 27 the parties proceeded a hundred miles to "Bloody Island" on the Missouri side of the Mississippi, duels being illegal in Illinois. Lincoln arrived first and killed time by trimming underbrush while humming "Yankee Doodle." Just as the duel was about to begin, Whig leader John J. Hardin (Mary Todd's cousin) and

Democrat Revel English showed up after a frantic two-day ride on horseback and offered to submit the case to impartial judges. Their plan was not followed, but it produced progress. Shields's friends, without his knowledge, declared his offending note withdrawn. Then Lincoln admitted writing "solely for political effect" with no intent of "injuring your personal or private character." Shields's supporters convinced him that the "apology" was sufficient, and all parties agreed to call the whole thing off. Major J. M. Lucas, a friend of Lincoln, said he had no doubt Lincoln meant to fight. Lincoln told him, "I did not intend to hurt Shields unless I did so clearly in self-defense. If it had been necessary, I could have split him from the crown of his head to the end of his backbone."[60]

Privately, Lincoln was ashamed. Guided as he was by unimpassioned reason, it was totally out of character for him to act on boisterous emotions. Mary, while touched by his chivalry, must have regretted her role in putting Lincoln's life on the line. Both of them agreed never to speak of it. When years later an Army officer teased Lincoln about fighting a duel "for the sake of the lady by your side," Lincoln's face flushed. "I do not deny it. But if you desire my friendship, you will never mention it again." Shields went on to become a Union general in the Civil War and the only person in American history to serve three different states in the U.S. Senate: first from Illinois, then from Minnesota, and finally from Missouri.[61]

Five days after the duel, John Hardin's sister Martinette, eighteen, married fellow Kentuckian Alexander McKee. Both Lincoln and Mary attended the ceremony but not together. Lincoln was with a young woman about half his age, eighteen-year-old Sarah Rickard, a close friend of Martinette and former sweetheart of Joshua Speed. Lincoln and Sarah had been seen together frequently.[62]

Six years earlier Lincoln met Sarah at the dining table in the home of her sister and brother-in-law, the William Butlers. Lincoln teased the young girl, then twelve, and grew fond of her. In a couple of years he started taking her to "little entertainments," including the first theater to play in Springfield. She liked him, too, but thought of him as a big brother and a friend of the family.[63]

When she was sixteen, he became even more attentive and teasingly proposed marriage, citing the Biblical Sarah becoming

Abraham's wife. Sarah considered herself too young to think much about matrimony. In later life she said, "I always liked him as a friend, but . . . his peculiar manner and his general deportment would not be likely to fascinate a young girl just entering the society world." She eventually married Richard F. Barret, son of a well-known Springfield family. She found him "much more graceful and attractive" than Mr. Lincoln.[64]

At the McKees' wedding dinner, Mary Todd sat directly across the table from Sarah and Lincoln. "They [Mary and Lincoln] spoke to each other [for the first time in months], and that was the beginning of the reconciliation," Sarah reported. Shortly thereafter, Mrs. Simeon Francis, wife of the editor of the *Sangamo Journal,* stepped in. She invited both Mary and Lincoln to a social affair without telling either about the other person coming. Once there, Mrs. Francis brought them together and advised, "Be friends again."[65]

John Hardin took a further step to unite the pair. He and his wife, Sarah, invited Mary and several other Springfield young people to Jacksonville for a visit. All but Mary were told to go for a carriage ride, and she was chagrined when they departed without her. Then, as if on cue, Lincoln drove up and asked for her. He said he had come to escort her to the party. She smiled triumphantly.[66]

Hardin, in just two months, had affected Lincoln's life dramatically. He had saved him from possible death in a duel, and he had lured him back into a relationship with Mary Todd. Mary, using every tactic at her disposal, had encouraged him to do so. A year younger than Lincoln, Hardin was one of the most admired men in Illinois. He served in the state legislature and would succeed John T. Stuart in Congress at the next election. Hardin seemed destined for greatness, possibly even the presidency. Tragically, his future ended with his death in the Mexican War in 1847. Had Hardin lived, Lincoln's political future might have taken a different course.

What definitely did change in the fall of 1842 was Lincoln's long and severe inner struggle. He could not live down his guilty feelings. He gave up. He would court Mary Todd, even if his heart was not in it. By doing so he would save his honor, but he would sacrifice his domestic happiness. So Lincoln proposed to Mary, and she was ecstatic.

Orville Browning, closely connected with both Mary and Lincoln,

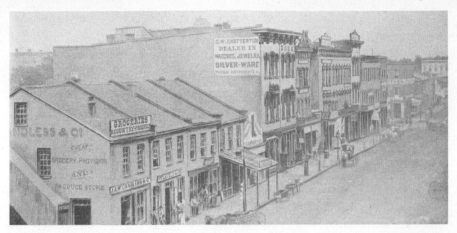

Springfield's west side of the town square in 1837 shows Chatterton's jewelry store where Lincoln later purchased Mary Todd's wedding ring. The Lincoln-Herndon law firm would be established in the same block. AUTHOR'S COLLECTION.

said, "There is no doubt of her exceeding anxiety to marry him." He added: "In this courtship, [Lincoln] undoubtedly felt that he had made [a mistake] in having engaged himself to Miss Todd. But having done so, he felt himself . . . honor-bound to act in perfect good faith towards her—and that good faith compelled him to fulfill his engagement with her, if she persisted in claiming the fulfillment of his word. . . . Had circumstances left him entirely free to act upon his own impulses, [I doubt] he would have voluntarily [proposed] to Miss Todd." Speed emphasized: "Lincoln [decided to marry] for honor—feeling his honor bound to her." Mary's cousin Elizabeth Grimsley cautiously acknowledged that Lincoln's feelings for Mary "had not the overmastering depth of an early love"—his love for Ann Rutledge.[67]

Mary apparently wanted to keep her engagement secret. Thus, if it did not work out, no one would know, and she would not be embarrassed. Further, she wanted to avoid a confrontation with her sister. Elizabeth Todd Edwards was angry with Lincoln and had bluntly told Mary that she and Lincoln "could not live happily as husband and wife." So Mary and Lincoln met secretly for about three weeks at the home of their friends, Simeon and Eliza Francis, who had no children and plenty of room for Mary and Lincoln to be together, alone and undisturbed.[68]

Granted, Mary may have wanted to keep it secret, but the ensuing chain of events seemed to carry secrecy far beyond what normal circumstances would dictate. Early on the morning of November 4, 1842, Lincoln dropped by the Reverend Charles Dresser's home. The Dresser family was eating breakfast when Lincoln reportedly announced, "I want to get hitched tonight." The surprised Episcopal minister checked his schedule and said he would be available. After stores opened, Lincoln dashed into Chatterton's jewelry shop and ordered a wide-band gold ring—perhaps according to Mary's instructions. It was to be inscribed: "A.L. To Mary, Nov. 4, 1842. Love is Eternal." At noon Lincoln visited James H. Matheny, a friend who was the son of the county clerk. "Jim, I shall have to marry that girl this evening. Will you be my best man?" Matheny agreed and thought that "Lincoln looked and acted as if he was going to the slaughter." Lincoln told Matheny he was "driven into the marriage." Mary Todd called on Julia Jayne, co-author of the "Lost Townships" letters, and asked her to be a bridesmaid. At about the same time, the couple's closest friends and relatives were notified, and Mary broke the news to her sister Elizabeth Edwards,

fueling the most memorable of the day's unforgettable exchanges. "How could you marry someone who humiliated you? He's white trash, a common person, a plebeian." But Mary would not back down. Elizabeth finally gave in but then attacked the timing: "You've only given me two-hours notice. I don't have time to prepare a suitable wedding feast. . . . I guess I'll have to send out for gingerbread and beer." "Well," Mary replied sarcastically, "that will be

Mary Todd Lincoln. LIBRARY OF CONGRESS.

good enough for plebeians, I suppose!" As Lincoln was dressing for the ceremony, his landlord's son asked him where he was going. Lincoln replied, "To hell, I suppose."[69]

On that cool November night, rain fell in torrents as Mary Todd, twenty-three, and Abraham Lincoln, thirty-three, exchanged marriage vows at the Edwards's mansion, with thirty friends attending. Among those present was Thomas C. Brown, a supreme court judge who tended to say what he thought without regard to place or surrounding. When Lincoln placed the ring on Mary's finger and said, "With this ring I thee endow with all my goods and chattels, lands and tenements," Brown blurted out, "God Almighty, Lincoln! The statute fixes that!" The flustered parson hastily pronounced them husband and wife.[70]

The newlyweds left to live in the Globe Tavern, a very ordinary Springfield boardinghouse that was a stopover for two stagecoach lines. They occupied a furnished second-floor room, eight by fourteen feet, and ate their meals in the common dining room. The total cost for room and board was four dollars a week. At bedtime, he would often go downstairs to fill a pitcher of water and then "sit on the steps of the porch and tell stories to whoever happened to be near." Mary would cough to signal that she wanted him; sometimes he "kept her coughing until midnight or after." One morning, in a rage, Mary flung hot coffee in his face. Another renter cleaned him up and treated the burns. A year later the Lincolns left the Globe and rented a three-room cottage.[71]

It is not known why the marriage announcement was so abrupt and the wedding so urgent. Perhaps they planned it that way to avoid opposition, or perhaps something significant occurred the night before to jar Lincoln and spur him into action. Mary was aggressive and determined to marry Lincoln. Did she lure him into bed, thereby forcing his commitment? Mary later admitted that during their courtship she had "trespassed, many times and oft, upon his great tenderness and amiability of character" and that she had used "all my friends and every art given to me."[72]

A week after the wedding, Lincoln wrote to a friend: "Nothing new here, except my marrying, which to me, is a matter of profound wonder." Indeed, it was profound. He had lost his one true love in New Salem. He had been rejected three times in Springfield—by Mary Owens, Matilda Edwards, and Sarah Rickard. He had agonized for months over the Todd situation. Then, suddenly, he had married Mary Todd.[73]

Their first son, Robert Todd Lincoln, was born on August 1, 1843, just three days short of nine months after the wedding. Lincoln later wrote to Speed: "[Robert] has a great deal of that sort of mischief that is the offspring of much animal spirits." Some historians insist he married to foster his political fortunes. Mary Todd was part of the Edwards-Stuart-Todd aristocracy. In marrying into this group, however, Lincoln had to constantly reassure his political base—the common people—that he was still one of them. His political opponents labeled him "the candidate of pride, wealth, and aristocratic family distinction"—a charge that prompted Lincoln to counter: "I am now and always shall be the same Abe Lincoln that I always was."[74]

Mary, on the other hand, soon felt she had tumbled from the aristocracy to the bourgeoisie or lower. Always afraid of poverty, she thought she was now experiencing it. Lincoln was still paying off his New Salem debts, so they had to pinch every penny. She had to cook, clean, and scrub—tasks slaves had done for her in the past. She believed her wealthy friends were snickering. It was a difficult time for this well-bred, sophisticated "creature of excitement."

9

"Lincoln's Wife Was a Hellion."

1844–61

By early 1844 Lincoln was earning a modest but respectable fifteen hundred to two thousand dollars a year from his law practice. From the Reverend Dresser, who had presided over their marriage, he purchased a one-and-a-half-story frame house in Springfield—with a stable and privies in back—for twelve hundred dollars. With a house of their own, the Lincolns could enjoy family life. Mary read reports and verse to him by lamplight, and on starry nights they sat on the porch and she pointed out planets and constellations. He chopped wood for the fireplace and stove, and she drew their water from a backyard pump and toted it into the house. She mended his clothes, sewed fine tucks in his shirts, and nagged him about his rumpled attire and untidy ways—sprawling around on the floor, wiping his mouth on his sleeves, and raking food from the meat plate with his knife. She was determined to improve his manners.

Coping with household chores, tending to baby Bobbie, making ends meet, and adjusting meals to Lincoln's irregular hours became more than Mary could handle. To get relief, she finally hired a maid, one of the lazy "wild Irish," as she called her. Even with help, Mary seemed overworked and exhausted. She suffered excruciating headaches that sent her to bed for days at a time, and she became anxious and had swift mood changes that were marked by vitriolic outbursts followed by dazzling charm and gaiety. The Lincoln-Todd "marriage of oppo-sites" was soon referred to by friends and acquaintances as "a state of mutual abuse," and their home was viewed by some as a suburb of Hades, where Mary served up steaming platefuls of invectives.[1]

The tongue-lashings that she dished out to maids, workmen, and her husband were widely discussed in Springfield. Turner R. King, register of the Springfield Land Office, said, "Lincoln's wife was a hellion—a she devil [who] vexed and harrowed the soul out of that good man [and] drove him from home, often and often." More than once Mary was seen chasing Lincoln from the house with a broom-stick. Once when he was half-dressed, their Irish house servant, Meg Ryan, brought him his clothes, and he dressed in the yard. He told Meg not to be scared, that Mrs. Lincoln would get over it. Another time Lincoln was observed fleeing out the door as Mary threw pota-toes at him. On other occasions she threw books. One Sunday morn-ing, Mary was observed chasing him through the yard with a knife. When Lincoln realized that passers-by were witnessing the scene, he abruptly wheeled on his wife and said, "You make the house intolerable, damn you, get out of it!"[2]

Servants were also harshly treated. When one threatened to leave unless her meager pay was raised by twenty-five cents to a $1.50 a week, Mary refused. "But Mother," Lincoln intoned, "I don't want her to leave. Pay the twenty-five cents. We can afford it." "No!" Mary defiantly resisted, "I won't do it!" Lincoln secretly told the servant, "Don't leave. Tell Mrs. Lincoln you've decided to stay, and I'll pay the extra twenty-five cents." Mary overheard them and stormed into the room: "What are you doing! I'm not going to be deceived. Miss, you can leave! And as for you, Mr. Lincoln, I'd be ashamed of myself!"[3]

With the rapid turnover of domestics, a friend of Lincoln, Jacob Taggart, volunteered his niece: "a fine girl, intelligent and industrious, who could satisfy anybody on earth." Mary hired her, and all went well for a while. Then one day, Mary insulted and slapped her, and she quit. Taggart went to see Mary and offered to make amends. "Mr. Taggart, how dare you bother me!" Mary raged. "You're a dirty vil-lain, a vile creature!" Then she struck him with a broom several times. Taggart looked up Lincoln in town. "You must punish your wife," he demanded. "She has insulted me and my niece. I demand an apology, and if I don't get it, I'll—" Lincoln interrupted, put his hand on Taggart's shoulder, and said mournfully: "Friend, can't you endure this one wrong done to you by a mad woman for our friendship's sake while I have had to bear it without complaint and without a murmur for lo these many years." Taggart immediately felt sorry for Lincoln, assured him of his continued friendship, shook hands, and left.[4]

On another day Mary angrily dismissed a servant boy and threw his suitcase out the window. Then she hired a woman to help two servants she already had—"but fired them all the next day." Her actions were consistent with two incidents reported by a local official, John B. Weber: "Once I heard a scream of 'Mr. Weber, Mr. Weber.' It was the voice of distress. I looked back and saw Mrs. Lincoln. She said, 'Keep this dog from biting me.' The dog was small and good natured and was doing nothing. . . . Another day I heard her scream, 'Murder! Murder! Murder!' and saw her up on the fence. I went to her. She said a big ferocious man had entered her home. I saw an umbrella man come out. I suppose he had entered to ask for old umbrellas to mend. He came out and said, 'Should be sorry to have such a wife.'"[5]

A neighbor, Elizabeth A. Capps, remembered that when Robert was a toddler, Mrs. Lincoln appeared in her front yard yelling, "Bobbie will die! Bobbie will die!" Elizabeth's father ran over to see what had happened. He found Bobbie "sitting by a lime box with a little lime in his mouth. He washed his mouth out, and "that's all there was to it." A political friend of Lincoln, Jesse K. Dubois, stopped by Lincoln's office early one morning just as he was leaving to go home with a package of meat for breakfast. "Walk with me, Jesse, we can talk on the way." Mary met them at the door, opened the package, and screamed at Lincoln: "You've brought the wrong kind of meat! I can't use this! I don't want this!" Then she struck Lincoln in the face. He wiped off the blood, motioned to Dubois, and they left.[6]

Vexed and harassed, Lincoln equipped his office with a six-and-a-half-foot-long couch and slept there on nights of domestic discord. He would often dine on cheese and crackers, rather than go home. Chased out of his home one morning, he took Bobbie to a restaurant. After they finished breakfast, Lincoln said: "Well, Bobbie, this ain't so bad after all, is it? If Ma don't conclude to let us come back, we will board here all summer."[7]

Turmoil often followed dinner parties. Mary would invite local aristocrats, but Lincoln would lead the men into a corner and swap stories until the party ended. After the guests left, Mary "would be as mad as a disturbed hornet," according to William H. Herndon, and would lecture Lincoln "all night, till he got up out of bed in despair and went whistling through the streets and alleys till daybreak." While Mary was hosting a party for society women one evening, Lincoln answered the door in his shirtsleeves. The two callers asked for Mary, and he told them he would "trot the women folks out." Mary cursed him when her guests departed, and he left the house until early the next morning.[8]

Sometimes he did not come home for days. One evening he dropped by a neighbor's house carrying "a prodigious carpet bag" and made a request: "Mary is having one of her spells, and I think I had better leave her for a few days. I didn't want to bother her, and I thought as you and I are about the same size, you might be kind enough to loan me one of your clean shirts! I have found that when Mrs. Lincoln gets one of these nervous spells, it is better for me to go away for a day or two." The postmaster reported a similar episode; Lincoln tarried at the post office one evening, swapping stories until eleven. "Well, I hate to go home," he finally admitted. "You can spend the night at my house, if you wish," Ellis offered, and Lincoln accepted.[9]

Mary's actions, regardless of their cause, were counter to the accepted rules for a wife's behavior in that period. Submissiveness, purity, and piety were expected. Mary's friend, Kentucky Sen. John Crittenden, advised his newlywed daughter accordingly: "I have never seen a wife who made her husband happy that was not happy herself. Remember this. Kindness and gentleness are the natural and proper means of the wife. There are wives who seek to rule, to make points with their husbands and complain—ay, scold. To love such a woman long is more than a mortal can do."

In 1844, Lincoln formed a law partnership with William H. Herndon. He was part of a small group of men whose company Lincoln enjoyed. They would sit around the potbellied stove at the drugstore, swap stories, and talk politics. "I don't like that man," Mary complained. "He's a drunkard, a 'dandy,' and a ladies' man.

Your partnership with him will be a disaster!" The partnership lasted twenty years—and was still in effect at the time of Lincoln's assassination—but Mary remained spiteful toward Herndon. Her hatred dated to 1837. As a visiting belle from Kentucky that year, she attended a ball at which Herndon asked her to dance. Intending to compliment her, he observed that she seemed to glide through the waltz "with the ease of a serpent." Mary, never known for a sense of humor, bristled at the reference to a serpent and stomped away.[10]

Lincoln covered his circuit by horseback or buggy for twenty years. He averaged a mile an hour in bad weather and thirty to forty miles a day in good weather. It got to the point where "he would refuse to go home," preferring weekends with tavern loungers to abuse from his wife. AUTHOR'S COLLECTION.

Matilda Edwards and Newton Strong reentered the Lincolns' life as newlyweds during the winter of 1844-45 with Strong's election to the legislature. They dined with the Lincolns and saw them at levees and soirees. Mary kept a close eye on twenty-three-year-old Matilda, not wanting to see her alone with Lincoln. From Mary's standpoint it was "good riddance" when the Strongs moved to Pennsylvania.

Lincoln rode the legal circuit in Illinois twice a year, traveling from courthouse to courthouse for three months in the spring and three months in the fall. His absences caused Mary to fret even though she knew it was financially necessary. While on the circuit he seldom wrote to her, and her letters to him were often more than a month apart. On weekends, other lawyers would go home, but Lincoln would often be away from home for as long as six weeks. In 1851, for instance, he was out of town from April 2 to June 4. Lincoln "would refuse to go home," said Illinois Judge David Davis. Lincoln preferred to spend his weekends with "tavern loungers."[11]

At a week's end on the circuit, Lincoln would join the "tavern loungers" and would frequently quote his favorite poem, "Mortality," by William Knox. He had learned it in New Salem and was said to have recited it often after Ann Rutledge's death. "I would give all I am worth, and go into debt," he would say, "to be able to write so fine a piece as I think that is." The fourth stanza may have reminded him of Ann: "The maid on whose brow, on whose cheek, on whose eye / Shone beauty and pleasure—her triumphs are by / And alike from the memory of the living erased / And the memory of mortals, who loved her and praised."[12]

Another poem Lincoln often recited, "The Last Leaf" by Oliver Wendell Holmes, may also have reminded him of Ann and her grave near New Salem: "The mossy marbles rest / On lips that he has pressed / In their bloom / And the names he loved to hear / Have been carved for many a year / On the tomb." According to Herndon, Lincoln would "recite it, praise it, laud it, and swear by it" and "tears would come unbidden to his eyes."[13]

Judge Davis, a powerful man who on the circuit shared more beds with Lincoln than any other judge, said, "Lincoln was a man of strong passion for women, but his conscience kept him from seduction. His [morals] saved many a woman." Lois Hillis, an itinerant performer with the Newhall Singers, was among the women who exhibited a special interest in Lincoln. She showed up in the country hotels on the circuit, and when she saw Lincoln, she greeted him warmly. "The emotions of his heart were deep and strong," observed Charles S. Zane, a Springfield attorney. "But they had the benefit of the light and wisdom of a great intellect, and the admonitions of a great conscience. He felt [obligated] to do what his conscience approved. He measured the morality of every action." He was never known to be unfaithful to his wife.[14]

Were his absences due to Mary's vitriolic outbursts and an unhappy married life, or were her outbursts due to his long absences? Historians differ. Mary told a neighbor, James Gourley, "If [my] husband had stayed at home as he ought to, [I] would love him better." Gourley, a deputy U.S. marshal, called Mary "a good friend" who "dared me once or twice to kiss her," but "I refused." Lincoln said that weekends on the road gave him time to think without family interruptions. On the circuit he was "as happy as he could be," said Judge Davis, "and happy no other place."[15]

Even when in Springfield Lincoln seldom spent his evenings at home. To reduce domestic conflicts, he often left for work around seven or eight in the morning and would not return until midnight or later. He read widely at the state library, broadening his knowledge of history, the Constitution, and the laws of human government. Thus his terrible domestic situation diverted him to studious pursuits which helped him to succeed in law and in politics.

On those rare occasions when Lincoln returned home early in the evening, he preferred to sit quietly by the fire and read. As he sat reading one evening while she cooked dinner, she warned him that the fire was about to go out. Absorbed in his reading, he did not respond. She called out again. No response. Furious, she grabbed a piece of firewood and struck him on the face, cutting his nose. Did her fits of violent anger probe Lincoln to ponder what might have been had Ann Rutledge lived? Reflecting on earlier times in Indiana and on his grandest love and most gripping tragedy, he penned a poem a decade after Ann's death. It read in part: "O Memory! thou midway world / 'Twixt earth and Paradise, / Where things decayed and loved ones lost / In dreamy shadows rise, / And, freed from all that's earthly vile, / Seem hallowed, pure, and bright, / Like scenes in some enchanted isle / All bathed in liquid light."[16]

In 1847, Lincoln was off to Washington, D.C. as a newly elected member of the U.S. House of Representatives. He, Mary, four-year-old Robert, and a new baby, Eddie, moved into a Washington boardinghouse. Throwing himself into his work, Lincoln spent very little time with Mary. She hindered him "in attending to business," he confided to a colleague. Most congressmen did not bring their wives to Washington, so Mary had few female friends. Further, she was appalled to discover that many legislators frequented saloons and brothels. Although Lincoln was a passionate man with strong attraction to the opposite sex, he also possessed extraordinary self-control. He was somewhat of an exception in prewar Washington. Prostitution was tolerated, and sexual escapades attracted little public attention in the press.[17]

Near the Capitol at 349 Maryland Avenue, a twenty-something entrepreneur by the name of Mary Ann Hall built and managed a top-of-the-line brothel, which offered fine food, expensive carpets, and plush, red furniture. It was a place where men of wealth and distinction were wined and dined, and sexually served by women noted for their youth, beauty, and social refinement. Lobbyists employed Miss Hall's lovelies and other prostitutes to influence legislators. During the Civil War, Gen. Joseph Hooker's troops bivouacked nearby and patronized a substantial number of the city's estimated five thousand prostitutes. The area was known as the "Hooker's Division" neighborhood, and the prostitutes became known as "hookers." When Miss Hall retired in 1876, she rented her property to a women's health clinic. After her death in 1886, the *Washington Evening Star* praised her civic character and "a heart ever open to appeals of distress."[18]

Mary Lincoln, however, found few pleasures in the nation's capital. She felt snubbed as the wife of a freshman congressman. She resented the complaints of other boarders about her noisy, undisciplined children. She was concerned about Eddie, who was sick much of the time. After three months of loneliness and boredom, she had had enough. She packed her boys and her bags and fled to her family home in Kentucky for the remainder of the congressional session. Lincoln missed them. "I hate to stay in this old room by myself," he wrote to Mary. "Having nothing but business—no variety—has grown exceedingly tasteless to me." He worried about the children and enjoined his wife, "Don't let the blessed fellows forget father." She responded: "How much, I wish instead of writing, we were together this evening. I feel very sad away from you." Mary's health improved in Kentucky, and for the first time since their wedding, she was entirely free from headaches. "That is good—good," wrote Lincoln. Teasing her, he added: "I am afraid you will get so well, and fat . . . as to be wanting to marry again. . . . Get weighed, and write me how much you weigh." If that did not irritate Mary, another situation certainly did.[19]

In his seat in the U.S. House of Representatives, Lincoln was just across the aisle from William Strong of Pennsylvania, the brother-in-law of Matilda Edwards, Lincoln's lost love from Springfield. Lincoln and Strong met at a congressional reception, where Lincoln asked about Newton and Matilda Strong. Later, after Congressman Strong mentioned to Lincoln that Matilda was planning a trip to Washington, Lincoln dashed off a letter to Mary: "A day or two ago Mr. Strong, here in Congress, said to me that Matilda would visit here within two or three weeks. Suppose you write her a letter, and enclose it in one of mine; and if she comes I will deliver it to her, and if she does not, I will send it to her."[20]

Mary ignored her lonely husband's request while intimating she wanted to return to Washington. Mindful of her tantrums and extravagances, Lincoln replied: "Will you be a good girl in all things, if I consent? Then come along . . . as soon as possible. . . . I want to see you, and our dear—dear boys very much." It has not been determined if Matilda came to Washington that year or if she ever saw Lincoln again. Three years later, while in Philadelphia, Matilda died suddenly from an undisclosed illness. She was only twenty-nine. Although she had lived in Reading just four years, the editor of the local newspaper wrote this unusual tribute:

> The sudden death of this most esteemed lady has awakened an unusual degree of sorrow in the circle of her friends. Her gentle temper, her conciliatory manners, and the sweetness of her heart made her dear to all who knew her. The memory of such as she cannot perish and it will be long ere her many friends shall cease to think of her virtues and grieve for her early death.[21]

In December 1848, Lincoln jumped into the congressional debates over slavery in the territories—and in the nation's capital. From Capitol Hill he could see the notorious "Georgia pen," which he described as "a sort of Negro livery-stable"—where "Negroes were collected, temporarily kept, and finally taken to Southern markets, precisely like droves of horses." He proposed a bill to free all slave children in the District and to compensate their owners, but when Southerners threatened to boycott Congress, Lincoln's backers abandoned him and he withdrew the bill.[22]

During his term in Congress, Lincoln's outspoken stand against President James K. Polk's support for the Mexican War alienated both friends and foes. The president, said Lincoln, provoked the war by announcing that Mexican troops had shed American blood on American soil in a border dispute. "Reveal the exact spot," demanded Lincoln, but Polk did not do so. Other Whigs failed to support Lincoln's efforts, and even in Illinois Lincoln was termed "misguided." Some critics even labeled him as "a second Benedict Arnold." "I neither seek, expect, or deserve" a seat in the next Congress, Lincoln confided to a friend.

With Gen. Zachary Taylor's election to the presidency, Lincoln expected to be rewarded with a cabinet post for his strong support of Taylor's candidacy. "Old Rough and Ready" ignored him, however, and Lincoln also lost a bid to become commissioner of the U.S. Land Office. The interior secretary offered to nominate him for governor of the Oregon Territory, but Mary adamantly opposed accepting the offer. She had had enough of frontier life; she feared Indians; and she was concerned about Eddie's health. Lincoln brooded over his stalled political life. "How hard it is to die and leave one's country no better than if one had never lived," he told Herndon. When an autograph collector requested his "signature with a sentiment," he wrote: "If you collect the signatures of all persons who are no less distinguished than I, you will have a very undistinguishing mass of names."[23]

In 1849, at age forty, Lincoln returned to full-time legal practice in Springfield. Haunted by his failure to achieve his political goals, he zealously focused on the law and intellectual pursuits. He mastered the abstract mathematical propositions in the first six books of Euclid and also resumed his study of Shakespeare. For five years, he avoided politics. By age forty-five his disciplined approach had produced a new maturity. He had become a statesman—while also facing personal tragedies.

In December 1849, three-year-old Eddie fell gravely ill. He was nursed day and night for nearly two months, but it was hopeless. On February 1, he died, probably of pulmonary tuberculosis. Lincoln was anguished, and Mary collapsed. She remained in her bedroom for weeks, crying much of the time. Lincoln tried to comfort her and tended to her every need. When she finally emerged, she was more temperamental and unstable than ever.

Dr. James Smith, pastor of Springfield's First Presbyterian Church, was the only person who seemed to be able to comfort her. He reassured her that God loved and cared for Eddie in heaven. Lincoln rented a family pew in the church so Mary could attend regularly. He occasionally accompanied her but refused to become a church member. Eleven months after Eddie's death, on December 21, 1850, Mary gave birth to William Wallace ("Willie") Lincoln, who was named after Mary's brother-in-law. That December Lincoln also learned from his stepbrother John Johnston that his father was terminally ill, but Lincoln made no effort to contact him. "Why haven't we heard from you?" Johnston wrote. "Because," said Lincoln, "it appeared to me I could write nothing which could do any good." Lincoln said he was unable to visit his father because of Mary's illness and other commitments. Finally, Lincoln sent a message:

> Tell him to remember to call upon, and confide in, our great, and good, and merciful Maker; who will not turn away from him in any extremity. He notes the fall of a sparrow, and numbers the hairs of our heads; and He will not forget the dying man who puts his trust in Him. Say to him that if we could meet now, it is doubtful whether it would not be more painful than pleasant; but that if it be his lot to go now, he will soon have a joyous [meeting] with many loved ones gone before; and where [the rest] of us, through the help of God, hope erelong [to join] them.[24]

Thomas Lincoln died on January 17, 1851, at age seventy-three. He had never seen his grandchildren or his daughter-in-law, Mary. He had sent a letter saying he "craved" to see his "only child," but Lincoln said he was too busy. A trip by buggy would take three days each way, and he had court cases daily. For the same reason, he did not attend the funeral.[25]

Mary gave birth to another baby boy on April 4, 1853, and they named him Thomas after Abraham's father. But they never called him by that name. Instead, he became "Tad" because he was born with an unusually large head and squirmed like a tadpole. The delivery was difficult, and for the rest of her life Mary suffered from what she called, with Victorian propriety, troubles "of a womanly nature." Still traveling the circuit at the time, Lincoln began to spend most weekends at home. The expansion of the railroads made the journey easier. Lincoln even helped with the baby-sitting—although it was an activity Mary apparently forced upon him. A neighbor claimed that Mary compelled Lincoln "to get up and get the breakfast and then dress the children, after which she would join the family at the table, or lie in bed an hour or two longer as she might choose. . . . It was [also his duty] to wash the dishes before going to his office." Another neighbor said she made him "take care of the baby," whom "he rolled . . . up and down in [the] baby carriage." He romped with the older children and chuckled at their misbehavior.[26]

The Lincolns allowed their children considerable freedom, encouraged them to ask questions, and held lavish birthday parties for them—all in stark contrast to Lincoln's childhood. He kept a promise he made to himself when he left his father's house—that his own children would be "free, happy, and unrestrained by parental tyranny" and that "love would be the chain to bind a child to its parents." He pulled Willie and Tad around in a little wagon, and when they were older, he took them to his law office on Sundays, much to the displeasure of Lincoln's law partner William Herndon. "These children would take down the books and empty ash buckets, ink stands, papers, gold pens, and letters in a pile and then dance on the pile. Lincoln would say nothing, [being] so . . . blinded to his children's faults. Had they s—t in Lincoln's hat and rubbed it on his boots, he would have laughed and thought it smart. I have felt many a time that I wanted to wring their little necks and yet out of respect for Lincoln I kept my mouth shut."[27]

Lincoln never had the daughter he wanted. Perhaps to fill that void, he developed a special fondness for Josie Remann, a little girl in his neighborhood. He carried her on his shoulders and took her to the circus with other children whose parents could not afford tickets. Son Willie was a near replica of his father. He was bright, articulate, compassionate, and gentle-mannered. He liked to read, and he memorized railroad timetables. He solved problems the way his father did. Lincoln told a visitor: "I know every step of the process by which [he] arrived at his satisfactory solution of the question before him, as it is by just such slow methods I attain results." Tad was like his mother—nervous, hyperactive, and affectionate. He was somewhat retarded—he had trouble dressing himself and learning to read— and he had a cleft palate and a speech impediment. "Pappa dear" sounded like "Pappy-day." Robert, the oldest, was never close to his father. During his childhood Lincoln was away much of the time, and Robert's main recollection of his father was watching him load his saddlebags in preparation for going on the circuit. Now he was jealous of his father's attention to Willie and Tad. "Robert is a Todd, not a Lincoln," said Herndon. "Robert is proud, aristocratic, and haughty." Lincoln had wanted to name him "Joshua" after his friend Joshua Speed but, instead, chose the name of Mary's father.[28]

Robert Todd Lincoln, oldest son of the president, was away at school during the White House years and seldom saw his parents. Completely undisciplined as a child, he frequently ran away from home. A late bloomer, he became a successful lawyer, held major governmental posts, and was the wealthy president of the Pullman Car Company. AUTHOR'S COLLECTION

To obtain the discipline unavailable at home, Robert was placed in a private school in Springfield. Even so, he failed fifteen out of sixteen entrance exams at Harvard. The Lincolns then sent him to Phillips Exeter Academy in New Hampshire for a year, where he excelled in athletics. At Exeter, Robert apparently matured. He was known as "a gentleman in every sense of the word, quiet in manner, with a certain dignity of his own." From there, he went to Harvard.[29]

By the early 1850s Lincoln was one of the most successful attorneys in central Illinois. It was a happy time for Mary. He pampered her more and more.

As an attorney Lincoln was at his best when he felt his client was oppressed. "When Lincoln attacked meanness, fraud, or vice, he was powerful and merciless in his castigation," said William Herndon. No case stirred him more than that of an elderly crippled woman who hobbled into their law office and told her story. She was the widow of a Revolutionary War soldier, and a pension agent had withheld one-half of her four-hundred-dollar pension as his fee. "Can you help me get what is due to me?" she asked Lincoln. He assured her he would do his best. Lincoln walked over to the agent's office and demanded that the money be returned to the widow. The agent, a Mr. Wright, refused. Lincoln filed a lawsuit and told Herndon, "I'm going to skin Wright and get that money back."[30]

In court the only witness he introduced was the old lady, who told her story through her tears. In his summation to the jury, Lincoln recounted the causes of the Revolution and drew a vivid picture of the hardships of Washington's army at Valley Forge. In minute detail he described the men, barefooted, leaving bloody footprints in the snow. Then he accused the defendant of fleecing the woman of her pension. His eyes flashed as he launched into Wright. "Never," said Herndon, "did I see Lincoln so wrought up." Before Lincoln closed, he drew an ideal picture of the plaintiff's husband, the deceased soldier, parting with his wife at the threshold of their home, and kissing their baby in the cradle, as he started for the war. "Time rolls by," he said in conclusion. "The heroes of '76 have passed away and are encamped on the other shore. The soldier has gone to rest, and now, crippled, blind, and broken, his widow comes to you and to me, gentlemen of the jury, to right her wrongs. . . . Out here on the prairies of Illinois, many hundreds of miles away from the scenes of her childhood, she appeals to us, who enjoy the privileges achieved for us by the patriots of the Revolution, for our sympathetic aid and manly protection. All I ask is, shall we befriend her?" The jury responded by awarding his client full restitution. Half of them were in tears, while the defendant sat writhing under Lincoln's scathing attack. Lincoln's interest in the widow did not stop there, however. He also paid her hotel bill and travel expenses—and charged nothing for his services.[31]

In another case Lincoln was sitting in the courtroom in Clinton, Illinois, when fifteen ladies were charged with trespassing. Objecting to a newly opened saloon, they had called upon the owner, a Mr. Tanner, and requested him to desist his liquor traffic. When he refused, they took the law in their own hands and dumped his liquor upon the ground. He filed a complaint. The ladies' attorney was less than convincing, and one of the women asked Lincoln to speak to the jury if he thought he could aid their cause. He was too gallant to refuse. Lincoln said he would "change the order of indictment and have it read 'The State versus Mr. Whiskey' instead of 'The State versus The Ladies.'" He spoke of the ruinous effects of whiskey on society and compared their act to that of "our forefathers in casting the tea overboard and asserting their right to life, liberty, and happiness." Lincoln then accused the saloon keeper of violating the moral law—"a law for the violation of which the jury can fix no punishment." After Lincoln had concluded, the judge, without awaiting the jury's return, dismissed the ladies, saying: "Ladies, go home. I will require no bond of you, and if any fine is ever wanted of you, we will let you know." The jury found them guilty, but the court fined them only two dollars. "Huzzah for the ladies," wrote the *Decatur Gazette*.[32]

After a day in court in Danville, Illinois, in 1854, Lincoln was informed that an elderly black woman, who had known him in Kentucky, wished to see him. Lincoln found her in a wretched hovel on the outskirts of town, sick and destitute. He gave her money and also engaged a physician to provide medical attention.[33]

In the fall of 1854, Lincoln charged back into politics after Congress passed the Kansas-Nebraska Act. Voiding a section of the Missouri Compromise banning slavery from these territories, the Act provided for "popular sovereignty"—leaving it to the people to choose for or against slavery. Opposing any extension of slavery, Lincoln ran for the Illinois legislature and was elected—but then resigned to seek election to the U.S. Senate. Election was determined by legislative vote, and in a close contest Lincoln gave up on the tenth ballot and directed his supporters to go for Lyman Trumbull, an antislavery Democrat. Trumbull was elected.

Meanwhile, "popular sovereignty" turned Kansas into a killing field as proslavers and abolitionists battled each other. In March 1855, five thousand heavily armed "Border Ruffians" from Missouri rode into Kansas, seized the polling places, voted in their own legislature, and imprisoned anyone who spoke against slavery. Abolitionist John Brown was infuriated. He stormed into Kansas and in May 1856 led a company of eight men toward the proslavery settlement on Pottawatomie Creek. In the middle of the night they banged on doors, ordered men outside at gunpoint, then split open their heads, cut off their arms, and threw their mangled bodies into the bushes. The massacre ignited a war lasting six months.

Amid these extraordinary events Lincoln decided to abandon the Whig party. He left the Whigs and became the principal architect of the new Republican Party in Illinois—a party with one major goal: opposition to the spread of slavery. At the national convention in 1856, Lincoln received 110 votes for the vice-presidential nomination, but the post went to William L. Dayton, a former New Jersey senator. The ticket was headed by the famous explorer John C. Fremont, who was a national hero. Lincoln campaigned wholeheartedly for the Republican ticket, but Democrat James Buchanan, the former secretary of state, was elected president. Despite his loss, Lincoln radiated a new enthusiasm for politics. No longer did he lament to anyone about his future, or grieve that he had done nothing to improve his country. He was focused and moving forward boldly.

In 1856, with assistance from her father, Mary Lincoln transformed the family's cottage into a handsome two-story Greek Revival home. She had it tastefully painted Quaker brown and equipped with dark green shutters. Construction was completed while Lincoln was on the circuit. When he returned he pretended to be puzzled. "Do you know where Lincoln lives?" he asked a neighbor. "He used to live here!" Their home was now one of Springfield's finest. It had a parlor, a large sitting room where the boys could play, a dining room, a library, and separate but connecting bedrooms for Lincoln and Mary—a fashionable arrangement that may have reflected their complex relationship. It also enabled Mary to indulge her favorite pastime—reading romantic novels in bed into the wee hours of the morning. "An air of quiet refinement pervaded the place," a visitor reported. "You would have known instantly that she who presided over [it] was a true type of American lady."[34]

Mary's behavior, however, continued to be unpredictable. When she got "the devil in her," James Gourley recalled, "Lincoln would pick up one of the children and walk off—would laugh at her, and go to his

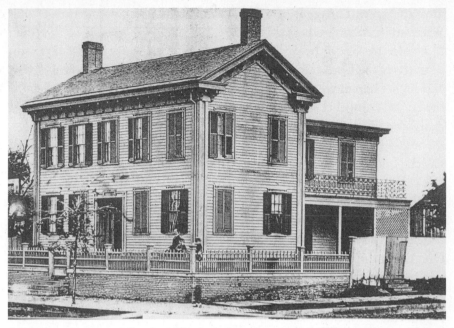

After extensive remodeling in 1856, including the addition of a second story, the Lincoln's home became one of Springfield's finest. AUTHOR'S COLLECTION.

office until she calmed down." When she was feeling well, she was an excellent neighbor. Shortly after Tad's birth she even breast-fed a sick neighbor's baby along with her own. To show off her "new" home—and perhaps to also enhance her husband's image—Mary entertained extravagantly. She hosted after-church "strawberry and ice-cream parties" and organized buffet suppers for as many as three hundred guests. She was a charming hostess, and her parties unquestionably helped Lincoln climb the steep passages through social classes.[35]

Circumstances brought an even better life a notch closer when the U.S. Supreme Court announced its Dred Scott decision in 1857. Confirming Northern fears, the decision proclaimed the constitutionality of slavery and guaranteed slaveowners the right to take their slaves into free states as well. The decision riled Lincoln and intensified his political drive. On June 16, 1858, his efforts paid off. It was to be the single most important day in his career—the day he was nominated by the Illinois Republican Convention to run against Sen. Stephen A. Douglas. Lincoln prepared his keynote speech and read a draft to a gathering of friends. All but one advised him to change it because it was "in advance of the times," but William Herndon, who had been sitting silently, sprang to his feet: "Lincoln, by God," he exclaimed, "deliver it just as it reads. If it is in advance of the times, let us lift the people to the level of this speech now, and higher hereafter. . . . It will aid you. . . . It will make you president of the United States." A key paragraph in the speech read: "A house divided against itself cannot stand. I believe this government cannot endure permanently half slave and half free. I do not expect the Union to be dissolved. I do not expect the house to fall, but I do expect it will cease to be divided. It will become all one thing or all the other."[36]

He gave the speech, and it sparked an explosion of controversy. A few days later an associate told him it would defeat him "for all offices for all times to come. . . . I wish it was wiped out of existence. Don't you now wish so?" Lincoln frowned, raised up his spectacles, and replied: "Well, if I had to draw a pen across and erase my whole life . . . and I had but one poor gift or choice left as to what I should save from the wreck, I should choose that speech and leave it to the world un-erased!"[37]

Lincoln engaged Douglas in a series of seven debates that left an indelible impression across the nation. "The prairies are on fire," wrote a New York reporter. At every place large crowds turned out to hear "the Tall Sucker and the Little Giant"—ten thousand at Ottawa and fifteen thousand at Freeport, sites of the first two debates. The sole topic was slavery and its effect on the nation's future.

The well-dressed Douglas, who through marriage owned a Mississippi plantation with 140 slaves, repeatedly quoted Lincoln's "house divided" speech and asserted that Lincoln was advocating war between the North and South. Why can't the nation exist "forever divided" on this issue, Douglas asked. He said the signers of the Declaration of Independence made "no reference to Negroes when they declared all men to be created equal. . . .They were speaking of white men." Injecting the female factor, Douglas thundered: "If you think that the Negro ought to be on a social equality with your wives and daughters, then support Mr. Lincoln!" Lincoln stated his opposition to racial equality and intermarriage, but made it clear that he believed slavery was "a moral, a social, and a political wrong" that was incompatible with America's ideals of freedom.[38]

Mary stayed home and rarely saw her husband that summer and fall. Lincoln gave sixty-three speeches and covered forty-two hundred miles, usually wearing a shabby old top hat, an ill-fitting frock coat, and unpolished boots. In the election, Lincoln outpolled Douglas by 4,085 popular votes, but the final outcome lay with the Democratically controlled legislature. There, Douglas had the upper hand. The final tally: Douglas, 54; Lincoln, 41. Lincoln said he felt like the Kentucky boy who stubbed his toe: "I am too big to cry about it, but it hurts too awful bad to laugh."[39]

The debates, however, propelled Lincoln into national prominence. As the state's leading Republican, he felt a huge obligation to keep the party's fragile coalition together and to plan for Republican victory in 1860. Although "absolutely without money" he spoke to far-flung crowds throughout the midwest, frequently traveling alone in an open buggy across windy plains. "Never forget," he said often, "we have before us this whole matter of right or wrong."[40]

Mary stayed in Springfield shopping on credit and spending lavishly. The amount she spent for one dress was equivalent to two months' pay for a typical Springfield family. Fearful of robbers and storms, Mary paid a neighbor's child to sleep in the back room or loft of the Lincolns' Springfield home. At various times all of her boys slept in her bed. She also solicited male neighbors, including James Gourley, to share a bed with her and Robert. She wanted companionship and protection even though her actions represented shameful impropriety.[41]

Wherever Lincoln went, he rose in political stature. "I suppose I am not the first choice of a great many," he said, but he suspected he could become an attractive compromise figure. Sen. William H. Seward of New York was the odds-on favorite, but Lincoln was touted by major newspapers as a possible vice president. "No, no," exclaimed Mary in a hard, bitter manner. "If you can't have the first place, you shall not have the second!"[42]

Lincoln received numerous invitations to speak. He accepted one in New York City—at the Cooper Union—after Mary urged him to go to Phillips Exeter Academy in New Hampshire to talk to Robert about his poor grades. Not only did the visit help Robert, but it also would later prove beneficial to Robert's roommate, George C. Latham, who was from Springfield. Lincoln befriended the young man, and a few years later wrote him a noteworthy letter about perseverance when he failed his entrance exams to Harvard:

I have scarcely felt greater pain in my life than on learning yesterday from Bob's letter, that you had failed to enter Harvard University. And yet there is very little in it, if you will allow no feeling of discouragement to seize, and prey upon you. It is a certain truth, that you can enter, and graduate in, Harvard University; and having made the attempt, you must succeed in it. "Must" is the word.

I know not how to aid you, save in the assurance of one of mature age, and much severe experience, that you can not fail, if you resolutely determine, that you will not.

The President of the institution, can scarcely be other than a kind man; and doubtless he would grant you an interview, and point out the readiest way to remove, or overcome, the obstacles which have thwarted you.

In your temporary failure there is no evidence that you may not yet be a better scholar, and a more successful man in the great struggle of life, than many others, who have entered college more easily.

Again I say let no feeling of discouragement prey upon you, and in the end you are sure to succeed.[43]

For his New York City address on February 27, 1860, Lincoln devoted more time for research and preparation than he had for any other address in his life up to that time. He even purchased a one hundred dollar black suit for the occasion. The capacity audience of fifteen hundred braved a raging snowstorm to see what one observer predicted would be "something weird, rough, and uncultivated" from Illinois. But when he spoke, he was proclaimed as better than New York's best. He was "the greatest man since St. Paul," an eyewitness told Noah Brooks, a New York Tribune writer. "His face lighted as with an inward fire. Forgetting myself, I was on my feet with the rest, yelling like a wild Indian, cheering this wonderful man." "No man ever made such an impression on his first appeal to a New York audience," Brooks wrote.[44]

With his usual eloquence Lincoln proposed that the North should accept slavery in the South but fearlessly persist in excluding it from

When Lincoln was in New York to speak at Cooper Union on February 27, 1860, he posed for this photograph in Matthew Brady's studio. Brady rearranged Lincoln's collar to make his neck look shorter. Lincoln was fifty-one. LIBRARY OF CONGRESS.

the territories. In splendid, spine-tingling form, he said: "Let us have faith that right makes might, and in that faith, let us, to the end, dare to do our duty as we understand it." As he finished, the audience stood, applauded thunderously, and waved hats and handkerchiefs all over the huge auditorium. Lincoln restated his position later to a questioner from the South: "There's only one difference between us. You think slavery is right and ought to be extended. I think it is wrong and ought to be restricted. For this, neither of us has any just cause to be angry with the other."

After the Cooper Union Speech Lincoln was known to the entire nation. In New England he gave eleven speeches in as many days and won support everywhere. At the Republican National Convention in Chicago, the primary objective of Lincoln's manager, Judge David Davis, was to secure at least a hundred votes on the first ballot as well as commitments from other delegates for support on the second ballot. If it worked, Lincoln would appear to be gaining momentum and still others would swing to him. Davis also arranged for Illinois railroads to offer special rates enabling thousands of Lincoln men to come to Chicago. Seward continued to be the favorite, and his supporters packed the hall on the day of the first ballot. Then something strange occurred. The tally sheets failed to arrive from the printer, and the delegates could not vote. The convention was adjourned until Friday. Lincoln's managers hailed the delay as an act of God. With thousands of Lincoln's supporters in Chicago, Davis's staff made bogus tickets for them and told them to come early to the convention hall, a large wooden structure known as the Wigwam. On Friday morning Seward's confident and jubilant followers marched in the streets, complete with a brass band. When they returned to the Wigwam, there was no place for them. The hall was already packed with Lincoln's people.

A total of 233 votes was needed to win the nomination. On the first ballot, it was Seward, 173 1/2, and Lincoln, 102, with others trailing far behind. On the second ballot the promised votes switched to Lincoln, and except for Seward, other candidates lost strength. The vote: Seward, 184 1/2; Lincoln, 181. On the third ballot, Seward retained his position, but nearly all other delegates flocked to Lincoln, and he had 231 1/2, needing only 1 1/2 votes. Then Ohio switched four votes to Lincoln, and others followed. Seward's men moved to make it unanimous. A tally official shouted: "Fire the salute! Abe Lincoln is nominated." A delegate wired to Springfield: "Abe, we did it. Glory to God!" Lincoln was the Republican candidate for president of the United States. Thus, a one-term former congressman who had not held office for a dozen years snatched the nomination from William Seward, the clear front-runner.

Was it Providence, strategic planning, or backroom politics? Lincoln simply said it was meant to be. In Springfield, the news reached Lincoln at the office of the *Illinois State Journal*. His supporters danced and sang, shouted and cheered. "Well, gentlemen," Lincoln said with a twinkle in his eye, "there's a little woman at our house who is probably more interested in this dispatch than I am, and if you will excuse me, I will take it up and let her see it."[45]

On May 19 a delegation headed to Springfield with the official notification. Mary prepared a fashionable table of cakes and sandwiches, two decanters of brandy, and a bottle of champagne. As soon as Lincoln saw the table, he objected to the liquor, knowing that several members of the delegation favored temperance. An argument ensued. Mary adamantly stressed that the delegates would expect liquor; Lincoln insisted that only ice water should be served. Mary yelled and screamed, and Lincoln left the house and walked around the block. He returned just as the delegation arrived. He introduced them to Mary, who now radiated Southern charm. She so wowed them with her conversation and poise that the head of the delegation, George Ashmun of Massachusetts, reported: "I shall be proud, as an American citizen, when the day brings her to grace the White House."[46]

Lincoln had three major opponents. A split in the Democratic Party resulted in the Northern wing nominating Douglas, while the Southern wing chose John C. Breckinridge of Kentucky, who was the current vice president under James Buchanan. A new National Unity Party—a reincarnation of the Whig and American Parties— nominated John Bell of Tennessee. In one of the ironies of history, Mary Todd Lincoln had been courted by three of the four candidates—all except Bell. If she had been a little older, she might also have had Jefferson Davis as a beau when he studied at Transylvania College in Lexington.

On election night—November 6, 1860—Lincoln joined fellow Republicans at the state capitol to hear the returns, which were relayed from the telegraph office. About two o'clock in the morning, the long-awaited news came over the wire: Lincoln had won. He hurried home to wake Mary, who had peevishly locked him out of the house. He used a spare key to let himself inside and woke her, saying, "Mary, Mary! We are elected!" The next day he told callers his wife had locked him out. "Shut your mouth," she admonished him. "Never tell that again!"[47]

Tired and weary the day after the election, Lincoln stretched out on a sofa in his Springfield home. Glancing into a mirror across the room—as he later told the story—he had two faces instead of one. Puzzled, he looked two more times; both times seeing two faces, one very pale. To Lincoln, it was an omen: He would be elected twice as president, he believed, but would not live through a second term.

His election to the presidency was highly gratifying to Mary, who was—said a Lincoln friend—"an ambitious little woman." Mary now became "pleasant and talkative and entertaining." To prepare for her new role, she traveled to New York in January and incurred a huge debt buying expensive clothes with which she hoped to impress Washington society. She concealed the staggering debt from her husband.[48]

At the end of January, after Mary returned from her New York shopping spree, Lincoln left for Farmington in Coles County to visit his seventy-three-year-old stepmother and his father's grave. As the short visit ended, his stepmother was in tears. "I didn't want Abe to run for president," she recalled later, "didn't want him elected—was afraid somehow or other that something would happen [to] him and that I should see him no more." "No, no Mama," he comforted her. "Trust in the Lord and all will be well. We will see each other again."[49]

Back in Springfield, Lincoln ran into an old friend from New Salem, Isaac Cogdal. A fellow Kentuckian and a former Whig, Cogdal was now a leading Republican. Feeling unusually nostalgic, Lincoln invited Cogdal to drop in at the statehouse that evening to talk over old times.

A tall, good-looking man, Cogdal had been a farmer and stonemason in New Salem before Lincoln encouraged him to study law. Recently admitted to the Illinois bar, he was destined to become a respected attorney.

That evening Lincoln immediately began reminiscing about New Salem families—the Greens, Potters, Armstrongs, and Rutledges, among others. Lincoln asked about them, and Cogdal reported what he knew. Lincoln was clearly in a retrospective mood, and Cogdal—he later claimed—asked if it were true that Lincoln fell in love with and courted Ann Rutledge. "It is true—true indeed, I did," Lincoln reportedly replied without hesitating. "I have loved the name of Rutledge to this day. I have kept my mind on their movements ever since." Lincoln then discussed his reaction to Ann's death, according to Cogdal. "I ran off the track," the president-elect reportedly admitted. "It was my first. I loved the woman dearly. She was a handsome girl; would have made a good, loving wife; was natural and quite intellectual, though not highly educated. I did honestly and truly love the girl, and think often, often, of her now."[50]

Eleven-year-old Grace Bedell set in motion a transformation of Lincoln's appearance that produced a new, lasting image for the new president. "You ought to grow a beard," she wrote on October

15. "All the ladies like whiskers, and they would tease their husbands to vote for you, and then you would be president. I have got four brothers, and part of them will vote for you any way, and if you will let your whiskers grow, I will try and get the rest of them to vote for you; you would look a great deal better for your face is so thin." He responded in his own handwriting: "My dear little Miss, Your very agreeable letter of the 15th is received. I regret the necessity of saying I have no daughters. I have three sons—one seventeen, one nine, and one seven years of age. They, with their mother, constitute my whole family. As to the whiskers, having never worn any, do you not think people would call it a piece of silly affectation if I were to begin to now? Yours very sincerely, A. Lincoln." A month later Lincoln was seen with stubble sprouting from his chin. Two days before his departure to the capital, the beard was fully grown. It gave him a more distinguished look, and he became the first president to have a beard.[51]

A crowd of Springfield residents gathered at the Great Western Railroad Depot to see Lincoln off on February 11, 1861. It was a cold, rainy morning as the president-elect climbed the steps to his private car and paused for a final good-bye to his neighbors—people from Springfield he had seen every day for years, as well as friends from the old days in New Salem. Did Ann Rutledge come into his mind as he pondered this dramatic departure from the people and places of his past? "My friends—No one, not in my situation, can appreciate my feeling of sadness at this parting," he told the crowd. "To this place, and the kindness of these people, I owe every thing. Here I have lived a quarter of a century, and have passed from a young to an old man. Here my children have been born, and one is buried."

Despite his reference to being "old," he would observe his fifty-second birthday the following day: he was one of the youngest presidents in American history at that time, and he was a generation younger than his predecessor. "I now leave," he continued, "not knowing when, or whether ever, I may return, with a task before me greater than that which rested upon Washington. Without the assistance of that Divine Being . . . I cannot succeed. With that assistance I cannot fail. . . . Let us confidently hope that all will yet be well. To

His care commending you, as I hope in your prayers you will com-mend me, I bid you an affectionate farewell."[52]

As the train passed through New York, it was delayed at Westfield, and Lincoln was called out by the crowd. In his remarks he noted that soon after the election he had received a letter from a little girl in that very town, suggesting he would be better looking if he would grow a beard. Then, stroking his face, he added, "I am following her advice." He asked if she were present, and if so, he would like to see her. She came forward, and he looked down at her. "You see," he said, "I have let these whiskers grow for you, Grace." Then he leaned over and kissed her.[53]

As Lincoln's train headed for Washington, an assassination plot was unfolding in Baltimore. Information about a possible plot was volunteered by a woman—social reformer Dorothea Lynde Dix—who alerted railroad officials of the threat. She said friends from the South had warned her of "an extensive and organized conspiracy to prevent Lincoln's inauguration." In response, the Pinkerton Agency was hired to protect Lincoln. Pinkerton assigned agents to infiltrate radical groups. A female agent, Mrs. Kate Warne, was paid to culti-vate the wives and daughters of known secessionists. Intelligence she and other agents gathered enabled Pinkerton to identify the potential assassins and to establish the time and place of the ambush.[54]

Pinkerton and Mrs. Warne rushed to New York City where the presidential train had arrived and urged the Lincoln party to change plans and travel to Washington immediately. Despite the dangers of delay, Lincoln insisted on a scheduled stop in Philadelphia. "I cannot go tonight," he declared. "I have promised to raise the flag over Independence Hall tomorrow morning and to visit the legislature at Harrisburg in the afternoon. Any plan that may be adopted that will enable me to fulfill these promises I will accede to, and you can inform me what is concluded upon tomorrow."[55]

At Independence Hall on February 22, he declared that all his political sentiments were drawn from the Declaration of Independence. Believing that threats of secession originated in oppo-sition to its principles of equality, he stated fearlessly: "I would rather be assassinated on the spot than surrender those principles so dear to me." Just two nights earlier thirty conspirators had reportedly met in

Baltimore and pulled slips of paper from a hat in a dark room. Whoever drew the red ballot was committed to kill Lincoln. But the group's leaders placed eight red ballots in the hat, rather than one. Thus, there would be eight sworn killers waiting for him in Baltimore. Lincoln, pushed by his advisers, turned himself over to the Pinkerton agency. Pinkerton's revised plans called for Lincoln and one companion to depart Harrisburg for Philadelphia in a special two-car train, ostensibly arranged to transport railroad officials back home. In Philadelphia, Lincoln would transfer to a sleeping car on the regular train leaving for Baltimore at 11 P.M. Mrs. Warne would reserve the rear half of the Pullman to accommodate herself and Lincoln—who was passed off as an "invalid brother." A curtain would separate them from other passengers.[56]

The strategy called for Mary Lincoln and the rest of the presidential party to follow the next day as previously scheduled. When Mary learned of the changes, however, she became unruly. She loudly insisted that she must accompany her husband and ignored all appeals to keep silent. Concerned for the president-elect's safety, officials finally hustled her into a locked room. One official—disgusted with her conduct—called her a "helpless fool." With telegraph wires disabled to prevent leaks to conspirators, Lincoln left his Harrisburg hotel at 5:45 P.M. wearing an unfamiliar soft felt hat positioned low on his head. A large

Social reformer Dorothea Lynde Dix apparently was the first person to alert authorities about the plot to kill Lincoln in Baltimore in February 1861. Later, as superintendent of women nurses for the Union, she accepted only "homely looking women" between the ages of thirty and forty-five. PHOTO FROM *LIFE OF DOROTHEA LYNDE DIX*, HOUGHTON MIFFLIN CO., 1918.

overcoat thrown over his shoulders concealed his long arms. He stepped into a carriage and was whisked to the special train, accompanied by his friend Ward Hill Lamon, who carried a personal arsenal of weapons. Pinkerton met them in Philadelphia at 10 P.M. and drove them in his carriage to the railroad depot. As they approached the train, Mrs. Warne came forward and greeted the president–elect as if he were her brother, and they entered the sleeping car. Several disguised guards also boarded the sleeper, but it was Mrs. Warne who was posted near the door to Lincoln's compartment. She carried a loaded revolver under her cloak.[57]

Soon the train was in motion and rolled unmolested to Baltimore's Calvert Street Station, where Lincoln was to have been assassinated. At 3:30 A.M. the station was nearly deserted. Lincoln's Pullman car was hitched to a team of horses and was pulled across town to the Camden Station—where it connected with the Baltimore & Ohio for the trip to the nation's capital. Waiting almost two hours in his berth, Lincoln regaled his tense, silent companions with homespun humor. Outside, a drunkard sang "Dixie." The deception worked perfectly, and Lincoln arrived in Washington around six o'clock in the morning.

10

"Mrs. Lincoln Is Involved in Corrupt Traffic."

In the White House Mary Todd Lincoln sought to be her husband's chief adviser on appointments. She would later boast, "My husband placed great confidence in my knowledge of human nature." Shortly after Lincoln's election, Mary began to accept gifts from people hoping to influence Lincoln. Isaac Henderson, publisher of the *New York Evening Post*, sent a diamond brooch to a Springfield jeweler to hold until Mary secured a post for him in the New York Custom House. When Lincoln objected, she lay on the floor in a hysterical fit until he finally relented. Henderson, an unsavory man, was later dismissed for accepting commissions from government contracts.[1]

As Lincoln debated cabinet appointments, Mary nagged him end-lessly. She was especially severe on William H. Seward—Lincoln's main rival for president and his preference for secretary of state. "He cannot be trusted," she said emphatically. "He has no principle." "Mother, you are mistaken," Lincoln replied. "Your prejudices are so violent that you do not stop to reason. Seward is an able man, and the country as well as myself can trust him." Mary was adamant: "It makes me mad to see you sit still and let that hypocrite twine you around his finger as if you were a skein of thread." "It is useless to argue the question, Mother," said Lincoln impatiently. "You cannot change my opinion!" Mary's hostility toward Salmon P. Chase was equally bitter, and she urged Lincoln not to appoint him as secretary of the treasury. She claimed that "he was a selfish politician instead of a true patriot," according to Elizabeth Keckley, Mary's seamstress and confidante. Mary warned Lincoln not to trust Chase either. "I do wish that you would inquire into [his] motives," she asserted.[2]

Mary apparently expressed no opinion about Lincoln's most questionable cabinet appointment, Sen. Simon Cameron, who was initially appointed as secretary of war. Even vice president–elect Hannibal Hamlin observed: "This appointment has an odor about it." Cameron had become a political boss through bribery and intimidation and had allegedly defrauded the Winnebago Indians of sixty-six thousand dollars during the Van Buren administration. Yet he was the key to delivering Pennsylvania to Lincoln. Lincoln's campaign chairman had vaguely promised Cameron a cabinet post if his delegates would vote for Lincoln after the first ballot, which they did. Lincoln never listened to Mary about major appointments, but—according to Herndon—he gave in on lesser positions. One he refused to move on was Mary's cousin, Elizabeth Todd Grimsley. Concerned about nepotism, he turned her down for the job of postmistress of Springfield. Mary stomped her feet and screamed but to no avail.[3]

Many residents of the District of Columbia regarded Lincoln with violent animosity—an odious embodiment of the abhorred principles of abolitionism. Curious to see a man represented to her as a monster, a proud, aristocratic South Carolina lady, a Mrs. Howard—the widow of a Northern scholar—called upon Lincoln. Seward, whom she knew, presented her to the president-elect. "I am a South Carolinian," she said. Lincoln addressed her with gentlemanly courtesy. Astonished, she said: "Why, Mr. Lincoln, you look, act, and speak like a kind, good-hearted, generous man." Lincoln asked if she had expected to meet a savage. "Certainly, I did, or even something worse," she admitted. "I'm glad I've met you, and now the best way to preserve peace is for you to go to Charleston and show the people what you are and tell them you have no intention of injuring them." Lincoln thanked her for her advice, and she returned home, where she found a group of secessionists. She told them: "I've seen him! I've seen him—the person you call a terrible monster. And I found him to be a gentleman, and I'm going to his first reception after his inauguration." They shook their heads in disbelief and left the house.[4]

At President Lincoln's first reception, Mrs. Howard showed up dressed in black velvet, with two long white plumes in her black hair. She looked striking and majestic. The president recognized her immediately. "Here I am again," she said, "that South Carolinian." "I am glad to see you," Lincoln said, "and I want to again assure you that the first objective of my heart is to preserve peace, and I wish that not only you but every son and daughter of South Carolina were here, that I might tell them so." In his inaugural address on March 4, Lincoln did indeed attempt to tell them so as he appealed to the South and held out a peaceful hand: "I have no purpose, directly or indirectly, to interfere with the institution of slavery . . . where it exists. I believe I have no lawful right to do so." He ended with this passage: "I am loth to close. We are not enemies, but friends. We must not be enemies. . . . The mystic chords of memory, stretching from every battlefield and patriot grave to every living heart and hearthstone, all over this broad land, will yet swell the chorus of the Union, when again touched, as surely they will be, by the better angels of our nature." His consuming goal was to preserve the Union.[5]

A month later, on Friday, April 12, Confederates bombarded Fort Sumter in Charleston harbor, sparking the Civil War. With the country in turmoil, Mary Lincoln shopped and partied for two weeks in Philadelphia and New York. She was accompanied by her cousin, Lizzie Todd Grimsley, and by William S. Wood, who supervised White House purchases. Mary, in fact, had secured Wood's appointment by locking herself in her room until Lincoln yielded. Wood supposedly rewarded Mary with a pair of fine horses, according to the *Washington Sunday Gazette*.[6]

The day after she returned from her shopping spree, she confronted the realities of war for the first time and responded poorly. With enemy territory just across the Potomac, Lincoln had ordered Federal occupation of neighboring Alexandria and Arlington Heights. Col. Elmer Ellsworth, twenty-four, a former clerk in Lincoln's Springfield law office, led a regiment across the river. Ellsworth saw a huge Confederate flag flying atop the Marshall House Hotel. "I'll take care of that," he vowed and entered the building with his troops. He climbed to the roof, cut down the flag, and proudly waved it over his head. As he came down the stairs with the flag, the secessionist proprietor killed him with a shotgun blast—and was killed in turn by one of Ellsworth's men. When news of Ellsworth's death reached Lincoln, he burst into tears. Ellsworth had accompanied him on his inaugural trip to Washington, and Lincoln was especially fond of the officer. Mary collapsed and was forced to bed for two days.[7]

To command all Federal forces in and around Washington, Lincoln turned to Gen. Irvin McDowell. Paris-educated, he spoke fluent French and played Mozart sonatas with the style of a professional pianist. To protect Washington against assault from the south or west, Lincoln ordered McDowell to secure the important railroads at Manassas Junction, Virginia, about twenty-five miles from the capital. McDowell's invading army was joined by a jubilant party-minded group of Washington celebrities and their wives, many of whom brought picnic baskets in their buggies.

On July 21, 1861, Federals forded Bull Run near Manassas and assaulted a Confederate army commanded by Gen. P. G. T. Beauregard. The Southerners fell back, and the Federals appeared to be on the verge of victory. The tide of battle shifted, however, and McDowell's army was turned back in a panicky retreat. In Washington Secretary Seward delivered the War Department dispatch to Lincoln: "The day is lost! Save Washington and the remnants of the army!" "If hell is [not] any worse than this, it has no terror for me," Lincoln said. But Washington wasn't attacked, and McDowell's shattered army streamed back into the capital.[8]

After Bull Run Lincoln replaced McDowell with the self-assured George B. McClellan, a superb organizer of troops. McClellan was a popular choice among the people and the soldiers but not with Mary Lincoln. "He is a humbug," she told her husband. "McClellan can make plenty of excuses for himself. . . . You will have to find some man to take his place if you wish to conquer the South." She would prove to be right.[9]

Needing fresh air and pampering, Mary decided to take a vacation, so she, Willie, and Tad left war-conscious Washington to spend much of August at Niagara Falls and ocean resorts in the northeast. As Mary and her children waited for a connecting train at Reading, Pennsylvania, a carload of miserably clad Confederate prisoners rolled into the same station and well-dressed Federal troops passed by heading south. On a nearby newsstand an issue of the *Reading Gazette* carried an article about the impact of the unexpected death of Sen. Stephen A. Douglas, Mary's old beau and Lincoln's political opponent. Douglas, forty-eight, had died on June 3 almost penniless, and the article requested contributions for his widow and child. Mary may not have seen the newspaper or contemplated the significance of what was happening around her or what had happened in this red-brick village surrounded by picturesque mountains—a village to which Newton and Matilda Edwards Strong had moved from Alton, Illinois, and where beautiful, young Matilda lay dead under the maples at Charles Evans Cemetery.

In Washington, on that same August morning, President Lincoln signed a proclamation declaring that "the inhabitants of the seceded states are in a state of insurrection against the United States and that all intercourse between them and the citizens of other parts of the United States is unlawful and forbidden." One journalist wrote: "[While her husband], a lonely man, sorrowful at heart, and weighted down by mighty burdens, bearing the Nation's fate upon his shoulders, lived and toiled and suffered alone, [Mary Lincoln relaxed] at the hotels of fashionable watering places. [She] seemed chiefly intent upon pleasure, personal flattery . . . and ceaseless self-gratification."[10]

By the fall of 1861, McClellan was being hounded by critics who complained he had not launched an offensive against the Confederates. "March on to Richmond!" demanded Horace Greeley. On October 21 McClellan sent part of his army across the Potomac to Leesburg. In a poorly planned advance, it met fierce Confederate opposition and was thrown back with heavy losses. Among the dead was another of Lincoln's longtime Illinois friends, Col. Edward D. Baker, a former senator from Oregon. When Lincoln heard the news, he wept uncontrollably. His second son, Eddie, was named after Baker. Willie, ten, who had inherited his father's literary talent, poured out his grief in a poem published in a Washington newspaper.

At the funeral, Mary shocked Washingtonians and her husband by wearing a lilac silk dress, with bonnet and gloves to match. A member of her social circle visited her the next day, and Mary greeted her by saying: "I am so glad you have come. I am just as mad as I can be. Mrs. Crittenden has just been here to remonstrate with me for wearing my lilac suit to Colonel Baker's funeral. I wonder if the women of Washington expect me to muffle myself up in mourning for every soldier killed in this great war?" "But Mrs. Lincoln," she replied, "don't you think black more suitable to wear at a funeral because there is a great war in the nation?" "No, I do not," Mary said indignantly. "I want the women to mind their own business; I intend to wear what I please."[11]

That same month Mary was back on the train to New York to buy china and glassware. This time her escort was John Watt, the White House gardener. A journalist wrote: "While her sister-women scraped lint, sewed bandages, and put on nurses' caps, and gave their all to country and to death, the wife of the president spent her time in rolling to and fro between Washington and New York, intent on extravagant purchases for herself and the White House. Mrs. Lincoln seemed to have nothing to do but to shop."[12]

Adding to his woes, the president received an anonymous letter about "the scandal of your wife and William S. Wood," the commissioner who had traveled occasionally with Mary to Manhattan. "If he continues as commissioner, he will stab you in your most vital part," the unknown correspondent warned. An Iowa dignitary later claimed that Mary "used to often go from the White House to the Astor House in New York to pass the night with a man [presumably Wood] who held a high government office in Washington." Lincoln spoke sharply to Mary about it. The Speaker of the House, Schuyler Colfax, called it "the war she had with Mr. Lincoln." He said the Lincolns "scarcely spoke [to each other] for several days." Wood later resigned under fire.[13]

Mary's alleged dalliances were apparently not limited to Wood. Two White House staffers—John Watt and doorkeeper Edward McManus—both later reported that "Mrs. Lincoln's relations with certain men were indecently improper." There were also rumors about a "Hungarian adventurer who very nearly succeeded in eloping with Mrs. Lincoln from the White House." Mary purportedly wrote to her confidant Abram Wakeman, "I have taken your excellent advice and decided not to leave my husband while he is [president]."[14]

Wakeman, an ambitious lawyer who was Lincoln's postmaster in New York City, craved the more prestigious post of port collector. He impressed Mary with his intelligence and his spiritualism, and she invited him to the White House frequently. A careful politician, he asked Lincoln's permission to "serve [Mary] in any way" when she was in New York. Soon Mary shared secrets with him. Then there was a "Mr. Dennison" (either William D., postmaster general in New York in 1864 and 1865, or George D., a naval officer in the New York Custom House). Something unsavory was going on between Mr. Dennison and Mary Lincoln, according to Sam Ward, a knowledgeable Washington insider.[15]

Mary's main project was refurbishing the White House. It resembled a rundown hotel with broken furniture, worn carpets, and peeling wallpaper. Delighted when Congress appropriated twenty thousand dollars to be expended over four years, Mary, of course, had to go to Philadelphia and New York to acquire suitable furnishings. Spending recklessly and compulsively, she bought everything she liked, including wallpaper imported from France, crimson Wilton carpet for the Red Room, and imported Brussels velvet green carpet for the East Room. She transformed the White House into a mansion stunning to behold. Guests at state dinners marveled at the elaborate Parisian upholstery, the French drapes and gold tassels, the Swiss lace curtains, and the expensive furniture. However, when the bills came in, Mary panicked. In less than a year, she had spent sixty-seven hundred dollars over the four-year appropriation. She knew Lincoln would be angry if he found out, so she launched a cover-up.

As a first step to cover the deficit, she authorized the sale of used furniture and of manure from the White House stables at ten cents a wagon load. John Watt advised her to pad household bills and to present vouchers for nonexistent purchases. Watt, himself, had accumulated a fortune stealing from the Mansion. Mary's mind went to work. She discharged the White House steward while on paper securing the job for Mrs. Watt, performing the duties herself and keeping the salary. Watt padded his own expense account and kicked back funds to Mary to help her pay her bills. He also made out fake bills for plants, pots, and services, and Mary certified them and drew the money. Included were bills for 517 loads of manure never delivered and the cost of a horse and cart for twenty-seven days to haul the manure to the White House. Newspapers reported that Mary also persuaded Watt to buy two cows and charge them to a fund to provide manure for the public lands. The Interior Department rejected the bill.[16]

Mary's dishonest financial manipulations were scandalous. In the summer of 1861, she claimed $900 for a $300 dinner for a visiting French dignitary, but Interior Secretary Caleb Smith rejected it after consulting with Secretary Seward, who knew the dinner's actual cost. A White House gatekeeper, James H. Upperman, complained to Secretary Smith about Mary's "deliberate collusion" and "flagrant frauds on the public treasury." Officials subsequently informed the President that "Mrs. Lincoln is involved in ethically insensitive conduct." Lincoln hung his head in shame and said he was convinced "her peculiar behavior is the result of partial insanity."[17]

To relieve Mary "from the anxiety under which she is suffering" and out of respect for the president, the Interior Department "measurably suppressed" the story, and Lincoln personally reimbursed the government. Nevertheless, gossip circulated throughout Washington's social circles. "I hope this calamity will be a lesson to her," Lincoln's friend David Davis said to his wife, "but I am afraid it won't." He was correct. Her extravagant behavior continued. The *New York World* reported that she ordered $800 worth of china but apparently tried to hide other purchases of $1,400 by having the total bill of $2,200 applied just to the china. A $6,000 bill for silverware was paid for by a bill charged against gas fixtures, and she attempted to disguise $500 in jewelry purchases by asking a New York merchant to charge $1,000 for a $500 chandelier for the White House.[18]

Mary cornered Isaac Newton of the Interior Department and implored him to pay her personal debts that were unknown to the president. Newton had been instrumental in efforts to prevent disclosures of her illegal dealings with Watt. She thought she could wring more help out of him, but Newton had no intention of getting involved. "She sat here on this sofa and shed tears by the pint," Newton said to Lincoln's secretary, John Hay in 1867. "There was one big bill for furs which gave her a heap of trouble, and she got it paid eventually by some of her friends."[19]

Still, the debt for White House furnishings had not been covered. So Mary called in Benjamin B. French, the commissioner of public buildings, who kept the White House accounts. She pleaded with him: "Mr. French, I have sent for you to get me out of trouble. If you will do it, I will never get into such a difficulty again. I want you to see Mr. Lincoln and tell him that it is common to overrun appropriations." Weeping, she begged, "Now do go to him and try and persuade him to approve the bill. Do it for my sake, but do not let him know that you have seen me." French reluctantly agreed to see the president, sensing that he would be upset.[20]

He was right. Lincoln was furious. He stormed back at the embarrassed Mr. French: "It can never have my approval. . . . It would stink in the nostrils of the American people to have it said that the president of the United States had approved a bill over-running an appropriation of $20,000 for flub dubs for this damned old house, when the poor freezing soldiers cannot have blankets!" He said he would pay for the overrun himself before requesting more funds. Congress, however, rescued Mary by burying two deficiency appropriations in the White House budget the following year, and Mary rescued Watt by securing an army commission for him. Lincoln forced his reluctant cabinet to approve it after Mary slept in a separate apartment for three nights. Shortly, Watt's commission was revoked. He tried to blackmail the president, demanding twenty thousand dollars for three letters in which Mary evidently asked Watt "to commit forgery and perjury for purposes of defrauding the government." Watt was warned to desist or be imprisoned. He panicked, gave up the letters, and settled for fifteen hundred dollars.[21]

Washingtonians sneered at Mary's wartime extravagance and maliciously accused her of being a Southern sympathizer. Newspapers ignored her good works, such as distributing fruit to the Union wounded—a thousand pounds of grapes in one week—and her compassion toward Washington's fugitive slaves. Instead, newspapers publicized her excesses and her Confederate ties in Kentucky. Lincoln was further embarrassed by information he received from the superintendent of the Old Capitol Prison, William P. Wood: "Mr. President, I hate to have to tell you this. But Mrs. Lincoln is involved in a corrupt traffic in trading permits, favors, and Government secrets." Wood described numerous shady practices. Among them, he claimed that Thomas Stackpole, a partisan Yankee Democrat, had won the confidence of Mrs. Lincoln and used her to gain trading permits, which he sold to a rabid secessionist and restaurateur John Hammack, and that Hammack, in turn, had peddled them to his customers. Wood said later that the president "exhibited more feeling than I believed he possessed."[22]

Mary's mischief was almost more than Lincoln could endure. Some historians suggest that dealing with his tempestuous wife prepared him for handling the troublesome people he confronted as president. Historian Benjamin Thomas concluded that "over the slow fires of misery that he learned to keep banked and under heavy pressure deep within him, his innate qualities of patience, tolerance, forbearance, and forgiveness were tempered and refined." Mary's temper tantrums, however, increased in frequency, and Lincoln became more distant. She flirted with other men, but flew into a rage when other women were around him. Women of all ages vied to be close to him, to hear him talk, and to be stared at by those tender, gray eyes. He, in turn, wanted their opinions and found it thrilling to be acquainted with some of the most beautiful women of the time. Mary scolded him: "I do not approve of your flirtations with silly women." To others, she expressed "great terror of strong-minded women" and said she would "never allow the president to see any woman alone."[23]

Kate Chase, daughter of Lincoln's treasury secretary, was Mary Lincoln's powerful social rival and the most talked-about woman in the city. LIBRARY OF CONGRESS.

Among those on Mary's "bad list" was the twenty-one-year-old daughter of Lincoln's treasury secretary, the lovely and bewitching Kate Chase. The *Boston Herald* described her face as "an enchanting and dangerous study to most men, who are pretty certain to fall in love with it." The wife of Congressman Roger A. Pryor wrote of Kate: "She was extremely beautiful. Her complexion was marvelously delicate; her fine features seeming to be cut from fine bisque, her eyes bright, soft, sweet, were of exquisite blue, and her hair a wonderful [red-gold] color like the ripe corn tassels in full sunlight. Poets sang then, and still sing, to the turn of her beautiful neck and the regal carriage of her head. She was as intellectual as she was beautiful. From her teens she was initiated into political questions, for which her genius, and her calm, thoughtful nature eminently fitted her."[24]

Miss Kate, as Lincoln called her, loved the stir of life, from learning new games and sailing riverboats to traveling widely and dabbling in politics. Coy and ambitious, with style and brains, Kate became social hostess for her widowed father at age seventeen when he was governor of Ohio. Swept into the whirl of receptions, dinners, and balls, she mastered the art of seducing men's minds—of steering social conversation into support for her father's causes and interests.

In Washington, when illness removed the wife of the secretary of state from the social scene, the honor of "First Lady of the Cabinet" went to the wife or hostess of the second highest ranking cabinet officer, the secretary of the treasury. That person was Kate Chase. She relished her new role and entertained diplomats and celebrities in lavish get-togethers. Prettier, slimmer, younger, and taller than Mary Lincoln, Kate was one of the most remarkable women ever known to Washington society. No one outshone Kate. Everything she did was done perfectly and splendidly.

Mary Lincoln could not tolerate being upstaged. She instructed her husband not to talk to Kate and other attractive women at a White House reception. Lincoln, with a mocked expression of gravity, asked: "Well, Mother, who must I talk with tonight—shall it be Mrs. D?" Mary responded: "That deceitful woman! No, you shall not listen to her flattery." "Well, then," said Lincoln, "what do you say to Miss C? She is too young and handsome to practice deceit." "No," said Mary, "she is in league with Mrs. D, and you shall not talk with her." "Well, Mother," said Lincoln exasperated, "I insist that I must talk with somebody. I cannot stand around like a simpleton and say nothing. If you will not tell me who I may talk with, please tell me who I may not talk with." Mary named "Mrs. D and Miss C," saying she detested both of them. "Mrs. B also will come around you, but you need not listen to her flattery. These are the ones in particular." "Very well, Mother," said Lincoln, "now that we have settled the question to your satisfaction, we will go downstairs." With "stately dignity, he proffered his arm and led the way," Elizabeth Keckley reported. Lincoln, however, continued to speak to all guests, including Kate Chase. Her sparkling conversation was a sweet diversion from the sour battlefield dispatches.[25]

At Kate's wedding in November 1863 to New England's richest bachelor—former "boy" governor, now thirty-three-year-old Sen. William Sprague of Rhode Island—all of Washington's elite were present, including Lincoln. Mary remained at home with a convenient chill and begged her husband to boycott the event. They argued, and her voice "penetrated the utmost end of the White House." As he left she charged after him and pulled out some of his whiskers.[26]

Sprague's wedding gift to his wife was a crown of matched pearls and diamonds costing more than fifty thousand dollars. Lincoln gave them an ivory fan. "I picked it out myself," he told Kate. "I like it. It is very beautiful," she said appreciatively. Lincoln kissed Kate on the cheek. He lingered at the reception an unusually long time for a busy president. When he returned to the White House, he could not get into his bedroom. Mary had locked him out.[27]

Kate's goal in life was to get her widowed father elected president so she could be White House hostess. Washington gossips claimed she had married Sprague for his money and political influence and was scheming to have her father replace Lincoln as the Republican candidate in 1864. Kate, the gossips concluded, never loved anyone except her father. Ironically, two of the men closest to Kate—her husband and Sen. Charles Sumner—both liked, and were liked by, Mary Lincoln. Yet both men were aware of the deadly dislike Kate and Mary had for each other. Such was the nature of Washington society. Mary was always suspicious of Kate's intentions and snubbed her everywhere, but Lincoln ignored Kate's political mischief and appreciated her quiet, contemplative demeanor. When Mary tried to prove to Lincoln that Kate and her father were their enemies, he replied: "Be good to them who hate you . . . and turn their ill-will into friendship."

Mary's suspicions were valid. In February 1864 the Chase campaign issued a pamphlet charging that the failures of the Union armies were due to "the feebleness of [Lincoln's] will" and his "want of intellectual grasp." The people "have lost all confidence in his ability to suppress the rebellion and restore the Union," it stated. A second publication, known as the *Pomeroy Circular,* declared that Lincoln's reelection was "practically impossible" and that Chase possessed "more of the qualities needed in a president." It was copied in newspapers throughout the country. Kate apparently was the queen bee in the nest of Chase supporters behind the strategy, but instead of producing political honey, they created political turmoil leading to political suicide. The publications placed Chase in an embarrassing dilemma. He appeared to be responsible for attacking an administration he was part of and a president he was obligated by his position to support. He apologized to Lincoln by letter. He denied knowledge of the *Pomeroy Circular* before its publication— possibly true, although the document's author said Chase fully approved its release. Chase then offered to resign. Lincoln formally acknowledged the letter, promising to answer fully when time permitted. A week later Lincoln wrote that he did not "perceive occasion for a change."[28]

As support for Lincoln's reelection soared, Maj. Gen. Frank P. Blair—a Missouri congressman on leave from his army command— fired back at Chase. Blair blamed him for corruption in the Treasury Department and criticized him for the Pomeroy Circular. Blair remarked: "It is a matter of surprise that a man having the instincts of a gentleman should remain in the cabinet after the disclosure of such an intrigue against the one to whom he owes his portfolio. . . . I presume the president is well content that he should stay; for every hour that he remains sinks him deeper in the contempt of every honorable mind."

Much to Kate's displeasure her father withdrew from the presidential contest on March 5. Chase, too, was miserable. He seldom spoke to Lincoln and skipped most cabinet meetings. Lincoln observed that

Chase was "irritable" and "uncomfortable." As for Kate, Chase's "earnest wish" was that she should "keep entirely aloof from everything connected with politics." That was like asking a cat to stop chasing mice. She was not about to follow her father's advice.[29]

Shortly after Lincoln was renominated in June, Chase precipitated another crisis. He attempted to fill the important position of assistant treasurer of the United States in New York City with one of his cronies. Lincoln said, "No." Chase reluctantly had the nomination withdrawn and then submitted his own resignation, expecting the president to reject it. This time the president accepted it, "having reached a point of mutual embarrassment in our official relation." Kate, incensed by Lincoln's action, fantasized that her father should run for president as an independent candidate. He did not do so, and both father and daughter had spells of illness off and on for weeks. Sprague took her on a cruise along the upper Atlantic to help her recover. By October Chase had reversed himself and was actively supporting Lincoln's reelection. In December, after the election, Lincoln nominated him for Chief Justice of the United States, and Chase proudly accepted the position. To Kate, it was Lincoln's way of getting her father out of politics, and nothing could have angered her more. After Chase's confirmation, Kate confronted her father's dear friend Senator Sumner with a comment reminiscent of Julius Caesar's retort to Brutus: "You, too, Mr. Sumner! You, too, in this business of shelving Papa! But never mind! I will defeat you all." As Chief Justice Chase administered the oath of office to Lincoln at his second inaugural, Kate's emotions veered from pride in her father to intense jealousy of Lincoln and a boiling frustration at her failure to make herself mistress of the White House.[30]

Kate and her husband continued as social leaders after the war. In 1868 she again led her father's campaign to become president. Proclaimed by Kate and his admirers as "the only man who can beat General Grant," Chase sought the Democratic nomination, but did not come close. Kate's marriage to Sprague soon deteriorated. He drank too much and frequently put her to shame in social functions at home, in society, and even at a state dinner during the Johnson administration. There, a guest advised Sprague he should not drink any more wine. Referring to Kate, the guest said, "There are a pair of bright eyes looking at you." "Damn them!" the excited man exclaimed as he refilled his glass. Kate fixed her eyes steadily on her husband and said earnestly: "Yes, they can see you, and they are heartily ashamed of you."[31]

By the early 1870s Chase's energy was gone, and in May 1873 he died. Kate had lost her beloved father, adviser, and hero. She turned to alcohol and carried on a scandalous affair with Sen. Roscoe Conkling of New York. Sprague discovered it, and his marriage to Kate dissolved in 1882. Kate withered as a lonely recluse and an eccentric and disappointed woman. Ironically, before marrying Sprague, Kate had been courted by Gen. James A. Garfield, who would become president in 1881. Kate could have been First Lady. But Garfield's wealth was only a tenth of Sprague's, and to her that was not enough.

Another captivating young woman despised by Mary Lincoln was Princess Agnes Salm-Salm, the adopted, foreign-born daughter of an American diplomat. Calling herself Agnes Leclercq before her marriage, the high-spirited girl briefly pursued a career as a circus acrobat, but then moved to Washington to meet leading politicians. Making it her business to know the right people, she moved from one influential circle to the next. Men loved her; women despised her daredevil spirit. The "Young Bohemienne," as she was called, cavorted with two female companions about the streets of the capital, took wild horseback rides past the White House, and visited soldiers at their campgrounds by the Potomac. Her shapely figure, wavy dark hair, and winsome smile caught the attention of Union officer Prince Felix Salm-Salm of Prussia, and he married her in August 1862. She stayed with him at military encampments and tended to the sick and wounded, even tearing up his sheets to use as bandages.

At a reception in Washington, Princess Agnes wrangled her way into a dance with Illinois Gov. Richard Yates. He found her so brilliant and bewitching that he commissioned her as an honorary captain. Always plotting mischief, she once bet an officer a bottle of champagne that she could place a kiss on Lincoln's lips. According to the story, when the president was seated at a luncheon she sauntered over to him and kissed him directly on the mouth. Lincoln reacted

High-spirited Princess Agnes Salm-Salm bet an army officer a bottle of champagne that she would kiss Lincoln on the lips.
COURTESY OF THE ATLANTA CENTURY.

with a reserved smile. Other female guests, inspired by the princess, repeated her performance, bringing rounds of laughter from all. Fortunately for everyone in the room, Mary Lincoln was not in town.

Princess Agnes earlier had antagonized Mary in a military procession by bolting ahead of the First Lady's carriage and cutting in front of her. Mary spoke to Gen. Joseph Hooker about it and urged him to remind the princess of her manners. With no patience for pettiness, the general ordered all women out of the camp, including the First Lady.

Except for social functions, Lincoln seldom saw Mary. He was running a war and working late into the night. Seeking companions, she entertained male friends in her Blue Room Salon. She chose "interesting men" no matter what their pasts—men who could talk engagingly about books, politics, war, and the latest gossip. Among them was Dan Sickles, a bawdy, rambunctious adventurer who escaped conviction for murdering his wife's lover on the then-novel ground of temporary insanity. Perhaps the most notorious was Henry Wikoff, a womanizer whose kidnapping of an American woman in Europe had landed him in jail on a charge of seduction. A flashy and cosmopolitan character, Wikoff once served as a secret agent in Paris for the British. Worming his way into the White House, he cultivated Mary Lincoln by conversing in French, and she responded by taking him on long carriage rides. He made himself very much at home in the Executive Mansion, lounging in the conservatory, smoking on the grounds, and spending long hours cozily seated wherever he pleased.

Washington society was distressed by their closeness. A reporter told his editor: "Mrs. Lincoln is making herself both a fool and a nuisance. Chevalier Wikoff is her gallant, and I have within the week seen two notes signed by him in her name sending compliments and invitations." Lincoln's secretary John Hay called Wikoff a "branded social pariah" and said it was disgraceful for him to be at large. Lincoln scolded Mary for her closeness to Wikoff, prompting the rogue to assure Lincoln he was just "teaching the madame a little European Court Etiquette."[32]

More trouble was brewing. Lincoln's first state of the union message was scheduled to be read to Congress by a clerk on December 3, 1861. Someone, however, leaked the tightly secured document to the *New York Herald*, which published excerpts. Other newspapers and the Congress were angry. The *Herald*'s source proved to be none other than its secret Washington reporter, Henry Wikoff. When the ever-alert *New York Tribune* accused Mary of giving Wikoff her husband's message, the House Judiciary Committee decided to investigate. The committee subpoenaed Wikoff, but he refused to disclose his source and was jailed overnight. The next morning he agreed to testify. "Who gave you the president's message?" asked a congressman. Without flinching, Wikoff said resolutely: "It was John Watt, the head White House gardener!" That was the same John Watt who had advised Mary on how to illegally secure funds and had been "repaid" by Mary with an army commission. The shocked committee came dreadfully close to investigating the White House. Lincoln, deeply embarrassed, appealed to Republicans to spare him from disgrace, and the committee dropped its inquiry.

In February 1862 the New York correspondent for the *Boston Journal*, Matthew Hale Smith, brought documented information to the president about Wikoff's scandalous activities. Lincoln learned that Wikoff had been hired by certain parties in New York to plant himself in the White House and wield influence that his backers might find useful. Wikoff was to "make himself agreeable to the ladies, insinuate himself into the White House, attend levees, show that he had power to come and go, and, if possible, open a correspondence with the ladies of the Mansion." He had succeeded far beyond his backers' expectations, thanks to Mary's support and close friendship. As Smith talked with the president, Wikoff was downstairs in the White House. "Give me those documents, and wait here until I return," demanded the incensed president as he "started out of the room with strides that showed an energy of purpose." Shortly, Lincoln returned, shook Smith's hand, and had Wikoff "driven from the Mansion that night."[33]

Another of Mary's companions was the handsome bachelor senator from Massachusetts, Charles Sumner, who once called Lincoln a "dictator." A brilliant orator with a sharp tongue, Sumner believed the greatest task on earth was to free the slaves and punish their masters. Some said he brought on the Civil War in an 1856 speech in which he cast dishonor on South Carolina Sen. Andrew Pickens Butler. Butler's enraged cousin, Congressman Preston Brooks, sneaked up on Sumner in a nearly empty Senate chamber and struck him mercilessly on the head with a thick cane. Sumner fell to the floor bleeding and unconscious, but Brooks continued to flail away until the cane broke. Plagued by severe wounds and posttraumatic shock, Sumner was absent from the Senate for three years while undergoing painful cures. Now he always smiled, but no one knew what it meant since he had no sense of humor.

Sen. Charles Sumner was called upon by Lincoln to comfort Mary after Willie's death and to escort her to the opera and theater. After the assassination, Sumner led senate efforts to award her a pension. NATIONAL ARCHIVES.

Sumner escorted Mary to the opera or the theater when Lincoln was unable or unwilling to go. The Lincolns had different theatrical tastes and often went to the theater with other companions. He preferred Shakespeare; she preferred Italian operas and German operettas. His musical tastes were simple and uncultivated, with a preference for old airs, songs, and ballads. He liked best the plaintive Scottish songs—the ones Ann Rutledge had often sung for him—"Annie Laurie," "Mary of Argyle," and "Auld Robin Gray." Newspaper correspondent Noah Brooks wrote:

> I remember that, one night at the White House, when a few ladies were with the family, singing at the piano-forte, he asked for a little song in which the writer describes his sensations when revisiting the scenes of his boyhood, dwelling mournfully on the vanished joys and the delightful associations of forty years ago. . . . There was a certain melancholy and half-morbid strain in that song which struck a responsive chord in his heart. The lines sunk into his memory, and I remember that he quoted them, as if to himself, long afterward. Lincoln perhaps was reflecting on his first true love, and as he repeated the lines in the song, tears came to his eyes.[34]

Lincoln brought to the White House its first guest artists. His choices suggested a partiality for young women: an American Indian singer named Larooqua, known as the "aboriginal Jenny Lind"; Teresa Carreno, the temperamental nine-year-old Venezuelan piano prodigy; and a beautiful twenty-year-old opera star, Spanish-born Adelina Patti, who was destined to become the world's most celebrated soprano and the most highly paid performer of her day. Patti, singing to the Lincolns after tea, had everyone in tears with "The Last Rose of Summer." When informed on one of her American tours that she made more money in one night than did the president in one year, she suggested, "Well, let him sing!"[35]

Among Willie and Tad's favorite playmates were Bud and Holly Taft, children of the chief examiner of the federal patent office. In 1861 their older sister, Julia, sixteen, often accompanied them to the White House in an attempt to supervise their behavior. In Julia's memoir, titled *Tad Lincoln's Father*, she recalled Lincoln telling stories to the children as they "perched precariously" on his knees and on the arms and back of his big chair. He held their attention with "tales of hunters and settlers attacked by Indians," and at the end of one story of frontiersmen chased by Indians, Lincoln drawled, "they galloped and galloped, with the redskins close behind." "But they got away, Pa, they got away," interrupted Tad. "Oh, yes, they got away." And then Lincoln stood and said, "Now I must get away."

Once, Julia heard "a terrible racket" in another room, and opening the door she beheld the president lying on the floor, grinning and enjoying himself, while the four boys were trying to hold him down. They called for Julia to help. "Come quick and sit on his stomach," Tad yelled. But Julia would not do that. She left the room and closed the door. "It struck me too much like laying profane hands on the Lord's anointed," she wrote in her memoir.

Julia remembered going into that same sitting room one morning looking for the boys and finding Lincoln there in the big chair with an old, worn Bible on his lap. She approached him, and in "an absent-minded sort of way" he clasped her hand and rested it on his knee as he stared out the window. Looking in the same direction she could not see anything but the tops of trees. Julia remained in that position for what seemed a long time. Her arm ached, and she grew restless. Finally, Lincoln turned to her and appeared startled: "Why, Julia, have I been holding you here all this time?" "Yes, you have, Mr. President," she responded. He released her hand, and she went off to find the boys.

Julia was much enamored by Kate Chase's then beau, the "boy governor," William Sprague. Mary Lincoln perhaps saw an opportunity to make Kate jealous or angry, and had the gardener make up a special bouquet for Julia to deliver to Governor Sprague with her compliments. Setting off for Sprague's office and rehearsing what she was going to say to him, Julia ran into Kate. Always inquisitive, Kate asked where she was taking the flowers, and Julia replied honestly that Mrs. Lincoln gave them to her to take to Governor Sprague. Kate grabbed the bouquet from Julia and said she would hand them to the governor herself. Julia went back to Mrs. Lincoln in wrath and tears.[36]

Eleven-year-old Willie, the idolized, model son, came down with a severe cold and fever in early February, just a few days before the scheduled White House reception on February 5, 1862. The physician saw no cause for alarm and advised the Lincolns to proceed with the party. Determined to make the reception memorable, Mary hired one of the nation's most expensive caterers for an elaborate midnight buffet with mounds of turkey, duck, ham, terrapin, and pheasant flanking sugary models of the Ship of State, Fort Sumter, and Fort Pickens. The Lincolns received their five hundred guests in the East Room while the Marine band played. The music included a sprightly new piece, "The Mary Lincoln Polka," written for the event.

Mary's sartorial taste was for dresses shorter at the top and longer at the train than was customary at the time. For this special evening she wore a white satin dress decorated with hundreds of small black flowers. It exposed a remarkably low décolletage and had a very long train. As she swept through the room, Lincoln remarked to her: "Whew! Our cat has a long tail tonight." She ignored him. Lincoln then glanced at her bare arms and neck, and remarked: "If some of that tail was nearer the head, it would be in better style." An Oregon senator, offended by the First Lady's revealing gown, told his wife that Mary "had her bosom on exhibition and a flower pot on her head." He added: "I can't help regretting that she had degenerated from the industrious and unpretending woman she was in the days when she used to cook Old Abe's dinner and milk the cows with her own hands. Now her only ambition seems to be to exhibit her own milking apparatus to the public gaze. I regret she couldn't have brought something like Republican simplicity to the White House." Mary, however, was proud of her elegant neck and bust, and unconcerned that her revealing clothes grieved the president greatly. Regardless, the party was a tremendous success. Dinner was served until three in the morning, and most guests did not leave until daybreak. The *Washington Evening Star* called it "the most superb affair of its kind ever seen here."[37]

Upstairs, Willie ran a high fever, and both parents spent time with him. In the ensuing days Tad, nine, also became ill, and Willie grew weaker, gasping for breath and finally becoming delirious. It was probably typhoid fever, caused by White House water piped in directly from the sewage-infested Potomac River. On February 20, Willie died—perhaps from the same illness that had taken Ann Rutledge and her father in 1835. In a voice choked with emotion, Lincoln told his personal secretary: "My boy is gone—he is actually gone!" Then he burst into tears. A nurse from Massachusetts was among those who attended Willie during his illness. To her, he said: "This is the hardest trial of my life. Why is it? Why is it?" The nurse, who had lost her husband and two children, said she saw the hand of God in her tribulations, and she loved Him much more than she ever had. "How is that?" asked Lincoln. "Simply by trusting in God," she said, "and feeling that He does all things well." "Did you submit fully after your first loss?" he asked. "No, not wholly," she responded, "but as blow came upon blow, and all were taken, I could and did submit and then was very happy." "I am glad to hear you say that," Lincoln said. "It is comforting to me. Your experience will help me to bear my affliction. I will try to go to God with my sorrows." Then he spoke of his mother: "I remember her prayers, and they have always followed me. They have clung to me all my life."[38]

Lincoln's growing belief in the sovereignty of God helped to cushion his sorrow. He believed that the Almighty controlled everyone's destinies and had, for His own reasons, taken Willie. More than ever, Lincoln saw himself as "an instrument of Providence" for God's own purposes. As he talked with friends, he quoted from Hamlet as he had in New Salem twenty-seven years earlier: "There's a divinity that shapes our ends, Rough-hew them how we will."

Mary suffered a nervous breakdown. She was so distraught she confined herself to her bed for three weeks and was unable to attend the funeral or to look after Tad, who was steadily improving. She screamed and moaned and acted as if she had lost all control. After one such attack Lincoln took her by the arm, led her to a window, and pointed toward a lunatic asylum: "Mother, do you see that large white building on the hill yonder? Try and control your grief, or it will drive you mad, and we may have to send you there." When she finally emerged from her room, she wore layers of black veils and crepes for weeks and suspended social functions for nearly a year. She spoke of seeing Willie's ghost: "He lives! He comes to me every night and stands at the foot of my bed with the same sweet, adorable smile. You cannot dream of the comfort this gives me." Mary never again entered the room where Willie died or the Green Room where he was embalmed.[39]

The president turned to Mary's friend Senator Sumner and asked him to spend more time with her—to discuss issues of the day and escort her to the theater. Mary dressed up and sat for hours in the Blue Room, receiving his calls. They wrote each other notes in French, and she sent him bouquets from the White House conservatory. Sumner made her happy, and when she was happy, Lincoln was less troubled than he otherwise would have been.

While Lincoln occasionally rebuked his wife, Mary seemed to be constantly griping about her husband's manners, even at official White House functions. When the president used official cutlery to feed a cat on a chair next to him at a dinner party, Mary asked a guest, "Don't you think it's shameful for Mr. Lincoln to feed Tabby with a gold fork?" Before he could answer, the president replied: "If the gold fork was good enough for Buchanan, I think it is good enough for Tabby." He fed the cat throughout the dinner. Working late in his office at the White House one night, Lincoln was resolving pressing business when the butler announced that dinner was ready. Lincoln ignored him. Then Mary entered the office "and in her emphatic tones of command, so characteristic of her when she was displeased," demanded that Lincoln join her for dinner. He calmly walked with her out of the room, then quickly reentered and closed and locked the door before she could follow him. He then resumed his meeting. Mary complained often that Lincoln did not doff his hat properly. She asked White House guard Ward Hill Lamon and Secretary Seward to instruct him how to do so. Despite their efforts, he never learned to do it right.[40]

One day, Francis B. Carpenter, a portrait painter residing in the guest quarters next to the master bedroom, overheard the following conversation: "No, Mr. Lincoln, you shan't have them!" "Now, Mother, you know I must have them!" "No, you can't have them until you promise me . . ." (The painter could not hear her demand.) "But Mother, you know that I need to . . . ." "You need to be taught a lesson! Promise me what I asked for, or I won't let go of them." "Mother, come now! Be reasonable. Look at the clock. I'm already late; let me have them—please! How do you reckon I can go to a cabinet meeting—without my pants!"[41]

They apparently compromised, and he hurried to the cabinet meeting where newly appointed Secretary of War Edwin Stanton had news about the military campaign in the West. Stanton reported that Gen. Ulysses S. Grant had captured thirteen thousand Confederate prisoners at Forts Henry and Donelson and gained control of the Tennessee and Cumberland Rivers. "Finally," rejoiced Lincoln, "we have a commander who gets things done!"

Later in the spring of 1862, Federal troops drove Confederate forces from Kentucky, most of Tennessee, and northern Arkansas, and took six thousand prisoners at Island Number Ten in the Mississippi River. The Battle of Shiloh in Tennessee was costly for both sides, with twenty-four thousand casualties—the greatest losses in American history to that time. The war in the East had begun with a demoralizing Northern defeat at Bull Run, but Northern successes in the war's Western Theater gave Lincoln reason for hope.

11

"Her Letter Had Been Carefully Treasured by Him."

*F*rowning and downcast, the president wandered into a White House room where Mary was being fitted for a dress by her personal seamstress, Elizabeth "Lizzie" Keckley, a former slave who had purchased her freedom. Mary asked if Lincoln had any news from the war. "Yes, plenty of news," he replied, "but no good news. It is dark, dark everywhere." Gen. George B. McClellan, with the Federal army of the Potomac, had driven up Virginia's peninsula toward Richmond, but when within sight of the Confederate capital's church spires, he and his huge army had been ingloriously repulsed by Confederate forces under a new commander: Gen. Robert E. Lee. Lee then followed up on his victory on the Peninsula by decisively defeating another Federal army under Gen. John Pope at the battle of Second Manassas in August 1862.[1]

Apparently dismayed by the course of the war, Lincoln picked up a small Bible and soon was absorbed in reading it. Fifteen minutes later he was more cheerful, and he walked from the room, leaving the open Bible on the table. Mrs. Keckley looked at the book and discovered he was reading about Job. She noted the passage: "Gird up thy loins now like a man: I will demand of thee, and declare thou unto me."

Mary, disturbed by the war news, left Washington in July for New York, ostensibly to raise money for army hospitals and to get Tad out

179

of a city ridden with smallpox and malaria. Lizzie Keckley joined her a few days later. New York was a major center of the occult spiritualist movement, which had become increasingly popular as Northern parents and wives sought to reach sons and husbands killed in the war. Mary spent much of her time in New York in darkened parlors trying to communicate with Willie. Lincoln himself appears to have shown no interest in spiritualism.

Lincoln fell into a deep depression as the war appeared to go against the North in 1862. In his office, beneath the globe of a gas lamp, Lincoln wrote an informal memorandum to himself that year. It echoed his personal philosophy: "I am almost ready to say . . . that God wills this contest, and wills that it shall not end yet. [God could] have either saved or destroyed the Union without a human contest . . . and having begun He could give the final victory to either side any day. Yet the contest proceeds. In the present civil war it is quite possible that God's purpose is something different from the purpose of either party."[2]

A delegation of Quakers—three women and three men—visited Lincoln on the morning of Friday, June 20, 1862, and urged a proclamation to emancipate the slaves. All six delegates were abolitionists and supporters of the Underground Railroad that offered temporary shelter for fugitive slaves on their journey North. Lincoln agreed with them that slavery was wrong, but said he differed with them in regard to the ways and means of its removal. A decree of emancipation would not be effective, he said, because it could not be enforced. "True, Mr. President," said Oliver Johnson, one of the delegates, "but we are solemnly convinced that the abolition of slavery is indispensable to your success." Another delegate then expressed an earnest desire that Lincoln might "under Divine guidance, be led to free the slaves and thus save the nation from destruction." Lincoln assured them he was "deeply sensible of his need of Divine assistance" in the troubles he faced. He was willing, he said, to be an instrument in God's hands for accomplishing a great work, but "perhaps . . . God's way of accomplishing the end [of slavery] . . . may be different from theirs." That afternoon, however, Lincoln signed a bill freeing slaves in the territories.[3]

Lee, meanwhile, had invaded Maryland. With a major confrontation imminent, Lincoln told his cabinet: "I made a vow, a covenant, that if God gave us the victory in the approaching battle, I would consider it an indication of Divine will, and that it was my duty to move forward in the cause of emancipation." The opposing armies clashed for fourteen hours on Wednesday, September 17, 1862, along the banks of Antietam Creek near Sharpsburg, Maryland. It was the bloodiest day in American history: 4,800 dead and 18,500 wounded, of whom 3,000 died. The South called it a draw, but McClellan had stopped Lee's invasion. If McClellan had been daring, he could, in fact, have smashed Lee's forces and ended the war. Overly cautious again, he allowed Lee to retreat to Virginia without pursuit—a mistake that led Lincoln to remove the general after the fall elections.[4]

Regardless, Lincoln viewed Antietam as a victory and, perhaps, as the omen he had sought. He drafted an Emancipation Proclamation, which was scheduled to go into effect on January 1, 1863. It irrevocably notified the world that now the war was being fought not just to preserve the Union but to put an end to slavery. It also secured support for the war from abolitionists and black leaders; it opened the army and navy to Negro volunteers; and it enabled Union armies to free thousands of slaves as they occupied Southern territory.[5]

As Lincoln grappled with these momentous wartime issues, no one exerted a more positive female impact on him

Eliza Gurney strengthened Lincoln's faith. They exchanged beautiful and revelatory letters. One of them may have been in Lincoln's pocket when he was assassinated. COURTESY OF THE QUAKER COLLECTION, HAVERFORD COLLEGE.

than did Eliza Gurney, the well-to-do Quaker widow of a British banker. In 1862, she felt driven by God to meet with Lincoln immediately, she later reported. To fulfill this compulsion, Gurney—an attractive widow—took three close friends and journeyed to Washington. Their Sunday morning appointment had been arranged by another friend, Isaac Newton, U.S. commissioner of agriculture.[6]

A driving rainstorm pelted Washington that morning. Lincoln had risen early after a sleepless night and worked for two hours before breakfast—an egg and a cup of coffee. He was back at his desk when the Gurney delegation arrived around ten o'clock, and he stood to receive them. "Deep thoughtfulness and intense anxiety seemed to mark his countenance," one of them later remarked. Lincoln had just returned from a visit to battle sites, and he was troubled by what he saw. McClellan's "over-cautiousness" had exhausted the president's patience and was playing havoc in the upcoming Congressional elections. Lincoln feared a severe rebuff at the polls—one that would materialize as Democrats capitalized on what Lincoln called "the ill success of the war." "Lincoln's introverted look and his half-staggering gait," one woman wrote, "were like those of a man walking in sleep," and his face "revealed the ravages which care, anxiety, and overwork had wrought."[7]

Drawing her chair next to Lincoln, Mrs. Gurney emphasized that they came "in the love of the gospel of our Lord and Savior Jesus Christ" to express "the deep sympathy we feel for you in your arduous duties." Speaking softly and compassionately she said: "Earnestly have I desired that . . . whatever the trials and perplexities you may have to pass through, the peace of God, which passeth all understanding, will [fill] your heart and mind." As she spoke the group later reported that Lincoln's anxieties appeared to vanish. He listened intently. She said she "rejoiced in the noble effort" he had made to "loose the bands of wickedness [and] to let the oppressed go free. I assuredly believe that for this magnanimous deed the children yet unborn will rise up and call you blessed in the name of the Lord. . . . May our Father in heaven guide thee . . . and bestow upon thee a double portion of [His] wisdom." After speaking for about fifteen minutes, she knelt in prayer "for her country and for the president."[8]

It was a touching scene. The others stood in reverential awe, and the president "appeared bowed in heart under the weight of his deep responsibilities." Apparently the experience deeply moved Lincoln: tears ran down his cheeks. After a solemn pause, he responded:

> I am glad of this interview. As an humble instrument in the hands of my heavenly Father, I have desired that all my words and actions may be in accordance with His will; but if after endeavoring to do my best with the light which He affords me, I find my efforts fail, then I must believe that, for some purpose unknown to me, He wills it otherwise. If I had had my way, this war would never have been; but, nevertheless, it came. If I had had my way, the war would have ended before this; but, nevertheless, it continues. We must conclude that He permits it for some wise purpose, though we may not be able to comprehend it; for we cannot but believe that He who made the world still governs it.

It was a theme Lincoln would use in his second inaugural address. As the delegation prepared to leave, the president took Mrs. Gurney's hand. He held it for a few moments in silence and then said resolutely: "I repeat that I am glad of this interview."[9]

A year later the president asked Commissioner Newton to entreat Mrs. Gurney to write to him as he felt the need of her spiritual help and reinforcement. She wrote immediately. Dated August 18, 1863, it was the first letter in a remarkable exchange. Addressing him as "Esteemed Friend," she expressed thanks for his "praiseworthy and successful attempts . . . to let the oppressed go free" and quoted Scripture: "May the Lord hear thee in this day of trouble, the name of the God of Jacob defend thee, send thee help from His sanctuary, and strengthen thee." She commended his "excellent proclamation appointing a day of thanksgiving" and his desire "that the whole nation be led through paths of repentance and submission to the Divine Will back to the perfect enjoyment of union and fraternal peace."[10]

In the following year, on September 4, Lincoln responded in a beautiful and revelatory letter:

> MY ESTEEMED FRIEND—I have not forgotten, probably never shall forget, the very impressive occasion when yourself and friends visited me on a Sabbath forenoon two years ago. Nor has your kind letter . . . ever

been forgotten. In all it has been your purpose to strengthen my reliance on God. I am much indebted to the good Christian people of the country for their constant prayers and consolations, and to no one of them more than to yourself. The purposes of the Almighty are perfect, and must prevail, though we erring mortals may fail to accurately perceive them in advance. We hoped for a happy termination of this terrible war long before this; but God knows best, and has ruled otherwise. We shall yet acknowledge His wisdom and our own error therein. Meanwhile we must work earnestly in the best light He gives us, trusting that so working still conduces to the great ends He ordains. Surely He intends some great good to follow this mighty convulsion, which no mortal could make, and no mortal could stay.

He signed it, "Your sincere friend, A. Lincoln." Mrs. Gurney, in her response, asked that God continue to sustain and strengthen him, and declared that nearly all Friends supported his re-election, believing that he is "conscientiously endeavoring, according to his own convictions of right, . . . to discharge the solemn duties of his high and responsible office, not with eye-service [or] as men-pleasers, but in singleness of heart, fearing God."[11]

Seventeen years after Lincoln's assassination, Mrs. Gurney's devoted friend, Joseph Bevan Braithwaite, wrote in London's *Annual Monitor* that she "had the mournful satisfaction of learning that her [first] letter to the president . . . had been carefully treasured by him, and was in his pocket when the fatal shot reached him." Braithwaite was in a position to know. He had written her late husband's biography at her request and corresponded with her regularly from England. When he arrived in America in August 1865—four months after the assassination—he went directly from his boat to her home. Eliza Gurney was not a braggart or publicity seeker, and it would have been uncharacteristic of her to have promoted stories about the incident. Braithwaite's account of it was published a year after Mrs. Gurney's death as part of her obituary in a Quaker yearbook. It was his way of putting it on the record although his documentation was never released. Mrs. Gurney's daughter repeated the story of the letter in Lincoln's pocket in magazine articles that appeared in 1910 and 1926.[12]

Other Quakers also visited Lincoln for prayer and spiritual communion. He expressed his appreciation in a letter to two of them—Isaac and Sarah Harvey of Ohio—saying tenderly: "May the Lord comfort them as they have sustained me." Lincoln sympathized with the Quakers, and he stretched his administrative powers to provide relief for their conscientious convictions. In early 1864 a clause was added to the enrollment bill declaring Friends to be noncombatants. It assigned all drafted Friends to hospital service or work among freedmen. It further provided for the exemption of Friends from military service on the payment of three hundred dollars into a fund for the relief of sick and wounded.

At the White House Lincoln walked over to the War Department almost every evening to read the latest dispatches. There was often more bad news than good.

Fall and Winter 1862: Western Front—The North slowly tightened a noose around the Confederacy with five victories, including the important railroad junction at Corinth, Mississippi.

December 13, 1862: Against Lincoln's advice, Gen. Ambrose Burnside (McClellan's replacement) took his troops to Fredericksburg and suffered the worst defeat in the history of the American army up to that time—12,653 dead, wounded, or missing.

January 2, 1863: At Murfreesboro, Tennessee, both sides lost a third of their armies in a three-day battle from December 31 to January 2. On the cold night before fighting started, only a few yards separated the opposing armies. Huddled around campfires they sang together to pass the time. As crickets chirped and men envisioned pain and death, they sang "Home, Sweet Home."[13]

May 6, 1863: At Chancellorsville "Fighting Joe" Hooker (Burnside's replacement) acted like "Chicken Joe" and stopped his ingenious advance in three directions against Lee's encampment. Lee then attacked on two fronts, and Hooker retreated after losing seventeen thousand troops.

After Fredericksburg Lincoln remarked to his friend, Sen. Orville H. Browning, "We are on the brink of destruction. It appears to me the Almighty is against us, and I can hardly see a ray of hope." After Chancellorsville, the president appeared broken, dispirited, and ghostlike. He clasped his hands behind his back and paced up and down the

John Hay was assistant secretary to and a close friend of President Lincoln. Hay screened visitors and mail and prepared daily news summaries. Dealing with Mary Lincoln's temperamental outbursts, Hay and John Nicolay, Lincoln's chief secretary, referred to her as "the Hellcat." PHOTOGRAPH BY ALEXANDER GARDNER FROM AUTHOR'S COLLECTION.

room, exclaiming, "My God! My God! What will the country say! What will the country say!"[14]

It was usually near midnight when Lincoln settled down in the White House living quarters. "I consider myself fortunate if at eleven o'clock . . . my tired and weary husband is resting in the lounge to receive me—to chat over the occurrences of the day," Mary lamented. The president, however, received little emotional support from his wife. Still grieving for Willie, she dressed in black, consorted with spiritualists, and held at least eight séances in the White House. She also traveled to Boston, where thousands of spiritualists were active. Although distraught and wallowing in self-pity, Mary remained concerned about her husband's health and poor eating habits but troubled him by stating her political views publicly through letters and conversations. From 1863 until his death, the Lincolns seemed to have drifted apart. She avoided him out of fear he might raise "forbidden subjects" such as her debts and extravagance. He was afraid to confide in her because he did not trust her eccentric judgment and did not want to disturb her fragile mental health. For a cultured woman brought up around successful politicians, she was strangely naive. She even chose as a close friend the wife of Judge James W. White, who led a petition drive to oust Secretary Seward from Lincoln's cabinet. Under such circumstances, Lincoln was not about to share sensitive information with Mary.

Lizzie Keckley wrote in her memoir: "When in one of her wayward, impulsive moods, Mrs. Lincoln was apt to say and do things that wounded him deeply. She often wounded him in unguarded moments." For the first time Mary became critical of him around other people and called an 1864 impromptu address "the worst speech I ever listened to in my life." Caught off-guard by the crowd's insistence that he speak while at a benefit for the Christian Commission, a wartime charity, he paid tribute to women active in war relief. Mary, perhaps in her own harsh way, tried to goad him to do better. She chided him: "How any man could deliver such remarks to an audience is more than I can understand. I wanted the earth to sink and let me go through." He did not reply.[15]

Lincoln's oldest son, Robert, was at Harvard College much of the year, but even when he returned to the White House during holidays, he did not provide much companionship. Their conversations were stiff and awkward. Lincoln's best support came from his private secretaries, John G. Nicolay and John Hay. They lived in the White House, and Lincoln dropped in on them at night to chat and review the day's news. Working side by side with them for long hours, Lincoln came to trust them with secrets of state. Hay, especially, was an intimate friend and was closer to Lincoln than was any other man during the war years.[16]

Occasionally, when Mary was out of town, Hay accompanied Lincoln to the theater. Hay, whose college roommate called him "a great favorite with the ladies," said it was a relaxing treat to watch "those Southern girls with their well-rounded forms, lustrous hair, and sparkling voices."[17]

Nicolay and Hay often clashed with Mary, whom Hay called "The Hellcat" or "The Madam." Their sharp conflicts were ostensibly over White House management but may have stemmed from jealousy over access to the president.

12

"The Best Abused Man of Our Nation."

Lincoln had endorsed women's suffrage during his campaign for reelection to the Illinois legislature in 1836. It pained him that women in America had almost no rights and few opportunities—including the right to vote. Wanting "to do right . . . in all cases with women," as he had stated years earlier, he startled the capital city by endorsing female employment in Federal offices, not just as temporary "government girls," but as a permanent part of the Washington scene. U.S. Treasurer Francis Spinner appointed the first female staffers, defended them against critics, and commended them for their efficiency. With Lincoln's backing, the Post Office Department continued to appoint postmistresses, especially when soldiers' widows had "claims and qualifications" equal to male applicants. When a man and woman applied for the postal position in Rockford, Illinois, Lincoln supported the woman because she was a war widow and had "the better right" to the job.

Despite Lincoln's progressive views, he was tormented by militant women and others who boldly demanded favors, privileges, or immunities and protested alleged injustices done to them. Generally, his manner toward them was kind and courteous, but there were exceptions. Lincoln lost his composure with Jessie Fremont, the wife of Gen. John C. Fremont. In a wartime meeting, she taxed Lincoln's patience so much he had to exercise extreme tact in dealing with her.

Lincoln had disagreed with her husband on several issues during the general's command in Missouri. In response, the general sent his politically powerful wife to Washington to present his case to the president. In a long discourse she forcefully defended her husband. Lincoln finally interrupted: "You are quite a female politician." She left in anger, prompting Lincoln to write a letter to her explaining he did not question her husband's "honor or integrity."[1]

Anna Elizabeth Dickinson, an outspoken young Quaker abolitionist, denounced Lincoln in 1862 as "an ass." Only twenty years old at the time, she had been writing and speaking about abolition for six years and was impatient with Lincoln's reluctance to free the slaves. Young, female, and an outspoken and skilled orator, she was a popular novelty in the North. In 1863, at age twenty-one, she was asked by the Republican Party to tour on behalf of its candidates. In New York an audience of five thousand hailed her as the Joan of Arc of the abolition cause. By then she was calling Lincoln "the wisest scoundrel in the country."[2]

Her shining moment came on January 16, 1864, when she addressed the House of Representatives on behalf of the Freedmen's Aid Society. Following a highly complimentary introduction by Vice President Hamlin, she launched a lowly, uncomplimentary two-hour tirade against Lincoln, who was seated directly in front of her. Then at the end of her speech, she reversed herself and endorsed his reelection, confusing everyone. Visiting Lincoln at the Executive Mansion, she urged him to do more to enforce the Emancipation Proclamation and called his reconstruction policy in Louisiana "all wrong, as radically bad as can be." He thanked her for her concerns but ended the visit by saying, "If the Radicals want me to lead, let them get out of the way and let me lead." Indignant, she stormed out of the White House.[3]

Another Anna—Anna Ella Carroll, the militant daughter of a former Maryland governor—wrote and distributed eloquent and persuasive pamphlets that supported Lincoln's policies and helped keep Maryland in the Union. Had Maryland seceded, the national capital would have been in great danger. "I am writing to aid my country," Carroll said, and no woman surpassed her as a political pamphleteer. In one of her pamphlets, Carroll defended Lincoln's controversial assumption of broad presidential war powers. Under these powers, Lincoln usurped what had been a Congressional responsibility and suspended the writ of habeas corpus, enabling Northern military leaders to arrest anyone thought to be aiding the Confederacy—including secessionist legislators in Maryland. For her effective but unsolicited public relations work, Carroll demanded fifty thousand dollars. It was twice Lincoln's annual salary, and he called it "the most outrageous demand ever made to any government upon earth." While rejecting her claim as exorbitant, he paid her "a very handsome compliment" in his cabinet meeting of April 14, 1862, citing her important "usefulness to the country." The following month he allegedly told several congressmen she would "stand a good deal taller" than her father, the former governor, when "the history of this war is written."[4]

Carroll's contributions as a military strategist are not as well defined and continue to be debated. But her devotees assert she did, indeed, frame plans that led to early Union victories and that her amazing accomplishments were concealed because she was a woman. In 1870—five years after the end of the war—she claimed she originated the plan adopted by General Grant in his successful Tennessee River campaign that contributed to the Confederacy's downfall. Petitioning Congress in 1870 for payment of $250,000 for the plan, she alleged that the War Department presented her proposal to Lincoln and secured his endorsement. Her demand was not met, even though Benjamin Wade, the abolitionist senator from Ohio, believed she had proposed "some of the most successful expeditions of the war," among them "the expedition up the Tennessee River." Illinois Sen. O. H. Browning, a close friend of Lincoln, wrote that her "suggestions [for] important military movements were among the meritorious services [Lincoln and Stanton] recognized as entitled to remuneration."[5]

Wanting to be accessible to all classes of citizens, Lincoln opened his office twice a week for those who might wish to speak with him. He was usually clad in a black broadcloth suit and neat cloth slippers and seated in an armchair beside a cloth-covered table. Each visitor was allotted a few minutes to state the object of his or her visit, and the president listened and decided each case. Southern women were frequently among the petitioners, and with them, Lincoln was sometimes brutally frank. To a Mississippi widow who asked for freedmen to run her farm, Lincoln replied: "I'd rather take a rope and hang myself than to do what you ask. There are a great many poor women who have

Abolitionist Harriet Beecher Stowe strongly supported Lincoln. Her anti-slavery novel *Uncle Tom's Cabin* was a potent abolitionist weapon in the North. NATIONAL ARCHIVES.

never had any property who are suffering as much as you are. Your condition is a necessary consequence of the rebellion." To a Baltimore woman who wanted a parole for her Confederate son, Lincoln said: "I can do nothing for your boy." To a couple who wanted a pardon for a convicted spy, he said sternly: "He was a spy, he has been a spy, he ought to have been hanged as a spy. . . . You ought to bless your stars that he got off with a whole neck; and if you do not want to see him hanged as high as Haman, do not come to me again."[6]

Lincoln warmly welcomed antislavery crusader Harriet Beecher Stowe in November 1862. According to family stories he greeted the author of *Uncle Tom's Cabin* by jesting, "So you are the little woman who wrote the book that made this great war." Her 1852 novel about brutal treatment of slaves may, indeed, have hastened the secession crisis. During their pleasant and candid conversation, Lincoln remarked, "Whichever way [the war] ends, I have the impression that I shan't last long after it is over." Perhaps Lincoln reminisced about Stowe's brother Edward Beecher, who was president of Illinois College in Jacksonville in 1835 when Ann Rutledge's brother David attended there. During his years in Springfield, Lincoln was surely aware of President Beecher and probably knew him. It was a remarkable coincidence that Beecher's sister and David Rutledge's anticipated brother-in-law were conversing twenty-seven years later in the White House.

Writing about her visit in Boston journals, Mrs. Stowe compared

Lincoln's "peculiar" strength to a wire cable that sways to every influence, but is "tenaciously and inflexibly bound to carry its great end." Lincoln was "the best abused man of our nation," she said. "He has seen the day when every man seemed ready to stone him, and yet, with simple, wiry, steady perseverance, he has held on, conscious of honest intentions and looking to God for help." She extolled him as "the safest leader a nation could have" in such perilous times—a leader who was "slow and careful in coming to resolutions" and "willing to talk with every person who has anything to show on any side of a disputed subject. . . . A ruthless, bold, theorizing, dashing man of genius might have wrecked our constitution."[7]

The mother of two men imprisoned for resisting the draft in western Pennsylvania—and the wife of one of them—came to Lincoln for help in freeing the men. Lincoln obtained a list of all draft resisters in prison in the region and asked a general if there were "any difference in the charges in degree of guilt." When he learned there were none, Lincoln said "these fellows have suffered long enough. . . . I will turn out the flock." The young wife ran forward and was about to kneel in thankfulness. "Do not kneel to me," said Lincoln. "Thank God and go." The older woman came forward with tears in her eyes. "Good-bye, Mr. Lincoln. I shall never see you again till we meet in Heaven." He instantly took her right hand in both of his. "I am afraid with all my troubles I shall never get there. But if I do, I will find you. That you wish me to go there is the best wish you could make for me. Good-bye."[8]

Lincoln's friend Joshua Speed had overheard the discussion from the waiting room. He approached Lincoln and said: "Lincoln, with my knowledge of your nervous sensibility, it is a wonder that such scenes as this do not kill you." Said Lincoln: "Things of that sort do not hurt me. For to tell you the truth, that is the only thing I have done today which has given me any pleasure. Those women were no counterfeits. The mother spoke out in all the features of her face. In doing right, I have made two people happy in one day. Speed, die when I may, I want it said of me by those who know me best that I always plucked a thistle and planted a flower when I thought a flower would grow."[9]

As Lincoln worried about pending battles in Pennsylvania and at Vicksburg that could determine the war's outcome, his health suffered.

A visitor noted "the drooping eyelids, looking almost swollen; the dark bags beneath the eyes; the deep marks about the large and expressive mouth." In 1863 Lee invaded the North again and headed toward Pennsylvania, pursued by Gen. George G. Meade and the Army of the Potomac. Despite the grave situation in Pennsylvania, Mary took Tad with her on a shopping binge to Philadelphia. While they were away, Lincoln dreamed Tad shot himself with a pistol Lincoln had permitted him to have—the gun was big enough to snap caps but not big enough for cartridges or powder. Rising early, Lincoln wired Mary: "Think you better put Tad's pistol away."[10]

On July 2, back from Philadelphia, Mary rode alone in the presidential carriage, returning to the White House from the Soldiers' Home, which served as Lincoln's summer retreat in Washington. Hearing a strange noise from the front, Mary looked up just in time to see the driver's seat and the coachmen fly off the carriage and fall in the road. The frightened horses bolted into a fast, uncontrolled gallop, with Mary screaming for help. On a curve in the road, the carriage struck a tree, throwing Mary to the ground. Her head hit a rock, and she was taken unconscious to an army hospital. Summoned from a White House meeting, Lincoln hurriedly drove to the hospital in his carriage. He whispered "Molly" into her ear—a nickname he often called her—but she did not respond. She did not regain consciousness until the next day. She was taken to the White House and remained bedridden for three weeks. An investigation found that the screws to the driver's seat had been removed by an unidentified culprit in an obvious attempt to injure the president. Mary's injury may have been more than physical. Robert Lincoln later said that his mother was never the same after this incident.

Her accident occurred as a great battle bloodied the Pennsylvania fields and ridges near Gettysburg. One-third of Lee's army—22,200—was lost in the three-day battle, and his crippled forces retreated southward toward Virginia. An equally important Northern victory occurred just one day after the fighting ended at Gettysburg: the mighty Confederate bastion at Vicksburg on the Mississippi surrendered to Grant's army. With the fall of Vicksburg (and Port Hudson five days later), the South was split asunder, with the Mississippi River totally under Federal control. Lincoln threw his arms around

Secretary of the Navy Gideon Welles and exclaimed, "I cannot, in words, tell you my joy over this result. The Father of Waters again goes unvexed to the sea! It is great, Mr. Welles, it is great!"[11]

As the war shifted in favor of the North, Lincoln sought relief from the intense pressures by spending more time at the Soldiers' Home. He was often alone. Meanwhile, Mary—now recovered from her accident—undertook the longest trip of her White House years. She and Tad vacationed in the White Mountains of New Hampshire. Lincoln corresponded with Mary by short, impersonal telegrams. On September 20, 1863, he wrote, "I wish you to stay or come just as is most agreeable to yourself." The next day he telegraphed: "I would be glad for you to come. . . . I would be glad [to] see you and Tad." Offended by these messages, Mary berated him, hoping "for one line to say that we are occasionally remembered."[12]

Lincoln seemed unable to resist indulging his wife and children. Ten-year-old Tad—loud, eccentric, and full of creative mischief— sprayed dignitaries with a fire hose, ran in and out of cabinet meetings, and after Lincoln created Thanksgiving Day, got his father to pardon the Thanksgiving turkey. When Tad pulled up some choice plants in the White House garden, the head gardener was irate and declared to his assistant he would tell the madam. "But remember," the assistant said, "he is the madam's son." Retorted the gardener: "He's the madam's wildcat." Mary thought otherwise. "I do not have any trouble managing Tad," she bragged. "He is my little troublesome sunshine."

To briefly free himself from troubling times, the president took Mary, Mrs. Hunter Cameron, and Nicolay and Hay to Ford's Theatre on November 9 to see John Wilkes Booth in *Marble Heart*. Lincoln applauded the actor rapturously and sent word backstage he would like to meet him. Booth declined the interview and told the messenger he would rather have "the applause of a nigger" than that of Lincoln.[13]

Back in the White House Lincoln worked on "a few appropriate remarks" for the dedication of the military cemetery at Gettysburg on November 19, 1863. On the day of his scheduled departure, family problems almost interfered. Tad was too sick to eat breakfast, and Mary screamed at her husband, demanding that he not leave her alone with the sick child. He said that the occasion was too important for him not to be there. He left at noon and arrived at Gettysburg around five o'clock. A telegram from Secretary of War Stanton relayed good news about Tad: "Mrs. Lincoln informed me that your son is better this evening." Lincoln was relieved, and he laughed and joked with his companions. Lincoln's short, ten-sentence speech followed a two-hour oration by Edward Everett, formerly a senator and president of Harvard College. Few remember Everett's remarks, but Lincoln's masterfully phrased comments became the most memorable speech in American history.

The Gettysburg Address was a fervent eulogy to the document that shaped Lincoln's political philosophy—the Declaration of Independence. Lincoln linked the nation's birth not to the year the Constitution was ratified but to 1776, the year of the Declaration. Lincoln saw the Constitution as flawed because it protected the interests of slave owners. But the Declaration proclaimed freedom and equality and that represented to Lincoln "a law higher than the Constitution." Lincoln was emphasizing that human equality was what the war was all about. By doing so he had changed the meaning of the war—he had placed the war on a higher moral ground.

In September the husband of Mary's youngest half sister, Emilie Todd Helm, was killed at Chickamauga. He was a Confederate general, and Emilie was outspoken in her loyalty to the South. She buried her husband in Atlanta and, with her six-year-old daughter Katherine, headed for Washington, hoping "Brother Lincoln" would help them get home to Kentucky. But when she refused to take an oath of allegiance to the Union, the army detained her at Fort Monroe. Lincoln was notified, and he wired back, "Send her to me." Lincoln and Mary welcomed Emilie with "the warmest affection" and sought to comfort her in her loss, she later wrote in her diary. Knowing her presence would be troublesome, the Lincolns tried to conceal her visit, but the embarrassing news leaked out, spawning scandalous stories. "You should not have that Rebel in your house!" exclaimed Gen. Daniel Sickles, who had lost a leg at Gettysburg. "My wife and I are in the habit of choosing our own guests," Lincoln responded. "We do not need advice or assistance in this matter."[14]

During Emilie's stay, she and Mary dined alone and talked about old friends and wept over family tragedies. Emilie wrote in her diary: "Sister and I cannot open our hearts to each other as freely as we would like. This frightful war comes between us like a barrier of granite closing our lips but not our hearts, for though our tongues are tied, we weep over our dead together and express through our clasped hands the sympathy we feel for each other." They avoided talk about the war, but Tad and little Katherine felt no constraints. Looking at newspapers on the floor of the sitting room, Tad beamed, "Oh, here's a picture of the president." "No, that's not the president. Jeff Davis is the president," Katherine asserted. As they were about to get into a tussle, Lincoln picked them up and placed them on his knees. "Well, Tad, you know who your president is," and then, looking at Katherine, he said with a chuckle, "I will just be your Uncle Lincoln."[15]

Later in the day Lincoln said to Emilie: "Little Sister, I hope you can come up and spend the summer with us at the Soldiers' Home. You and Mary love each other. It is good for her to have you with her—I feel worried about Mary; her nerves have gone to pieces; she cannot hide from me that the strain she has been under has been too much for her mental as well as her physical health. What do you think?" Emilie admitted that she too was concerned about Mary. "She does seem very nervous and excitable," Emilie said, "and once or twice the frightened look in her eyes has appalled me. She seems to fear that other sorrows may be added to those we already have to bear. I believe if anything were to happen to you or Robert or Tad it would kill her." Lincoln, shaking his head sorrowfully, said: "Stay with her as long as you can."[16]

Emilie stayed only a week. With a pass from Lincoln to cross army lines, she returned to Kentucky, where she resumed her pro-South behavior. Lincoln reacted by revoking a previous order to shield her from arrest. In a message to the Federal commander of the District of Kentucky, he wrote: "If the papers given her by me can be construed to give her protection from [disloyal] words or acts, it is hereby revoked pro tanto. Deal with her for her current conduct just as you would with any other." Emilie's visit, however, helped to bring Mary out of her shell and her mourning clothing. At the 1864 New Year's Day reception in the White House, Mary appeared in a purple dress trimmed with black velvet. Both the president and the First Lady showed more enthusiasm than had been evident in months. For the first time in American history the guests presented to the president at the reception included what one newspaper described as "four colored men of genteel exterior, and with the manners of gentlemen."[17]

When Lincoln's secretary, John G. Nicolay, produced the guest list for the annual cabinet dinner on January 14, Mary struck off Treasury Secretary Salmon P. Chase, whom she regarded as a political enemy, as well as his daughter Kate and his son-in-law William Sprague. Lincoln ordered the names restored, and "her Satanic Majesty," as Nicolay once called Mary, went on a rampage, according to Nicolay. Mary attempted to handle the dinner arrangements herself, but on the afternoon of the dinner, she realized she was unable to manage. She apologized to Nicolay and requested his help. "I think," reported Nicolay, "she has felt happier since she cast out that devil of stubbornness."[18]

Throughout the war years, Lincoln apparently continued to occasionally dwell on the memory of Ann Rutledge.

Artist Francis B. Carpenter lived in the White House while working on portraits of Lincoln and sometimes shared evenings with the president. On one occasion in 1864, Lincoln leaned back in his armchair and discussed poetry with Carpenter. "There are some quaint, queer verses written, I think, by Oliver Wendell Holmes," Lincoln said. He named "The Last Leaf," as one he found "inexpressibly touching." He recited part of it: "The mossy marbles rest / On the lips that he had pressed / in their bloom / And the names he loved to hear / Have been carved for many a year / On the tomb." As he finished the verse, Lincoln said in his emphatic way: "For pure pathos, in my judgment, there is nothing finer than those six lines in the English language!" Memories haunted Lincoln. Did he think of Ann Rutledge when he quoted romantic poetry to Carpenter? Was it Ann Rutledge whose lips he "pressed in their bloom" and whose name he "loved to hear"?

Mary disliked Ulysses S. Grant, whom Lincoln named as general-in-chief of the Federal armies in 1864. Engaging Lee in a bloody series of battles in Virginia in the dreadful summer of that year, Grant was relentless despite severe Federal losses. At the battle of the Wilderness, Grant lost 17,000 to Lee's 11,000; at Spotsylvania, 11,000 to 4,000. At Cold Harbor, near Richmond, Grant sustained his worst defeat of the war, losing 7,000 in a controversial assault. In six weeks of incessant fighting, Grant incurred almost 100,000 casualties—which was a number greater than the troops in Lee's Army of Northern Virginia. Grant had literally marched in blood and agony from Northern Virginia to the James River and had few victories to show for it. However, he had forced Lee to fall back step by step to a line near the Confederate capital. A weary Johnny Reb pondered the superior numbers of Grant's army: "What's the use of killing those fellows? Kill one and half a dozen take his place." Grant remained determined despite his horrendous losses. "I propose to fight it out on this line if it takes all summer," he wired Washington. "He has the grit of a bulldog!" Lincoln said admiringly. "Once let him get his 'teeth' in, and nothing can shake him off." Grant eventually besieged Lee at Petersburg, and the campaign fell into bloody, prolonged trench warfare. Inflamed at the heavy loss of life, Democrats began calling Grant and Lincoln "widow-makers." Grant was "a butcher [who] is not fit to be at the head of an army," proclaimed Mary. "Well, Mother, suppose we give you command of the army," Lincoln replied. "No doubt you would do better than any generals I have tried." The awful bloodshed also troubled Lincoln. He and Mary often visited army hospitals together. She brought delicacies from the White House kitchen; talked to the men; read to them; wrote letters for them; and endured the blood, the smells, and the groans of the wounded. Somehow she got through it, and so did Lincoln. "I cannot pretend to advise," he told Grant at one point, "but I do sincerely hope that all may be accomplished with as little bloodshed as possible."[19]

In July 1864 Confederate Gen. Jubal A. Early crossed the Potomac with twenty thousand troops and advanced on Washington. Early's army damaged railroads, destroyed telegraph lines, and stripped the countryside of food and military equipment. In Washington, some frightened inhabitants fled to Georgetown and slept in the streets. Lincoln, Mary, and Tad were hustled back to the White House from the Soldiers' Home, and a naval vessel stood by in the Potomac to evacuate them if necessary.

On July 11 Early's forces marched through Silver Spring and approached Fort Stevens on the outskirts of the capital. Smoke darkened the sky as Lincoln arrived at the fort to assess the situation. The next day Lincoln returned to the fort with Mary, who thought a military outing would clear her aching head. On Gen. Horatio Wright's reckless suggestion, the president mounted a parapet for a clear view, and a surgeon standing near him was shot. "Get down, Mr. President!" Wright exclaimed. "But I want to watch the action," Lincoln countered. "Step down, now, or I will have you forcibly removed," Wright said in exasperation. "Alright," Lincoln conceded, "I will stand behind the parapet." Moments later, as the president turned to speak to a nearby officer, a bullet smashed the man's face, and he fell dead beside the president. Another soldier shoved Lincoln to the ground. As the day ended, the reinforced Federals prevailed, and Early's army retreated. Wright made a lackadaisical move to chase them but stopped, "for fear he might come across the Rebels and catch some of them," Lincoln said angrily. Lincoln's encounter at Fort Stevens was the only time a sitting American president and First Lady were together while under enemy fire in battle.[20]

Mary, still spending lavishly to ornament herself, told Lizzie Keckley that she was terribly worried that Lincoln might not be reelected. "To me, to him, there is more at stake in this election than he dreams of." "What can you mean, Mrs. Lincoln?" asked Keckley. "I don't comprehend." "Simply this," responded Mary. "I have contracted large debts of which he knows nothing, and which he will be unable to pay if he is defeated. They consist chiefly of store bills. I owe altogether about $27,000. You understand, Lizabeth, that Mr. Lincoln has but little idea of the expense of a woman's wardrobe. He glances at my rich dresses and is happy in the belief that the few hundred dollars that I obtain from him supply all my wants." Justifying her debt, Mary said she "must dress in costly materials" because being from the West, she is subjected to "more searching observation. . . . To keep up appearances, I must have money—more than Mr. Lincoln can spare for me." "He does not suspect how much you owe?" Lizzie asked. "God, no! And I would not have him suspect," Mary exclaimed. "He does not know a thing about any debts, and I value his happiness too much to allow him to know anything. This is what troubles me so much. If he is re-elected, I can keep him in ignorance of my affairs; but if he is defeated, then the bills will be sent in, and he will know all."[21]

Sojourner Truth, reared as a slave, became a national figure in anti-slavery and women's rights causes. She told Lincoln that he was "the best president" in American history. COURTESY OF SUNY COLLEGE AT NEW PALTZ.

Mary had ample reason to be worried. Lincoln himself had all but conceded defeat. The country was war-weary. "Negotiate to end the killing" was a common cry. The Union armies appeared stalemated, and the Republicans were badly divided. It was no wonder that a visitor found Lincoln deeply depressed, "indeed quite paralyzed and wilted down." General Grant wrote to a friend: "I think . . . for [Lincoln] to attempt to answer all the charges the opposition will bring against him will be like setting a maiden to work to prove her chastity."[22]

Early's advance on Washington in the summer of 1864 had alarmed politicians and fueled war weariness in the North. Under pressure from Lincoln, Grant sent Gen. Philip Sheridan and his Federal cavalry to the Shenandoah Valley in August 1864 with orders to destroy Early's army and render the region unfit to supply further Confederate operations. When Sheridan's campaign ended, much of the Shenandoah Valley lay in smoldering ruins.

A former slave, bought and sold three times on the auction block, visited Lincoln on October 29, 1864, to thank him for the Emancipation Proclamation. This tall, slender woman was an illiterate but intelligent grandmother who had risen magnificently to become a legend in her own time. Legally freed with all slaves in New York State in 1827, she announced one night at a prayer meeting: "I am no longer Isabella (her name as a slave). I am Sojourner Truth, an instrument for the Lord's bidding." Traveling throughout the land as a Methodist evangelist, the eloquent "African prophetess" moved friend and foe alike with her "heart of love and tongue of fire." Soon she was a national figure loathed and feared by Southerners and Northern conservatives for her "-isms"—radicalism, abolitionism, and feminism.

At a women's rights convention, she responded to a clergyman who argued that women should not have as many rights as men "because Christ was not a woman." With her eyes piercing the preacher, she asked him: "Where did your Christ come from?" Raising her voice still louder, she repeated: "Where did your Christ come from? [He came] from God and a woman! Man had nothing to do with Him!" The entire crowd responded with deafening applause.[23]

In the war's early stages, Sojourner Truth had been troubled by Lincoln's goal of preserving the Union rather than freeing the slaves. But after his Proclamation, she felt that "God's hand is in this war, and it will end in the destruction of slavery." In 1864, at about the age of sixty-seven, she resolved to visit Lincoln and made the long journey from her home in Battle Creek, Michigan. Lizzie Keckley helped arrange the appointment. A respected Negro leader, Sojourner Truth was president of the Ladies' Contraband Relief Association. It was dedicated to finding food and jobs for fugitive slaves. Mary Lincoln was among its contributors.[24]

"I am pleased to see you," Lincoln said as he stood and extended his hand to Sojourner Truth. He thanked her for her work against slavery and for assisting freed blacks who had rushed to Washington seeking refuge. She said she appreciated him, "for you are the best president who has ever taken the seat."[25]

Lincoln showed her an elegantly bound Bible presented to him by Baltimore's black community. Removing it from its silk-lined walnut case, he handed it to her. "It is beautiful beyond description," she said, admiring its velvet lining, banded-gold corners, and heavy gold clasps. "Isn't it ironical," she said, "that colored people gave this holy book to the head of the government—a government that once sanctioned laws prohibiting them from learning enough to be able to read this book. Indeed, it's a beautiful gesture on their part to give such a valuable book to you."

"I told them," said Lincoln, "that the Bible is the best gift God has given to man. . . . But for this book we could not know right from wrong. All things most desirable for human welfare, here and here-after, are to be found portrayed in it. Their gift of this book to me is one of my greatest treasures." Lincoln then autographed a book she carried. As she was taking her leave, he took her hand and said he would be pleased to have her call again. She later said: "I never was treated by anyone with more kindness and cordiality than were shown to me by that great and good man. I felt I was in the presence of a friend."

Other writers have stated that Sojourner Truth advised Lincoln on such issues as the cruelty of slavery, freeing the slaves, and enlisting blacks in the Union army. Such claims "have not been substantiated and in any case seem inherently improbable," wrote her biographer Carleton Mabee. Lincoln may have been influenced by articles he read about her, but by her own words, they did not meet before October 1864. By that time Lincoln's positions on those issues were well established.[26]

While the blacks praised Lincoln for the Emancipation Proclamation, the Democrats attacked him for it. During the political campaign of 1864, they publicized rumors of young white women parading the streets with banners inscribed, "Fathers, Protect Us From Negro Equality" and of sixty-four white schoolteachers at Port Royal, South Carolina, giving birth to mulatto babies. The Democrats also coined a new word, "miscegenation," and explained it with an illustration in a pamphlet showing a Negro man and a white woman in fond embrace. McClellan, the Democratic candidate, had pledged to end the war by suspending the Emancipation Proclamation. He wanted an immediate armistice. The country's future was at stake. If McClellan had won, the South would have won its independence and kept its slaves. Thus the election marked the beginning of a seventy-five-year affiliation of black people with the Republican Party.[27]

After the election Lincoln pressed for an amendment to the constitution banning slavery forever in every part of the nation. It required a two-thirds majority in the House of Representatives. Lincoln worked the Congress one-by-one, cajoling, arm-twisting, and using all of his political skills to secure the necessary votes. He was successful, but just barely. The measure passed by three votes.

When the final tally was announced, "there was a moment of utter silence," wrote correspondent Noah Brooks. "Then there was an explosion, a storm of cheers, the like of which probably no Congress of the United States ever heard before. Strong men embraced each other with tears. The galleries and aisles were bristling with standing, cheering crowds . . . women's handkerchiefs waving and floating . . . arms around each other's necks, and cheer after cheer . . . burst after burst." "The great job is ended," Lincoln exclaimed in the White House. It is a "great moral victory," he said. That night Lincoln slept better than he had in years.

Newspapers ran a popular cartoon showing a black man who said, "Now I's nobody's nigger but my own." In mass meetings, blacks sang, "Jehovah has triumphed, His people are free." Before the Thirteenth Amendment could go into effect, it had to be ratified by twenty-seven of the thirty-six states. Lincoln's home state of Illinois began the process, and the amendment soon was well on its way to becoming the law of the land.

When Robert Lincoln came home for Christmas in 1864, he repeated a request he had often made: "I want to enlist in the army." He had graduated earlier that year from Harvard and was now studying law. Critics had called him a "shirker" for not serving his country. Mary was against it at first, but now acknowledged that Robert's plea "was manly and noble, and I want him to go . . . but I am so frightened he may never come back to us." "Many a poor mother has had to make this sacrifice," Lincoln said, "and has given up every son she had—and lost them all." Mary's voice quivered: "Before this war is over I may be like . . . my poor mother in Kentucky with not a prop left in her old age." Lincoln asked General Grant to find a place for Robert with some nominal rank, and offered to pay his official expenses. He became an aide to Grant. He would never be exposed to battle. He would witness Lee's surrender.[28]

Lincoln's heart went out to mothers who suffered multiple losses— women such as Sarah Mills of Des Moines, Iowa, who lost her husband, father, and brother at the battle of Corinth, Mississippi, and Polly Ray, a widow in North Carolina whose seven sons were all killed in the war. Lincoln had recently written a compassionate and masterful letter to a Massachusetts woman, Lydia Bixby, who said five of her sons had been killed:

> I have been shown in the files of the War Department a statement of the Adjutant General of Massachusetts that you are the mother of five sons who have died gloriously on the field of battle.
>
> "I feel how weak and fruitless must be any words of mine which should attempt to beguile you from the grief of a loss so overwhelming. But I cannot refrain from tendering to you the consolation that may be found in the thanks of the Republic they died to save.
>
> "I pray that our Heavenly Father may assuage the anguish of your bereavement, and leave you only the cherished memory of the loved and lost, and the solemn pride that must be yours, to have laid so costly a sacrifice upon the altar of Freedom." [29]

It wasn't until years later historians discovered that Mrs. Bixby was a Confederate sympathizer who ran a whorehouse and that she had lied about her sons. She actually lost two, not five. Of the three others, one had deserted the army, another may have deserted, and the third was honorably discharged. Despite the mythology of her case, Lincoln's letter to her would enter American history and folklore as a classic example of presidential compassion.

While Lincoln's attention was riveted on the war and reelection, two congressional friends dropped in to ask him to pose for a seventeen-year-old female sculptor, Miss Vinnie Ream. He refused, saying he did not have time. "But, Mr. President," one of them argued, "she's a poor girl from the Wisconsin Territory." They explained that she was struggling on her own and had done fine work for others, including a number of congressmen. They pointed out that she was being tutored by Clark Mills, a famous sculptor, who had talked about her "remarkable ability." Mills' studio was in the Capitol basement, and congressmen could not help but notice his beautiful young apprentice. Smitten by the young woman, they willingly posed for her. To some of them she expressed an interest in doing a bust of the president. Looking at them with her sparkling brown eyes and gleaming smile, she knew they would help. Now two of them were trying to. They noted that Ream's father was a land surveyor who had brought his family to Washington

Vinnie Ream, a seventeen-year-old sculptress and art prodigy, convinced Lincoln to pose for her. Fortunately for Lincoln, his wife never learned he was alone with the attractive teenager. After Lincoln's death Vinnie was chosen to do his life-size statue for the U.S. Capitol. LIBRARY OF CONGRESS.

in 1861 and acquired a government job. Ream, then not quite fifteen, applied at the Post Office Department and was hired as a clerk in the dead-letter office. To get the job the precocious girl swore she was over sixteen. "She feels she can do better, and she has faith in herself," said one of the congressmen. Lincoln knew that Mary would not think much of him posing for a young, single woman, but he could relate to, and sympathize with, a poor, struggling person from the West. He said he would try to arrange his schedule to see her.[30]

As time passed and Ream heard nothing from the White House, she began haunting the upstairs corridor near Lincoln's private office. She sat there among hordes of office seekers and, with sketch pad in hand, captured a few details of Lincoln's face as he passed in the hallway. One day, Lincoln noticed her presence and paused in front of her. He asked her what brought her there. She replied that she was a sculptor. He asked if she was the young lady from Wisconsin who wanted to do a bust of him. She said that she was. He told her that they should discuss the matter in his office.

Rising to her full height of only five feet, the petite ninety-pound girl looked up and was instantly "under the spell of his kind eyes and genial presence." She followed him to his office. They made an indelible impression on each other. He was struck by her drive and determination and by her graceful manner and lively nature. Like him, she had resolved at an early age to take charge of her life and to make something of herself. That rang a familiar chord. She later recalled: "And so it was, the great heart which vanity could not unlock opened with the sympathy that recalled to him his own youth."[31]

He also learned that she composed both poetry and music, sang at concerts in military hospitals, helped wounded soldiers write letters, and did charity work for the blind. Lincoln recognized that this prairie Cinderella and child genius was certainly worthy of his time. He acceded to her wishes and allowed her to work in a corner of his office during his rest periods.

Some congressional patrons escorted her on her first three visits. On the third day Lincoln quipped: "Why do you always come with Miss Ream? It is not often that I get to see a pretty woman alone." From then on the escorts stayed away. With death threats increasing daily against the president, Ward Hill Lamon, the U.S. marshal for Washington, arranged a new passage for Lincoln to enter his office unseen. It helped to ensure his safety. It was also used by Ream, and it kept the sittings secret from Mary.[32]

Using the sittings as a time to relax during his torturous eighteen-hour work days, Lincoln often slouched in his chair, with head bowed in deep thought. One day, he looked out the south window where he had often watched Willie and Tad play on the White House lawn, and then he dropped into a chair and sobbed. Drying his eyes, he reminisced: "I was thinking of Willie." "Never was there grief like Lincoln's," Ream said later. "He was still suffering from the blow of that child's death while great affairs convulsed the nation. . . . He seemed an absolutely heartbroken man. Sometimes at these sittings his face wore a look of anxiety and pain. . . . At other times he would have that far away dreamy look that somehow presaged the tragic fate awaiting him; and again, those quiet eyes lighting up, a radiance almost Divine would suffuse those sunken cheeks, and the whole face would be illuminated with the impulse of some Divine purpose. . . . I was modeling him in clay, but all the time his personality was sinking deeper into my soul, being engraved deeply upon my heart."[33]

The half-hour sittings continued through the cold winter months of

Lincoln poses for sculptress Vinnie Ream.
COURTESY OF LLOYD OSTENDORF.

1864–65, and Lincoln and Ream became warm friends. The finished bust was a masterpiece that bore a striking resemblance to the president. He liked it. Others also praised it, and in 1866, after the assassination, Ream sought the ten-thousand-dollar commission offered by Congress for a life-size marble statue of Lincoln for the Capitol. She was supported by a petition signed by President Andrew Johnson, members of his cabinet, 31 senators, 110 current and former representatives, and 31 other dignitaries. The House of Representatives approved Ream by a vote of 67 to 7, but she ran into trouble in the Senate. Mary expressed her strong disapproval, as did Mary's long-time companion, Sen. Charles Sumner, who tried to block the commission. "This candidate is not competent to produce the work," he argued in the Senate debate. "She may make a statue, [but] she cannot make one that you will be justified in placing in this national Capitol." Jumping to his feet Sen. James Nesmith of Oregon disagreed vehemently. Scorning Sumner's admiration for anything European, Nesmith rallied support for Ream: "If this young lady and the works which she has produced had been brought to his notice by some near-sighted, frog-eating Frenchman, with a pair of green spectacles on his nose, the senator would . . . vote her fifty thousand dollars!" The final vote was 23 for, 9 against.

Winning over distinguished male sculptors, Ream became the first woman and, at nineteen, the youngest artist ever awarded a Federal commission for a statue. Explosive reactions erupted across the country, with female reporters in the forefront, all questioning how a young girl could be awarded so important a prize. She has "never

Vinnie Ream's Lincoln statue in the U.S. Capitol. COURTESY OF ARCHITECT OF THE U.S. CAPITOL.

made a statue," wrote Jane Swisshelm, who summed up Ream's professional work as a few "plaster busts on exhibition, including her own minus clothing to the waist." Undaunted, Ream set up shop in the Capitol basement. She wanted to sculpt Lincoln in an authentic suit and wrote to Mrs. Lincoln asking if she could borrow the clothes he wore on the night of the assassination.

The response of September 10, 1866, was a resounding "No!" Assuming Ream had never met the president, Mary stated bluntly: "As every friend my husband knew was familiar to me, and as your name was not on the list, consequently you could not have become familiar with [his] expression[s]." On the same day Mary wrote to Senator Sumner: "Nothing but a mortifying failure can be anticipated . . . and the country will never cease to regret that your wise admonitions were disregarded." Ream eventually obtained Lincoln's daytime clothes worn on April 14 from White House doorman Alphonse Dunn, to whom Mary supposedly had given them.[34]

Three years later, in 1869, Ream completed the model and accompanied it to Italy to be rendered in marble. It was returned to Washington late in 1870 and unveiled at a Capitol ceremony on January 25, 1871. As the flag rose from the statue, the audience applauded loudly, and Ream stood and bowed as the applause continued for some time. "This is Mr. Lincoln," said Senator Trumbull of Illinois during the ceremony. Reviews were generally positive, calling the statue a remarkably true and awesome representation. But women writers, especially those who had been critical of Ream's commission, labeled the statue as "frightful" and "lifeless."[35]

Ream, whose talents included poetry, penned these stirring lines a few weeks after the unveiling: "O, Lincoln, prophet, hero, friend! / You clasped the hands so long estranged / You healed the wounds— you broke the chains / You honored all our silent slain." She went on to sculpt more than a hundred pieces, many of them of major military and political figures. She designed the first free-standing statue of a Native American (Sequoyah) placed in the Capitol, and, with the support of Gen. William T. Sherman, she won the twenty-thousand-dollar commission to sculpt the city's prestigious memorial to Adm. David Farragut. The town of Vinita, Oklahoma, was named in her honor.

13

"That Woman Is Pretending to Be Me!"

On March 23, 1865, Lincoln, Mary, and Tad cruised down the Potomac on the *River Queen* to General Grant's headquarters at City Point. White House guard William H. Crook said Tad "studied every screw of the engine and knew and counted among his friends every man of the crew." The First Family was warmly welcomed with luncheons, dinners, parties, and dances. Lincoln visited all hospitals in the area and shook hands with thousands of wounded. In a strategy meeting to discuss peace terms, Lincoln emphasized to Generals Grant and Sherman and Adm. David Porter that his objective was more than peace. He wanted reconciliation. This requires generous terms, he said, to "get the deluded men of the Rebel armies disarmed and back to their homes. . . . Let them all go, officers and all; I want submission, and no more bloodshed. . . . I want no one punished; treat them liberally all round. We want these people to return to their allegiance to the Union and submit to the laws."[1]

It was not a view Mary supported. She blamed the South for the war—a war that had torn asunder and decimated the Todd family. Her stepmother, her brother George, all her half-sisters, and all but one of her half-brothers remained loyal to the South. Four brothers and half-brothers and four brothers-in-law fought for the Confederacy. Dead in battle were three half-brothers and the husband of her youngest sister. She wanted the South punished.

To witness a grand review of the Federal Army of the James, now commanded by Gen. O. C. Ord, Lincoln and the generals rode on horseback to the main encampment. Mary and Mrs. Grant followed in a converted ambulance over muddy, bumpy roads. They sat together on the rear bench, clutching the side of the lurching wagon. One of Grant's aides sat opposite them. Mary, not wanting to be late for the review, complained about the slow speed. "Faster!" she demanded. "We must go faster!" The driver slapped the horses, and as they responded, the front wheels struck a felled tree barely visible in the thick mud. Both women bounced off the bench simultaneously, striking their heads against the roof. Their large, well-decorated hats cushioned the blow, but knocked the wax cherries on Mary's hat to the floor. Mary's head throbbed. Her nerves tightened. Her hands twitched. She was set to explode.

The detonation came moments after they arrived at the reviewing stand, when Mary realized the review had begun without her. Fuming over being "left out," Mary went berserk when she saw another woman riding along the lines with Lincoln. It was General Ord's young, attractive wife. "Look!" Mary exclaimed to Julia Grant, "that woman is pretending to be me. The soldiers will think that vile woman is me!" Mrs. Grant tried to reassure her: "No, no, Mrs. Lincoln, that's Mrs. Ord, and she's riding with her husband." Shaking with anger, Mary blurted out: "Does she suppose that he wants her by his side?" Mrs. Ord was there as the general's wife, Mrs. Grant calmly tried to explain, not as the president's wife. Mary turned on Mrs. Grant. "I suppose you think you will get to the White House yourself, don't

The wife of General Edward Ord riled Mary Lincoln by riding near the president during a troop review. LIBRARY OF CONGRESS.

you?!" she said accusingly. Mrs. Grant replied evenly, "No, Mrs. Lincoln, we are quite happy where we are." Inconsolable, Mary was in a towering rage as the unsuspecting Mrs. Ord rode to the reviewing stand. "Welcome, Mrs. Lincoln," she said cheerfully. "You whore!" Mary shouted, adding expletives in a vicious tirade. "How dare you follow up the president?!" Mrs. Ord burst into tears.[2]

Adam Badeau, secretary to General Grant, said Lincoln bore it "with an expression of pain and sadness that cut one to the heart . . . and he walked away hiding that noble face that we might not catch the full expression of its misery." Badeau later said: "I never suffered greater humiliation than when I saw the Head of State, who carried all the cares of the nation at such a crisis—subjected to this inexpressible public mortification. But he bore it with supreme calmness and dignity."[3]

At dinner that night aboard the *River Queen,* Mary continued her attack, first lambasting her husband for "flirting with Mrs. Ord" and then, while seated next to General Grant, demanding that he remove General Ord from command. "He is unfit for his place, to say nothing of his wife!" Mary grumbled. "I need him," Grant replied assuredly. "He is an excellent officer." Lincoln, embarrassed, tried to ignore Mary, but she persisted late into the night. Feeling ill, she spent several days in her cabin; then on April 1, she left suddenly for Washington. Although no one could have predicted it, her actions would contribute to her husband's assassination.

On April 2, following a disastrous defeat at the battle of Five Forks, Lee abandoned Petersburg and Richmond, and retreated westward. Federal forces marched into Richmond the following day. Lincoln was eager to visit the fallen capital of the Confederacy. As he walked through the streets with Tad, jubilant blacks thronged around him. "Thank God I have lived to see this," Lincoln said. "It seems to me I have been dreaming a horrid nightmare for four years, and now the nightmare is over." At the Confederate White House, he sat at Jefferson Davis's desk. Outside, Federal troops cheered.

Mary, feeling left out of a great moment in history, rushed back on April 6 to see Richmond for herself. She was accompanied by her frequent companion, Senator Sumner, as well as Lizzie Keckley and others. Mrs. Keckley, once a slave, sat in Davis's chair in the Senate chamber. That night, aboard the *River Queen,* an officer casually remarked to Mary: "You should have seen the president on his triumphal entry into Richmond. . . . The ladies kissed their hands to him, and greeted him with the waving of handkerchiefs. He is quite a hero when surrounded by pretty young ladies." With eyes flashing, Mary turned to him and curtly said that his familiarity was offensive to her. "Quite a scene followed," said Keckley, "and I do not think the captain will ever forget [it]." Mary's dressmaker would later write that she had never seen "a more peculiarly constituted woman" than Mrs. Lincoln.[4]

On the Lincolns' last night aboard the *River Queen,* the ship was decorated with multicolored lights and a military band performed for officers and dignitaries. At about ten o'clock the president was asked to speak. He politely declined, saying he was too tired, but added: "Now, by way of parting from the brave soldiers of our gallant army, I call upon the band to play 'Dixie.' It has always been a favorite of mine, and since we have captured it, we have a perfect right to enjoy it." When the music ended, everyone applauded. Then the last goodbyes were spoken, and the *River Queen* headed back to Washington. On the return trip, Mary, still seething with jealousy and resentment, reportedly struck her husband in the face and cursed him. While driving from the wharf to the White House, a calmer Mary said, "This city is filled with our enemies." Lincoln looked at her with surprise: "Enemies! We must never speak of that."[5]

Later that Palm Sunday night of April 9, Lincoln learned of Lee's surrender at Appomattox. He was also told that Capt. Robert Lincoln was on the porch of the McLean House while Lee and Grant conducted surrender arrangements. Washington lit up with fireworks and exploding rockets. A banking house signaled "Glory to God" in gold stars. At General Lee's Arlington mansion, Freedmen marched on the lawn chanting "The Year of Jubilee." By Lincoln's wish the bands kept playing both "Dixie" and "Yankee Doodle."[6]

The bloodiest war in American history was over, and Lincoln had emerged as the grandest figure of that terrible war. Now it was Lincoln's dream that brotherhood, not bloodshed, would become the American way of life and that America would become a land fulfilling the Declaration of Independence—a land where "all men are created equal"—a Declaration that was Lincoln's political chart and inspiration. With victory, emancipation, and a restored Union, Lincoln's desire for a noble destiny was fulfilled. This plain man of the people had not only persevered. He had prevailed.

On Tuesday night, April 11, great crowds gathered in front of the White House to hear the president speak. He was greeted with thunderous applause but was hard to see, and voices shouted, "More light! More light!" A lamp was brought out, and little Tad rushed to his father's side: "Let me hold the light, Papa! Let me hold the light!" His wish was granted.[7]

During his remarks Mary embarrassed him again. She and some female friends chatted and laughed loudly from an adjacent window, drowning out Lincoln's voice. At first the listeners tolerated it, but several of them finally hushed the women emphatically. Lincoln at first thought something he said had caused the demonstration, but then realized that Mary again was the problem. An expression of pain and mortification came over his face, but he resumed his reading.

Lincoln's powerful statement projected his vision of a united America without slavery. He said he would not accept a policy of anger and rejection toward the South because it would be "discouraging and paralyzing" for both races. Standing in the shadows that night was John Wilkes Booth. As Lincoln talked about suffrage for educated blacks or those who had served in the military, Booth grumbled to his friends Lewis Paine and David Herold, "That means nigger citizenship." Vowing "that is the last speech he will ever make," Booth urged Paine to shoot Lincoln now. Paine refused, and Booth turned away in disgust and exclaimed, "By God, I'll put him through."[8]

Earlier on Tuesday Lincoln had related a dream to Mary and a few friends. In his dream he heard sobs in the East Room of the White House. He saw "a corpse wrapped in funeral vestments . . . soldiers who were acting as guards [and] a throng of people . . . weeping pitifully." Lincoln demanded of the soldiers, "Who is dead?" "The president," was the answer. "He was killed by an assassin." Then, Lincoln said, "a loud burst of grief [came] from the crowd, which awoke me from my dream."

The day after the dream Lincoln opened the Bible and read Jacob's dream in Genesis, chapter twenty-eight. Everywhere he turned in the

Bible his eyes fell upon an account of a vision or a supernatural visitation. As the president's self-appointed bodyguard Ward Hill Lamon prepared to depart for Richmond, Lincoln told him about his dream and Bible readings. "It seems strange to me how much there is in the Bible about dreams," Lincoln said. "There are, I think, some sixteen chapters in the Old Testament and four or five in the New in which dreams are mentioned; and there are many other passages scattered throughout the book which refer to visions. If we believe in the Bible, we must accept the fact that in the old days, God and His angels came to men in their sleep and made themselves known in dreams. [The dream I had] has haunted me. Somehow the thing has got possession of me, and like Banquo's ghost, it will not let go." It undoubtedly reminded Lincoln of election night five years earlier in Springfield, when he saw double images of himself in the mirror—one face robust, the other ghostly·pale, which he had interpreted as an ominous sign if he had a second term. Lamon, a huge and commanding-looking Virginian, was one of Lincoln's most devoted friends. He pleaded with the president: "Promise me you won't go out after nightfall while I'm gone, particularly to the theater." Lincoln would not fully agree. "Well, I promise to do the best I can towards it," he said.[9]

On Thursday Mary asked General Grant to escort her to view the city's illuminated buildings. Lincoln urged him to accept, and he did. As Mary and Grant entered their coach, the crowd shouted "Grant" nine times. Mary was upset and directed the driver to let her out. Then the crowd cheered for Lincoln, and she gave orders to proceed. This routine was repeated at different stages of the drive, and Mary was angry that Grant was always cheered first.[10]

On Good Friday morning, April 14, Lincoln and Mary enjoyed a relaxing breakfast together and spoke affectionately. Earlier, he had sent Mary a note about taking a carriage ride that afternoon. It was "playfully and tenderly worded," she said later. Robert joined them for breakfast, and they talked about his future. Lincoln encouraged him to finish Harvard Law School and to read law for three years. That, Lincoln said, should help us determine "whether you will make a good lawyer or not."[11]

At 11 A.M. Lincoln met with Grant and the cabinet, with reconstruction in the South the principal order of business. Stanton, whom Lincoln had asked to draft a plan for cabinet consideration, remarked that the president was "grander, graver, more thoroughly up to the occasion than he had ever seen him." All members expressed "kindly feeling toward the vanquished . . . with as little harm as possible to the feelings or the property of the inhabitants." "There must be no bloody work," Lincoln said. "No one need expect me to take part in hanging or killing these men, even the worst of them." "If we are wise and discreet," he said, "we shall reanimate the states and get the governments in successful operation, with order prevailing and the Union established, before Congress comes together in December." He expressed concern about "men in Congress . . . who possessed feelings of hatred and vindictiveness." Stanton proposed martial law with the South ruled by military governors until civilian rule could be reestablished. The military would preserve order while the federal departments carried out their various functions. These suggestions met with general approval, but another Stanton proposal to combine Virginia and North Carolina into a single military unit under the War Department (and Stanton) was controversial. Lincoln asked all members to consider carefully the matter of reconstruction. "No greater or more important [subject] could come before us or any future cabinet," he emphasized. The discussion was to be continued at next Tuesday's meeting.[12]

Lincoln skipped lunch and ate an apple as he went back to his office and summoned Vice President Johnson. They talked for about half an hour. Lincoln wanted to be sure Johnson understood his wishes regarding reconstruction. Lincoln then labored over pardons and reprieves and contended with numerous callers. Alone at his desk, Lincoln heard a ruckus outside his door. "For God's sake! Please let me see the president!" shouted a female voice. Lincoln opened the door and saw a guard barring a former female slave from seeing him. "Let the good woman in," Lincoln said. The distraught woman, Mrs. Nancy Bushrod, told Lincoln she and her husband had been freed as slaves on a plantation near Richmond. He had enlisted in the Army of the Potomac, but his pay was not coming through, and they had many children to support. "Can you help us, Mr. President?" Lincoln looked at her compassionately and replied: "Come back around this time tomorrow, and the papers will be signed and ready for you."[13]

About noon on Friday, April 14, John Wilkes Booth stopped by Ford's Theatre to pick up his mail. The ticket seller, Thomas Raybold, handed him a pile of letters and told him the president was coming that night. Booth asked if he was sure, and Raybold said it had been confirmed. At about eight o-clock, Booth met with fellow conspirators George Atzerodt and Lewis Paine. They were assigned, respectively, to kill Vice-President Johnson and Secretary of State Seward. Booth would kill the president. All assassinations were to occur at 10:15 P.M. Booth later wrote in his diary that the country's troubles were caused by Lincoln and "God

John Wilkes Booth, the twenty-six-year-old assassin of President Lincoln, was killed on April 26, 1865, at the Garrett farm in Caroline County, Virginia. Booth had written in his diary that the country's troubles were caused by Lincoln and "God simply made me the instrument of his punishment." LIBRARY OF CONGRESS.

simply made me the instrument of his punishment. . . . I struck for my country and that alone. A country groaned beneath this tyranny and prayed for this end."[14]

Late in the afternoon Lincoln and Mary rode in an open carriage to the Navy Yard. He seemed "cheerful, almost joyous," she later recalled, and she said to him, "You almost startle me by your great cheerfulness." He responded: "And well I may feel so, Mary. I consider this day the war has come to a close." He then offered a challenge to both of them: "We must both be more cheerful in the future—between the war and the loss of our darling Willie—we have both been very miserable." They talked about traveling abroad. He especially wanted to visit Jerusalem and Europe. They also planned to visit the American West. Then he would resume his law practice in

Illinois and argue cases before the Illinois Supreme Court. He looked forward to quieter and happier times.[15]

Working into the evening Lincoln wrote the final letter of his life to Gen. James H. Van Alen, who had warned him to be more careful when going out in public. Lincoln, in his response, said he would use "due precaution." His final sentence was: "I thank you for the assurance you give me that I shall be supported by conservative men like yourself in the efforts I may make to restore the Union, so as to make it, to use your language, a Union of hearts and hands as well as of States."

That night, the Lincolns were scheduled to attend a performance at Ford's Theatre, but by dinner Mary had developed a headache and preferred to stay home. Lincoln insisted that they go. The newspapers had announced their presence, and he could use some comedy in his life, he said. To him, the theater was a refuge—a relaxing escape from the reality of war, ruthless men and women, and even the bruising bouts with his rambunctious wife. Without the theater Lincoln said he "could not go on." He went so often—at least twelve times—that newspapers accused him of trivializing wartime.

Together, Mary and Lincoln had seen the piquant comedy of Maggie Mitchell in her signature role of Fanchon, the Crickett, and the foremost tragedian of the time, Charlotte Cushman, in the role of Lady Macbeth. Miss Cushman was introduced to Lincoln at the White House by Secretary Seward, her close friend. A feminist and strong supporter of the war effort, she gave five benefit performances for the American Sanitary Commission, a civilian effort that mobilized women to help soldiers by knitting sweaters, folding bandages, and serving as nurses. She had played opposite both John Wilkes Booth and his brother Edwin. She described Edwin as "living proof of how short the country was of gentlemen" and John as a strange, daring man who demanded complete realism on stage. Often his sword thrusts and fisticuffs left scars and bruises—in return for which he, too, was cut many times and slept bandaged in steak and oysters. Now, Lincoln wanted to see Laura Keene in *Our American Cousin* at Ford's Theatre. The London-born actress had been an instant success in comedies in New York and was well received wherever she went. She was the first woman to manage a theater in the United States.

Lincoln asked the Stantons and the Grants to accompany them. The secretary of war refused for several reasons: his wife did not like Mrs. Lincoln; he did not approve of the theater; and he wanted to discourage Lincoln from going. "Mr. Lincoln ought not to go," he warned. "It was too great an exposure." General Grant initially accepted, but then declined. He did not want to incur Mary's displeasure again, and Mrs. Grant, after her horrid experience with Mary at City Point, did not want to be confined for hours in a theater box with "that crazy woman." Seeking a valid excuse, Mrs. Grant decided to visit her children in Burlington, New Jersey, and the general asked to be excused so he could be with her. If Mary's rude outbursts had not occurred, the Grants likely would have accepted, and Grant would have had a large military guard for protection. Lincoln

Julia Grant's horrid experience with Mary Lincoln at City Point, Virginia, led to her refusal to be confined in a theater box with "that crazy woman." LIBRARY OF CONGRESS.

might not have been assassinated that night at Ford's Theatre.[16]

That morning Lincoln walked across the White House lawn to Stanton's office and asked for special protection at the theater. He told Stanton he had seen his man Eckert break five cast-iron pokers by striking them over his arm, one after the other, "and I'm thinking he would be the kind of man to go with me this evening. May I take him?" Lincoln was referring to Maj. Thomas T. Eckert, chief of the War Department's Telegraph Office. Stanton shrugged. "I cannot spare him. I have important work for him this evening." "I will ask him myself," Lincoln replied. "He can do your work tomorrow." The president walked into the adjoining cipher room and extended the invitation to Eckert. "Now, Major," he cajoled, "come along. Mrs. Lincoln and I want you with us." Eckert knew Stanton's wishes and was not about to cross him. He declined the president's request, citing the pressing work he had to do for Stanton. "Very well," Lincoln said, "I will take Major Rathbone along, but I should much rather have you." Rathbone, slender and dapper, was a ladies' man incapable of breaking a poker over his arm. Actually, the Lincolns had already invited Major Rathbone and his fiancée, Clara Harris, whose father was a senator from New York. Rathbone, however, would go unarmed, and his attentions would be centered not on Lincoln but on Clara. Shortly after the president left the War Department, Stanton reportedly told Eckert he had changed his mind about needing him to work that night. "The work can wait until tomorrow," he allegedly said. They both went home.[17]

Stanton's behavior prompted at least one researcher to attempt to link him to the conspiracy to kill Lincoln. All such efforts, however, have been discredited. Stanton was a peculiar man. Grant said of him: "It seemed to be pleasanter to him to disappoint than to gratify." David Homer Bates, manager of the War Department's Telegraph Office, thought Stanton was by nature "haughty, severe, domineering, and often rude." Bates likened him to the characterization of Napoleon by Charles Phillips, the Irish orator: "Grand, gloomy, and peculiar." When Stanton's little daughter Lucy died in 1841, he had her body exhumed and kept the coffin in his own room for two years. And when his wife died in 1844, he dressed and re-dressed her in her bridal clothes. Such was the man who advised Lincoln to avoid the theater, but then failed to provide adequate protection when Lincoln chose to go. At his disposal were all the U.S. military forces in Washington, as well as the Secret Service and the provost marshals with their army police and detectives. Stanton, however, did nothing. Some historians say it was his way of trying to discourage Lincoln from going to Ford's Theatre.[18]

White House guard William Crook, about to go off duty, also begged Lincoln to avoid the theater, but Lincoln would not hear of it. "Then let me stay on duty and accompany you," Crook insisted. "No, Crook," Lincoln said kindly but firmly, "you have had a long, hard day's work already, and you must go home to sleep and rest. I cannot afford to have you get tired out and exhausted." As Crook was leaving, Lincoln neglected for the first time to say good night to him. Instead, he turned to him and said, "Good-bye Crook."[19]

At 8:15 the Lincolns climbed into the presidential carriage and headed for Senator Harris's home to pick up their guests, accompanied only by the coachman and Lincoln's personal attendant, Charles Forbes. A heavy fog drifted throughout the city as the group arrived late at Ford's Theatre. As they entered, the play stopped, the audience stood, and the orchestra struck up "Hail to the Chief." The presidential party proceeded to the State Box overlooking the stage.

One solitary man—John Parker—stood guard over their box. He was a low-life member of the Metropolitan Police Force with many reprimands on his record. He had been cited for unbecoming conduct, insubordination, and loafing and drunkenness while on duty. He also habitually arrested streetwalkers who refused to grant him their favors gratis. So, who was responsible for assigning such a man to the White House detail? To a large extent, the blame can be placed on Mary Lincoln. Earlier that month, Parker was up for the army draft and wanted to avoid it. He did, thanks to a letter Mary wrote on April 3 sponsoring his transfer to the White House guard and then another letter the following day to have him "exempted from the draft." She made these requests shortly after her return from City Point. Now, through Mary's involvement, Parker stood guard at Lincoln's box at Ford's, Theatre.

Lincoln and Mary appeared to be enjoying the play, with Lincoln laughing heartily and Mary applauding often. During the third act, she put her hand in his and moved closer to him. "What will Miss Harris think of my hanging on to you so?" she whispered. "She won't think anything about it," he replied. Meanwhile, true to form, guard John Parker left his post, apparently to go outside for a drink, although he later told William Crook he went to find a seat "so that he could see the play." His absence was never adequately explained. All facts related to his movements were conveniently "lost" in the files of the official investigation. When Mary's sponsorship of Parker came to light, nobody wanted to pursue it. Her actions, Stanton's inaction, and Parker's incompetence had made it incredibly easy for John Wilkes Booth, or anyone, to kill the president at Ford's Theatre that night.[20]

Thus, shortly after 10 P.M. Booth entered the president's unguarded anteroom and barred the door behind him so as not to be disturbed. Quietly, he reached into his pocket for a small brass derringer. It was a single-shot weapon loaded with a lead slug about the size of a marble. Booth awaited a line in the play that he knew would draw applause and laughter. The play was about an American bumpkin, Asa Trenchard, who goes to England to claim riches inherited from a noble relative. A fortune-hunting Englishwoman follows him, hoping he will marry her daughter. When the Englishwoman, played by Laura Keene, learns that Trenchard has given away his inheritance, she denounces him and makes a haughty exit. He responds: "Don't know the manners of good society, eh? Well, I guess I know enough to turn you inside out, old gal—you sockdologizing old man-trap." Booth stepped quickly behind Lincoln, who was leaning forward with his chin in his right hand and his arm on the balustrade. At a distance of two feet, Booth pointed his pistol at the left side of the president's head, and fired. It was 10:13 P.M.

Mary screamed in deranged, impenetrable terror and ran around the box like a caged tiger. Clara Harris shouted repeatedly: "They have shot the president! They have shot the president!" Rathbone sprang toward Booth and seized him, but Booth freed himself and made a violent thrust with a razor-sharp hunting knife at Rathbone's arm, cutting an artery, nerves, and veins. As Booth leaped to the stage, Rathbone cried out: "Stop that man!"[21]

Two young physicians ran to the box and found Lincoln paralyzed, with no pulse. They removed the blood clot, applied mouth-to-mouth resuscitation, and restored his breathing. Laura Keene, the star of *Our American Cousin*, was just off the stage when the shot was fired. Hoping she could be helpful, she brought a glass of water to the president's box. By this time, Lincoln had been placed on the floor, with a white handkerchief under his head. The actress reportedly received permission to place his head in her lap. She dabbed water on his forehead as blood soiled her yellow satin skirt.

Shortly, other physicians made their way into the box, and with the assistance of men from the audience they carried Lincoln across the street, through the eerie mist, to a boardinghouse owned by William Petersen, a merchant-tailor. In a shabby room down a narrow hallway, they laid the president on a bed that was too short for his six-foot-four-inch frame. He had to be placed diagonally, with his feet dangling on the side.

Lincoln lay there for nine hours, never regaining consciousness.

Mary, distraught, sat beside him and called on him to speak to her. She showered his face with kisses and spoke words of endearment. She wanted to fetch Tad, thinking Lincoln would speak to him, but the physicians advised against it. Robert came in with Senator Sumner, saw his mother's desperate condition, and with the help of Sen. James Dixon's wife, one of Mary's closest friends, persuaded her to retire to the parlor—but she returned hourly.

Stanton quickly took charge and dictated telegrams. He ordered all bridges out of the capital closed, and initiated a massive manhunt. Soon, he learned of the two other planned assassinations. Atzerodt, however, had disobeyed Booth and had not attacked the vice-president, but Paine had savagely assaulted Secretary Seward in his bed and left him barely alive. Both Atzerodt and Paine were captured within days. It took nearly two weeks to find Booth at a Virginia farm, where he was shot and killed.[22]

As Mary sat beside her husband, he suddenly made a heavy snoring sound, and she jumped with a piercing cry and fainted. Stanton demanded: "Take that woman out and don't let her in again!" However, she was allowed to return and again seated herself by the president, kissing him and beseeching him: "Love, live but one moment to speak to me once—to speak to our children." As he neared death, she was led back to the front room. Resting on a sofa, she recalled Lincoln's prophetic dream, cried pitifully, and begged God to take her too. Shortly after 7:22 A.M. the physicians came in and told her: "It is all over! The president is no more!" Robert cried aloud and leaned on Senator Sumner. Stanton asked the pastor of the New York Avenue Presbyterian Church to say a prayer. Then Stanton said: "Now he belongs to the ages."[23]

The fog had turned to a heavy rain as Robert assisted his grieving mother into a carriage, and the horses pulled them through the rough muddy streets back to the White House. Mary wept hysterically and made unearthly shrieks. Except for her family, the only companion she wanted was her dressmaker Lizzie Keckley. An optimistic woman of tact and poise, Mrs. Keckley was the perfect companion to calm Mary's emotional imbalance. She finally arrived around eleven o'clock and bathed Mary's head with cold water and comforted her. Tad hugged his mother's neck and pleaded: "Don't cry so, Momma!

Don't cry, or you will make me cry too! You will break my heart!"
When he pleaded, she composed herself as best she could and clasped
her child in her arms.[24]

Stanton, meanwhile, ordered the rocking chair in which Lincoln
was shot brought to his office. He kept it there for a year, looking at
it daily.

A few hours after Andrew Johnson was sworn in as president,
Radical Republicans caucused to discuss the rosy picture they now
expected for their program of vengeance against the South. They had
been diametrically opposed to Lincoln's "soft" peace plan and his reconstruction proposals. They wanted Rebel property confiscated and the
conquered South treated as a prize of war. Johnson, they felt, would be
more supportive of their position. They had rejoiced when earlier that
month he went to Lincoln with demands that Confederate leaders be
executed. Representative George Julian of Indiana later wrote that
"while everybody was shocked at [Lincoln's] murder, the feeling was
nearly universal that the ascension of Johnson to the presidency would
prove a godsend to the country." Sen. Zachariah Chandler of Michigan
intoned that God had placed a better man in Lincoln's place.[25]

Mary was emotionally unable to attend the funeral in the White
House on Wednesday, April 19. She remained upstairs, weeping hys-
terically, with Mrs. Keckley at her side. In the hushed and dimmed
East Room, Lincoln's casket rested on a flower-covered catafalque.
Robert stood at the foot of the coffin; General Grant sat at the other
end, his moist eyes focused on a cross of lilies. Some six hundred
Washington dignitaries crowded into the room for the eleven o'clock
service. Only seven women were among them: the bewitching Kate
Chase Sprague, whom Mary regarded as a heartless wretch and who
for years had belittled Lincoln behind his back; Kate's younger sister
Nettie; Mrs. Gideon Welles, who was Mary's friend and whose husband, the secretary of the navy, had sat by the head of the president's
bed most of the night after the assassination; Mrs. Edwin Stanton,
who disliked Mary and had campaigned without success to get
Lincoln to appoint her husband as chief justice; Mrs. John Palmer
Usher, wife of the secretary of the interior; and Mrs. William
Dennison, wife of the postmaster general, and their daughter. The
supportive women in Lincoln's life were not there—probably because

they had not been invited—women such as his "esteemed friend" Eliza Gurney, author Harriet Beecher Stowe, "African prophetess" Sojourner Truth, and sculptress Vinnie Ream.

Later, while Tad was being dressed, he looked up at his nurse and said: "Pa is dead. I can hardly believe that I shall never see him again. I must learn to take care of myself now." He thought for a moment and then added: "Yes, Pa is dead, and I am only Tad Lincoln now, little Tad, like other little boys. I am not a president's son now. I won't have many presents any more. Well, I will try and be a good boy, and will hope to go some day to Pa and brother Willie, in heaven."[26]

At dawn on Friday, April 21, Lincoln's body left Washington in a nine-car funeral train decorated with Union flags and accompanied by three hundred dignitaries. Willie's coffin was moved from its Georgetown grave and placed beside his father for the seventeen-hundred-mile journey taking them home to Springfield. A million Americans in a dozen cities would look upon Lincoln's face. "No common mortal had died," said Lizzie Keckley. "The Moses of my people had fallen in the hour of triumph." Lincoln's stepmother sighed on hearing of his murder: "I know'd they'd kill him." A neighbor said, "She never had no heart after that to be 'chirp' and 'peart' like she used to be." Sarah, too weak to attend services in Springfield, died four years later at her Goosenest Prairie cabin.[27]

The procession from the Illinois State House in Springfield to Oak Ridge Cemetery was the largest one ever seen in the West. Ann Rutledge's brother Robert was among the planners and the mourners. During the Lincoln administration he had been appointed provost marshal of the First Congressional District of Iowa. President Johnson never expressed sympathy for Mary Lincoln's grief or the loss of her husband. He never called on her, never wrote to her, and never inquired about her welfare. When she finally left the White House forty days after the assassination, no one told her good-bye. She descended the public stairway; entered her carriage; drove to the depot; and with Lizzie Keckley, Robert, and Tad, boarded a train for Chicago. Seventeen more years of heartaches and trouble lay ahead for the last woman in Lincoln's life.

Epilogue

"Beloved of Abraham Lincoln."

*A*nn Rutledge was reinterred in 1890, fifty-five years after her death. It was the result of a commercial venture by a local undertaker and civic-minded citizens in Petersburg, Illinois, a town located near New Salem. The undertaker, Samuel Montgomery, was an investor in the newly established Oakland Cemetery. To boost the sale of cemetery lots, he proposed moving Ann Rutledge's remains to Oakland. McGrady Rutledge, then seventy-six, was Ann's only Rutledge relative in the Petersburg area. He initially opposed the idea, as did Ann's sister Nancy, then living in Iowa. "Ann's remains should stay where those of her family were buried," she declared. Montgomery persuaded McGrady to change his mind, however, arguing that the grave would receive better care at Oakland than at the cemetery where she had been buried—which was abandoned.

On May 15, 1890, Montgomery, McGrady Rutledge, two laborers, and a nine-year-old boy attempted to reinter Ann's remains. When they dug up her badly decayed wooden coffin at Old Concord Cemetery, all they reportedly found were some pearl buttons, long strands of hair, a few bones, and a small silver buckle. These items, along with a few shovelfuls of dirt from her grave, were placed in another wooden box, loaded onto an open flatbed wagon, taken to Petersburg, and buried the next day at Oakland.

As mementos of his favorite cousin, McGrady kept several other items: a small button covered in cloth of faded rose, a bow four-inches wide made of silky ribbon, a two-foot-long strip of black lace,

The remains of Ann Rutledge were moved from Old Concord to Petersburg's large burial ground, Oakland Cemetery, in 1890. COURTESY OF SHARON L. SCHIRDING.

and a lock of hair. He later gave these relics to his brother Jasper, who passed them down to his daughter—a namesake of Ann. Eventually, the artifacts came into the possession of Jasper's great-granddaughter Margaret Richardson. A photograph of the items appeared in an 1893 booklet, *Menard-Salem-Lincoln Souvenir Album,* which was published by a local women's club.

Eventually, an impressive granite monument was erected at Ann's new gravesite in Oakland Cemetery. Engraved on it is an epitaph by Edgar Lee Masters:

> Out of me unworthy and unknown
> The vibrations of deathless music!
> "With malice toward none, with charity for all"
> Out of me forgiveness of millions toward millions,
> And the beneficent face of a nation
> Shining with justice and truth.
> I am Ann Rutledge who sleep beneath these weeds,
> Beloved of Abraham Lincoln,
> Wedded to him, not through union,
> But through separation.
> Bloom forever, O Republic,
> From the dust of my bosom!

For more than a century-and-a-half, the former site of Ann's grave at Old Concord was identified by a simple wooden sign. In 1996 Rutledge descendants replaced it with a granite headstone etched on both sides. The front of the stone reads: "Original Grave of Anna Mayes Rutledge, Jan. 7, 1813–Aug. 25, 1835. Where Lincoln Wept." On the opposite side: "Ann Rutledge. 'I cannot bear to think of her out there alone in the storm.' A. Lincoln."

Mary Todd Lincoln lay in bed in the White House forty days after Lincoln's assassination and even tried to contact her dead husband through bedside séances conducted by spiritualists. Finally eased out, she moved to Chicago. She begged friends for money, tried unsuccessfully to sell her elaborate wardrobe under a false name, and became the object of ridicule and humiliation. Her hysteria intensified when her husband's law partner William Herndon uncovered the story of Lincoln's love for Ann Rutledge and spoke and wrote about it. Mary threatened Herndon and insisted that Lincoln's heart had not been "in any unfortunate woman's grave—but in the proper place with his beloved wife and children."

In 1868 Mary left America and withdrew to Germany, taking her youngest son Tad with her. They returned three years later after she was awarded a long-sought government pension. Unfortunately, the cold ocean crossing was too much for Tad, who shortly developed pleurisy or pneumonia and died at age eighteen in Chicago in 1871. Mary then moved into a spiritualist commune and claimed to communicate with her dead husband. Signs of mental instability became evident. She entered a hotel elevator half-dressed, thinking it a lavatory; she bought three hundred pairs of gloves, a hundred shawls, and yards of expensive drapery for which she had no use; and she wandered around Chicago with thousands of dollars in securities sewn in her dress. In 1875 her only living son, Robert, gave up on her and had her committed to a sanitarium for well-to-do women. She had been there only a short time when she was declared sane and released. As might be expected, Mary severed all ties with Robert. He is a "wicked monster," she wailed. She had now lost everyone she ever really cared about. She left the country again. For three years she lived in a dingy hotel in southern France. She developed severe arthritis, suffered from a series of crippling falls, and became partially paralyzed. Returning to Springfield, she moved into the home of her sister Elizabeth Edwards. It was the same mansion where she had married Lincoln. With her bedroom shades always drawn, she packed and unpacked her sixty-four trunks of clothing by candlelight. She slept on just one side of the bed to leave a place for her husband. On July 16, 1882, she died after suffering a stroke. She was sixty-four.

Robert Todd Lincoln was admitted to the bar in Illinois in 1867 and became a corporate lawyer. In 1868 he married Mary Harlan, daughter of U.S. Sen. James Harlan of Iowa, but it was a difficult marriage. She suffered from nervous debility and was reclusive. They had a son, who died of blood poisoning at seventeen, and two daughters, one of whom eloped after Robert disapproved of her choice for a husband. Robert Lincoln served as secretary of war under Presidents James Garfield and Chester Arthur (1881–1885) and as minister to Great Britain (1889–1893) under President Benjamin Harrison. He witnessed the fatal shooting of two presidents: Garfield, at the Washington railroad station on July 2, 1881, and William McKinley, at the Pan-American Exposition in Buffalo, New York, on September 6, 1901. Robert was twice named as a contender for the presidency, but he never ran for public office. He was the wealthy president and chairman of the board of the Pullman Company from 1897 until 1911. He died at eighty-three of a cerebral hemorrhage at his Vermont estate on July 26, 1926, and was buried at Arlington National Cemetery. His wife, Mary, died on March 31, 1937, at the age of ninety.

Abraham Lincoln now lies in an ornate granite mausoleum in Oak Ridge Cemetery in Springfield, Illinois—buried within a block of concrete eight feet square by fifteen feet deep. Fearful his body might be stolen, the family entombed Lincoln beneath an insurmountable obstacle. Mary Todd Lincoln and three of the four Lincoln children are buried there. About twenty-two miles northwest lie the remains of the first love in Lincoln's life—Ann Rutledge.

Notes and Sources

$\mathcal{C}$itations may be fully identified by reference to the bibliography. The frequently cited source, Wilson & Davis, relates to their major work, *Herndon's Informants* (1998), which, for the first time, provides all letters, interviews, and statements about Lincoln collected by his law partner, William H. Herndon (WHH), and Herndon's collaborator, Jesse W. Weik (JWW), for a biography of the martyred president.

CHAPTER 1:
"ALL THAT I AM OR EVER HOPE TO BE I OWE TO HER."

1. Basler, 1:118 (Lincoln to Mrs. O. H. Browning, Springfield, April 1, 1838); Herndon & Weik, 3; Boritt & Boritt, 228.

2. Herndon & Weik, 3; Ward Hill Lamon Papers, Henry E. Huntington Library, San Marino, Calif. (WHH to Ward Hill Lamon, Springfield, Ill., March 6, 1870; WHH to JWW, Springfield, Jan. 19, 1886; WHH to Charles H. Hart, Springfield, March 2, 1867); Hertz, *HL*, 63, 139, 411-412 (Herndon's memoir on Nancy Hanks, Greencastle, Ind, Aug. 20, 1887).

3. Herndon & Weik, 2-3.

4. See James A. Peterson, *In re Lucey Hanks* (Yorkville, Ill., privately published, 1973), chapter 5.

5. Beveridge Papers, Library of Congress, Washington, D.C. (J. Edward Murr to Albert J. Beveridge, New Albany, Ind., Nov. 21, 1924); Lamon Papers, Henry E. Huntington Library (WHH to Charles H. Hart, Springfield, Ill., Dec. 28, 1866 and WHH to Ward Hill Lamon, Springfield, Feb. 25, 1870).

6. Wilson & Davis, 67 (Samuel Haycraft to WHH, June 1865).

7. Hertz, *HL*, 204 (WHH to Truman Bartlett, Sept. 25, 1887); Ibid., 138-39 (WHH to JWW, Jan. 19, 1886); Wilson & Davis, 615 (John Hanks to JWW, June 12, 1887); Ibid., 37 (Dennis F. Hanks to WHH, Chicago, Ill., June 13, 1865); Linder, 39.

8. Tarbell, *Footsteps*, 93; Barton, *Paternity*, 182-83 (Robert Enlow, grandson of Abraham Enlow, to Barton, May 20, 1920).

9. Garrison, 7.

10. Hertz, *HL*, 63 (letter from WHH to Ward Hill Lamon, Feb. 25, 1870); Herndon said he "was convinced that the weight of evidence is that Mr. Lincoln was an illegitimate. The evidence is not conclusive, but men have been hung on less evidence."

11. Herndon & Weik, 12; Wilson & Davis, 67 (Samuel Haycraft to WHH, Elizabethtown, Ky., June 1865); Wilson & Davis, 675 (Charles Friend to WHH, Aug. 20, 1889); Ibid., 612 (Judge Alfred M. Brown to JWW, March 23, 1887); Barton, *Paternity*, 20-1.

12. Wilson & Davis, 612 (Judge Alfred M. Brown to JWW, March 23, 1887); Ibid., 675 (Charles Friend to WHH, Aug. 20, 1889). (Note: Charles Friend, postmaster of Sonora, Kentucky, said he was present when "Old Uncle Abe Enlow" was asked if he was Abraham Lincoln's father, and Enlow said, "I never touched more than her hand in my life, never had carnal knowledge of her or intercourse with her in my life."); Ibid., 87 (Presley Nevil Haycraft to John B. Helm, July 19, 1865); Ibid., 82 (John B. Helm to WHH, Aug. 1, 1865); Ibid., 613 (Lizzie Murphy to JWW, March, 1887); Ibid., 82 (John B. Helm to WHH, Aug. 1, 1865).

13. Hertz, *HL,* 63 (WHH to Ward Hill Lamon, Feb. 25, 1870).

14. Ibid., 18; Wilson & Davis, 235 (Charles Friend to WHH, March 19, 1866); Tarbell, *Footsteps,* 103; Burba (Austin Gollaher to Howard Burba).

15. Herndon & Weik, 51.

16. Ibid., 55-6.

17. Rankin, 325.

18. Lamon, *Life of AL*, 40n and Chapter 2; Wilson & Davis, 38 (Dennis F. Hanks to WHH, June 13, 1865).

19. Hertz, *HL*, 279-81; Herndon & Weik, 27.

20. Warren, *Lincoln's Youth*, 58; Temple, 11; Browne, 59-61 (quoting Dr. J. G. Holland); Burlingame, *Inner World*, 137-39.

21. *Shelby County* (Ill.) *Leader*, March 19, 1931 (address by Clarence W. Bell in Mattoon, Ill, Feb. 11, 1931; Bell was the grandson of Elisha Linder, a friend of Lincoln and a neighbor of Thomas Lincoln in Illinois).

CHAPTER 2:
"SHE WAS DOUBTLESS THE FIRST PERSON WHO EVER TREATED HIM LIKE A HUMAN BEING."

1. Herndon & Weik, 29-30 (quoting Sarah's granddaughter, Harriet Chapman).

2. Ibid., 28.

3. Ibid.

4. Wilson & Davis, 41 (Dennis Hanks to WHH, June 13, 1865); Ibid., 82 (John B. Helm to WHH, Aug. 1, 1865); Ibid., 107-08 (Sarah Johnston Lincoln to WHH, Sept. 8, 1865); Rice, 468.

5. Basler, 4:62.

6. Wilson & Davis, 112 (Nathaniel Grigsby to WHH, Sept. 12, 1865).

7. Hertz, *HL*, 280-01; Herndon & Weik, 38; Hertz, *HL*, 279.

8. Murr, 57 (quoting Polly Richardson Agnew); Wilson & Davis, 113 (Nathaniel Grigsby to WHH, Gentryville, Ind., Sept. 12, 1865).

9. Conway, 87; Gridley, 136 (quoting Mrs. Samuel Chowning).

10. Conway, 76; Warren, *Lincoln's Youth*, 157.

11. Papers of the Southwest Indiana Historical Society, Evansville Central Library (Nora Bender, granddaughter of Elizabeth Tuley, to an unidentified correspondent); also *Chicago Times-Herald*, Dec. 22, 1895 (interview with Elizabeth Tuley); Conway, 89; Wilson & Davis, 126 27 (Elizabeth Crawford to WHH, Sept.16, 1865).

12. Wilson & Davis, 131 (Anna Roby Gentry to WHH, Rockport, Ind., Sept. 17, 1865).

13. Ibid.; *Los Angeles Times,* Feb. 12, 1929 (statement by Dennis Franklin Johnston, son of John D. Johnston); Herndon & Weik, 49, 55.

14. Wilson & Davis, 110 (Matilda Johnston Moore to WHH, Sept. 8, 1865); Herndon & Weik, 31.

15. Wilson & Davis, 126 (Elizabeth Crawford to WHH, Sept. 16, 1865); Hertz, *HL*, 367.

16. Donald, n605, 33; Wilson & Davis, 134 (A. H. Chapman to WHH, Charleston, Ill., Sept. 28, 1865); Ibid., 107 (Sarah Johnston Lincoln to WHH, Sept. 8, 1865).

17. Ibid., 119-20 (Joseph C. Richardson to WHH, Sept. 14, 1865).

18. Ibid.; Herndon & Weik, 44-7; Wilson & Davis, 113 (Nathaniel Grigsby to WHH, Sept. 12, 1865); Herndon & Weik, 41.

19. Herndon & Weik, 61.

CHAPTER 3:
"TEACH ME, O LORD, TO THINK WELL OF MYSELF."

1. Ann Rutledge's birthdate is recorded in the Rutledge family Bible, now pre-served at Lincoln's New Salem State Historic Site in Illinois; Wilson & Davis, 382 (Robert B. Rutledge to WHH, Nov. 1, 1866); for information on the early history of Henderson County, Ky., see Bergevin et al., 21 (as described in a letter from a traveler addressed to "Friend" and signed "C.S." in October, 1807).

2. The marriage date is cited in the Henderson County (Ky.) Marriage Register, with certification by James McGready; 1810 Census of Henderson County.

3. Author's telephone conversation with genealogist George Rutledge, July, 1999; letter from Rutledge researcher C. V. Mayes to Ralph E. Winkler on Aug. 1, 1985, states that the *History of McLean County, Illinois*, 1887, con-tains a biography of Robert H. Rutledge, grandson of John J. Rutledge, indi-cating that John J. Rutledge was "born in Ireland, reared in Dublin, where he . . . learned the trade of shoemaker." Robert H. Rutledge (born March 21, 1810 in Henderson County, Ky.) was the son of Thomas Officer Rutledge (born Oct. 17, 1768 in or near Charlestown, S.C.).

4. In the letter cited in #3, Mayes indicates, apparently from the same source, that "Rutledge's bride, formerly Jennie Officer, was a lady of most excellent family of Irish descent, and highly educated and accomplished." Also, "Descendants of James Officer 1690-1980," by George H. Rutledge, pri-vately published, Hanover, Pa., Nov. 1982; James Officer Descendants *Family Newsletter*, Vol. 3, No. 1, p. 2; and *Family History: Lest We Forget, 1720–1800*, by Kenneth A. Unico, privately published, LDS Film #1035658, Item 2. Except for Jennie, the Officers spent the rest of their lives in Chester and Cumberland Counties in Pennsylvania.

5. Land, "Letter," 2; Bergevin et al., 190.

6. Note: While Rutledge was making shoes in Charlestown, another John Rutledge (an attorney) and his four brothers (Andrew, Edward, Hugh, and Thomas) lived luxuriously. Andrew was the largest retail merchant in the Carolinas. John would become one of the fifty-five signers of the U. S. Constitution. Edward, at age twenty-six, would become the youngest signer of the Declaration of Independence. Their father, John Rutledge, Sr., a sur-geon born in County Tyrone or County Cavan in Ireland, immigrated around 1735 and married fourteen-year-old Sarah Hext in Charlestown on Christmas Day, 1738. The relationship, if any, between the two Rutledge families has not been determined.

7. Bergevin et al., 4; Land, "Seven Mile Prairie," 1; Land, "Letter," 1; Bergevin et al., 4 (Thomas Camron received a land grant of 450 acres in Craven County on Nov. 19, 1772. Fairfield County was formed from Craven County at a later

date, and then Craven County ceased to exist. The 1790 Census for Fairfield County lists one male under sixteen and four females in the household of Thomas Camron and a wife in the household of Thomas Camron, Jr. Four other Camrons, believed to be sons of Thomas Camron, Sr., were listed as heads of households.); Hammand; Bergevin et al., 180; Obituary of Mary Ann (Miller) Rutledge, *Birmingham* (Iowa) *Enterprise*, Jan. 2, 1879; further documentation appears in "The Rutledge Family of New Salem, Illinois" by James Rutledge Saunders, the oldest child of Ann Rutledge's youngest sibling, 1926.

8. Rouse, *Planters and Pioneers,* 200.

9. Rouse, *Great Wagon Road,* 53.

10. Bergevin et al., 6 (Camron appeared personally and listed a sworn claim for recompense against the State of South Carolina on Feb. 1, 1784; the claim amounted to "Eight Pounds, Eight Shillings Sterling" and was granted to Camron and signed for by John Cook on April 12, 1785.); Land, "Letter."

11. Obituary of Mary Ann (Miller) Rutledge, op. cit. The exact dates each family arrived in Georgia are uncertain, but legal records show Thomas Camron, Sr., there by Dec. 7, 1793. He stated on that date that he was a resident of Elbert County when he deeded to William Richardson of Fairfield County, S.C., 110 acres of land for the sum of Forty-five Pounds Sterling. It was part of a tract of 260 acres granted to Camron by His Excellency William Moultrie on Feb. 6, 1766. In 1795 Camron purchased 1,856 acres on Beaverdam Creek, Elbert County, from his son-in-law, Robert Hawthorn, who was headed for Kentucky.

12. Bergevin et al., 26.

13. Land, "Seven Mile," 1; Bergevin et al., 3, 21, 26, 180; Brown, 30. (According to Bergevin et al., in 1791, a legal document from Elbert County, Ga., shows the names of John Hawthorn, John Camron, and Peter Miller, with Miller as testator to a land sale.)

14. Bergevin et al., 9, 195. (They note that the 1810 Census of Henderson County, Ky., lists the Camrons, Rutledges, Hawthorns, and Peter Millers. Also, Mrs. Land quotes James Mayes Rutledge in her article, "Interesting Incidents of History Recalled In Account On Enfield": "There was a regular clan of us living down in Kentucky, as Scotch and Presbyterian as any parish in Scotland—the Rutledges, the Millers, the Camrons, the Mayes, the Hawthornes, the Veatchs, etc. They were nearly all Aunts, Uncles, and Cousins to me. Good people they were, too, smart and well-educated. . . ."); Drake, 19-20.

15. Drake, 21-2; Hammand; Bergevin et al., 26.

16. Land, "Enfield Township," 1, "Seven Mile Prairie, 2 (Mrs. Land lists the members of the traveling group.).

17. Ibid.; Bergevin et al., 193.

18. Land, "Seven Mile," 2.

19. Land, "Enfield Township," 2; State Memorial Highway Marker on Illinois Route 45 in White County. According to Mrs. Land ("Seven Mile Prairie," 4), the log church was built on land belonging to Thomas Rutledge in Section 21 of what is now called Enfield Township. The history of the church is also described in an undated booklet, *Norris City and Indian Creek Township, Illinois,* by Edward Oliver, sponsored by the Norris City Lions Club.

20. Shere; Brown, 34.

21. Shere; Brown, 34; letter from Mrs. C. Land to C. Vale Mayes, Dec. 16, 1964.

22. "Memoirs of James McGrady Rutledge;" Bergevin et al., 40–1; Pond, 87.

23. Land, "Seven Mile," 3; Bergevin et al., 193.

24. Pickard, 28-9.

25. Hay, 25.

26. Land, "Enfield Township," 2-3.

27. Bergevin et al., 26, 192; Drake, 38.

28. Bergevin et al., 26.

29. Drake, 44.

30. Allen.

31. Drake, 45.

32. Reep, 6; Thomas, *LNS,* 7.

33. Reep, 9.

34. Ibid., 9-11; Bergevin et al., 192.

35. Reep, 117-18.

36. For the early history of New Salem, see the works by Barton, Chandler, Onstot, Reep (9–17), and Thomas, *LNS* (5–17).

CHAPTER 4:
"THERE'S MORE IN ABE'S HEAD THAN WIT AND FUN."

1. Thomas, *LNS,* 45–6; Hay, 24.

2. Duncan & Nickols, 100.

3. Ibid., 95, 98.

4. Ibid., 91.

5. Wilson & Davis, 242-43 (Mentor Graham to WHH, April 2, 1866); Ibid., 21 (William G. Greene to WHH, May 30, 1865); Ibid., 383 (Robert B. Rutledge to WHH, Nov. 1, 1866).

6. Ibid., 527 (Esther Summers Bale interviewed by WHH, 1866); Ibid., 374, (Caleb Carman to WHH, Oct. 12, 1866); Ibid., 253 (John McNamar to G. U.

Miles, May 5, 1866); Ibid., 242 (Mentor Graham to WHH, April 2, 1866); Ibid., 80 (Lynn McNulty Greene to WHH, July 30, 1865); Ibid., 21 (William G. Greene to WHH, May 30, 1865). For additional descriptions, see pages 73, 80, 242–44, 250, 253, 374, 604; also see Donald, *Lincoln,* 56; Oates, 19; Herndon and Weik, 106-07; Walsh, 96; and Sandburg, *AL,* 140.

7. Wilson & Davis, 409 (Robert B. Rutledge to WHH, Nov. 21,1866); Drake, 72.

8. Reep, 104.

9. Thomas, *LNS,* 24; Onstot, 114.

10. Herndon & Weik, 62–3.

11. Josiah G. Holland Papers, New York Public Library (quoted by Erastus Wright to Josiah G. Holland, July 10, 1865).

12. Miers, 1:14.

13. Herndon & Weik, 63–4; Wilson & Davis, 457–58 (John Hanks to WHH, 1865–66).

14. Mearns, 1:151 (based on interview with William Butler, May, 1860).

15. Herndon & Weik, 67; Wilson & Davis, 69 (J. Rowan Herndon to WHH, July 3, 1865).

16. Wilson & Davis, 73 (James Short to WHH, Petersburg, Ill., July 7, 1865); Ibid., 170 (Abner Y. Ellis to WHH, Jan. 23, 1866); Ibid., 387 (Robert B. Rutledge to WHH, Nov. 1, 1866).

17. Ibid., 74 (James Short to WHH, July 7, 1865).

18. Bergevin et al., 27; Drake, 52, 65, 77. (The quotes attributed to Lincoln in this section come from letters written by children and grandchildren of John Miller Camron and given to Julia Drake, Camron's biographer. Julia Drake's notes were shared with me by her niece, Sharon Schirding, who is a cousin of John Miller Camron's wife, Polly Orendorff.)

19. Ibid., 60–1, 79; Bergevin et al., 29.

20. Drake, 57; Bergevin et al., 35 (from a letter from a granddaughter of John Miller Camron—Mrs. W. R. Waters, nee Olive Thompson—to an unidentified person).

21. Onstot, 77.

22. Thomas, *LNS,* 145.

23. Reep, 55; Onstot, 86.

24. Wilson & Davis, 385 (Robert B. Rutledge to WHH, Nov. 1, 1866); Tarbell, *Early Life,* 191.

25. Wilson & Davis, 90 (N.W. Branson to WHH, Aug. 3, 1865).

26. Ibid., 387 (Robert B. Rutledge to WHH, Nov. 1, 1866); Wilson, *Honor's Voice* (see pages 21-51 for a critical analysis of conflicting accounts of the wresting match).

27. Wilson & Davis, 189-90 (Abner Y. Ellis to WHH, Feb. 1, 1866); Herndon & Weik, 97.

28. Thomas, *LNS*, 48; Wilson & Davis, 546 (John McNamar to WHH, Menard County, Ill., Jan. 20, 1867).

29. Ibid.; Reep, 102; Duncan & Nickols, 123.

30. Reep, 54; Wilson & Davis, 374 (Caleb Carman to WHH, Oct. 12, 1866); Thomas, *LNS*, 70; Herndon & Weik, 38; Wilson & Davis, 118 (John Romaine to WHH, Sept. 14, 1865).

31. Thomas, *LNS*, 45; Wilson & Davis, 540 (Jason Duncan to WHH, 1866-67); Pond, "Intellectual New Salem" lecture; Wilson & Davis, 384-85 (Robert B. Rutledge to WHH, Nov. 1, 1866).

32. Thomas, *LNS*, 121; Reep, 68; Tarbell, *Early Life,* 192.

33. Reep, 119.

34. Burlingame, *An Oral History,* 19 (William Butler to John Nicolay, June 13, 1875); Wilson & Davis, 69 (J. Rowan Herndon to WHH, Quincy, Ill., July 3, 1865); Ibid., 557 (Elizabeth Abell to WHH, Feb. 5, 1867).

35. Stevens, 8.

36. Wilson & Davis, 370, 365 (Johnson Gaines Greene to WHH, Oct. 10, 1866, and Oct. 5, 1866); Ibid., 367-68 (William G. Greene to WHH, Oct. 9, 1866); Ibid., 421 (John McNamar to WHH, Nov. 25, 1866).

37. Ibid., 383, 409 (Robert B. Rutledge to WHH, ca Nov. 1, 1866, and Nov. 21, 1866).

CHAPTER 5:
"HE HAS DUMPED HER—HO, HO, HO."

1. Herndon & Weik, 71; Hertz, *HL,* 314, 252-53 (McNamar to G. U. Miles, May 5, 1866).

2. Ray P. Basler, ed., "James Quay Howard's Notes on Lincoln," *Abraham Lincoln Quarterly* 4 (Dec. 1947): 391.

3. Wilson & Davis, 481 (John T. Stuart to WHH, 1865 or 1866).

4. Basler, 4:64-5 (from autobiography written by AL for John L. Scripps, June, 1860).

5. Reep, 49.

6. Herndon & Weik, 108-09; Wilson & Davis, 383 (Robert B. Rutledge to WHH, Nov. 1, 1866).

7. Lamon, *Life of AL,* 161; Reep, 105. The acknowledgment of the deed for one-half of the Rutledge farm was before Bowling Green, J. P. (Transcript Record A, page 183, Menard County, Ill.) On Jan. 20, 1833, James Rutledge

and wife sold the remaining forty acres of his farm to John Jones for $300 (Transcript A, page 239, Menard County, Ill.) Thus, when Ann and her father died, James Rutledge owned no real estate. The entire eighty acres was regarded as poor farming land.

8. Barton, *The Women Lincoln Loved,* 174–75.

9. Shere; Barton, *San Diego Sun.* Shere's lengthy feature article on Ann Rutledge was based on numerous interviews of Rutledge-family relatives and descendants of close friends of the family. He also reviewed letters written from New Salem from 1832 to 1835.

10. Drake, 46.

11. Wilson & Davis, 170 (A. Y. Ellis to WHH, Jan. 23, 1866); Herndon & Weik, 95–6.

12. Based on recollections of Sarah Rutledge Saunders, as told to Bernie Babcock and reported in her book on page 48.

13. Wilson & Davis, 10 (Mentor Graham to WHH, May 29, 1865); Duncan & Nickols, 128.

14. Flindt, *Chicago Inter-Ocean,* Feb. 12, 1899 (interview with Nancy Rutledge Prewitt, Ann's sister); Hammand (Sarah Rutledge Saunders to Jane E. Hammand, March 28, 1921, for the Decatur Lincoln Memorial Collection; Barton, *San Diego Sun.*

15. Walsh, 131–32.

16. Flindt.

17. Ibid.

18. Herndon & Weik, 89; Tarbell, *Footsteps,* 217.

19. Basler, 4:65.

20. Thomas, 94; Herndon & Weik, 110; Carnegie, *The Unknown Lincoln,* 26.

21. I am indebted to Historian Michael Burlingame for sharing the Parthena Nance quotation with me. It comes from her rare volume, *A Piece of Time.* See also Herndon & Weik, 109.

22. Nance, *A Piece of Time,* 26; Wilson & Davis, 374 (Caleb Carman to WHH, Oct. 12, 1866); Ibid., 545–546 (McNamar to WHH, Jan. 20, 1867, in which he says Ann "undoubtedly was about as classic a scholar as Mr. Lincoln").

23. Carnegie, *The Unknown Lincoln,* 26.

24. Wilson & Davis, 383 (Robert B. Rutledge to WHH, Nov. 18, 1866); see also 13, 21, 25, 67, 80, 175, 325, 374, 387, 402–3, 409, 440, 520, 541; Carnegie, *The Unknown Lincoln,* 28; Walsh, 157; Chandler, 503.

25. Herndon & Weik, 98; Tarbell, *Early Life,* 181.

26. Barton, *Women,* 187–88; Wilson & Davis, 374 (Caleb Carman to WHH, Oct. 12, 1866); Ibid., 364–65 (Johnson Gaines Greene to WHH, Jan. 23, 1866).

CHAPTER 6:
"MY COMFORT BY DAY, AND MY SONG IN THE NIGHT."

1. Wilson & Davis, 557 (Elizabeth Abell to WHH, Feb. 15, 1867).

2. Tarbell, *Footsteps*, 199.

3. Hertz, *HL*, 233–34; Wilson & Davis, 90 (N.W. Branson to WHH, Aug. 3, 1865).

4. Wilson & Davis, 73 (James Short to WHH, July 7, 1865); Walsh, 70-2; Drake, 90; Basler, 1:48; also see Helen Ruth Reed, "A Prophecy Lincoln Made," *Boston Herald*, Feb. 9, 1930. The endorsement came during his re-election campaign for the Illinois legislature. He received the most votes of the seventeen Sangamon County candidates on election day, Aug. 1.

5. Wilson & Davis, 423 (John M. Rutledge to WHH, Nov. 25, 1866); Herndon & Weik, 112; letter from A. M. Prewitt, son of Nancy Rutledge Prewitt (Ann Rutledge's sister) to Miss J. E. Hamand.

6. Hertz, *HL*, 138.

7. Herndon & Weik, 106; Wilson & Davis, 591, 605-06 (Elizabeth Herndon Bell to JWW, Aug. 24, 1883 and to WHH, March, 1887). Elizabeth Bell was the daughter of the schoolmaster, Mentor Graham.

8. *The Prairie Picayune*, Lincoln's New Salem Newsletter, 1996 (quoting from Englishman William Oliver's account in *Eight Months in Illinois*. I am grateful to New Salem Volunteer Carol S. Jenkins for this information.

9. Onstot, 125-26.

10. Saunders, 3 (from a paper, "The Rutledge Family of New Salem, Illinois," compiled in 1926 by James Rutledge Saunders, the oldest child of Ann Rutledge's youngest sibling).

11. Ibid., 2; Wilson & Davis, 358–60 (Mary Todd Lincoln to WHH, Sept. 1866); Basler, 1:382; Hertz, *HL*, 406; Wilson & Davis, 506 (Joseph Gillespie to WHH, Dec. 8, 1866). Lincoln, in his race for Congress in 1846 publicly stated he was "not a member of any Christian Church." His stepmother told William H. Herndon on Sept. 8, 1865, "Abe had no particular religion."

12. Maltby, 31; Mearns, 1:154 (William G. Greene to James Q. Howard, May, 1860); Ibid., 74-6; Wilson & Davis, 70 (J. Rowan Herndon to WHH, July 3, 1865).

13. Drake, 82; Land, "Enfield Township," 2; Wilson & Davis, 172 (A. Y. Ellis to WHH, Jan. 23, 1866); Herndon & Weik, 102.

14. Wilson & Davis, 578 (Jesse W. Fell to Ward Hill Lamon, Sept. 22, 1870).

15. Ibid., 13 (Hardin Bale to WHH, May 29, 1865); Ibid, 62 (John Hill to WHH, June 27, 1865); *The Index*, 5, Feb. 18, 1870 (WHH to Francis E. Abbot); Wilson, *Honor's Voice*, 81; Wilson & Davis, 441 (Isaac Cogdall to

WHH, 1865/66); Stevens, 11-12; Wilson & Davis, 472 (James H. Matheny to WHH, 1865/66); Ibid., 576 (John T. Stuart to WHH, March 2, 1870).

16. Basler, 1:382; Speed, 32-3.

17. Wilson & Davis, 464 (James W. Keyes to WHH, 1865 or 1866); *Bicentennial Collection of Quotes*, Salesian Missions, New Rochelle, 1976.

18. Wilson & Davis, 501 (A. Y. Ellis to WHH, Dec. 6, 1866).

19. Duncan & Nickols, 156.

20. Wilson & Davis, 426 (Robert B. Rutledge to WHH, Nov. 30, 1866); Herndon & Weik, 92.

CHAPTER 7: "ANNIE'S WHOLE SOUL SEEMED WRAPPED UP IN LINCOLN."

1. Wilson & Davis, 236 (George U. Miles to WHH, March 23, 1866, quoting Mrs. Bowling Green); Ibid., 402-3 (Robert B. Rutledge to WHH, Nov. 18, 1866); Herndon & Weik, 112; Wilson, *Civil War History;* Wilson & Davis, 383 (Robert B. Rutledge to WHH, Nov. 1, 1866); Tarbell, *Early Life,* 218 (quoting Jean Rutledge Berry). One cannot state precisely when and where Lincoln proposed to Ann Rutledge. Wilson, in *Honor's Voice*, page 117, said "the engagement was most likely agreed to sometime in the first half of 1835" after Lincoln had returned in February from his legislative session.

2. Herndon & Weik, 111; Wilson & Davis, 402-3 (Robert B. Rutledge to WHH, Nov. 18, 1866); Sandburg, *AL*, 186; Walsh, 35-6; Wilson & Davis, 383 (Robert B. Rutledge to WHH, Nov. 1, 1866); Flindt; Shere.

3. Flindt; Wilson & Davis, 409 (Robert B. Rutledge to WHH, Nov. 21, 1866, corroborated by McGrady Rutledge who reported that Ann told him that as soon as certain studies were completed and Lincoln "was admitted to the bar," they would be married); Herndon & Weik, 112.

4. Drake, 94, 83.

5. Rankin; Tarbell, *Footsteps*, 218; Walsh, 107.

6. Wilson & Davis, 21 (William G. Greene to WHH, May 30, 1865); Ibid., 80, Lynn McNulty Greene to WHH, July 30, 1865); Ibid., 243 (Mentor Graham to WHH, April 2, 1866); also Harvey Ross, *Early Pioneers* (Ross carried mail between Springfield and Lewistown, passing through Lincoln's Post Office at New Salem four times a week.); Wilson & Davis, 423 (John M. Rutledge to WHH, Nov. 25, 1866); Herndon & Weik, 112 (Herndon reported that, according to Ann's brother John, Ann sang this hymn to Lincoln early in her illness, and that it was "the last thing she ever sung."); Sandburg, *AL*, 186.

7. Barton, *The Women Lincoln Loved*, 82-3. Between the pages of the Rutledge family Bible, Ann's sister, Nancy Rutledge Prewitt, found this letter from David. Nancy gave the letter to her youngest sibling, Sarah, and Sarah shared it with historian William Barton when he interviewed her in California. The letter provided evidence that Ann wanted to prepare herself to be a lawyer's wife before marrying Lincoln. Barton first mentioned it in a talk at New Salem in May of 1926.

8. Wilson & Davis, 604–05 (Parthena Nance Hill to WHH, March, 1887).

9. Walsh, 133–34.

10. Wilson & Davis, 604–05 (Parthena Nance Hill to WHH, March, 1887); letter from John Hill to Ida M. Tarbell, Feb. 6, 1896, original in Ida M. Tarbell Papers, Allegheny College Library.

11. Shutes, 45 (quoted from the doctoral dissertation of Lorenzo D. Matheny, a Springfield resident studying for his medical degree, 1836).

12. Donald, *Lincoln*, 57; Carnegie, *The Unknown Lincoln*, 31.

13. Thomas, *LNS*, 46–7; Herndon & Weik, 112; Herndon's lecture of Nov. 16, 1866; Thomas, *LNS*, 123.

14. Flindt; Herndon & Weik, 112; Wilson & Davis, 606–07 (Jasper Rutledge to WHH, March 9, 1887); letter from A. M. Prewitt (son of Nancy Rutledge Prewitt) to Miss J. E. Hammand, Nov. 7, 1921, for the Decatur Lincoln Memorial Collection.

15. Reep, 75 (based on statement from Berry's daughter, Mary, who was 13 at the time).

16. Drake, 95; Flindt; Herndon & Weik, 112; Manfrina, *News-Press*; Cook, *Lompoc Record.*; Walsh, 15-6 (quoting from William H. Herndon's lecture of Nov. 16, 1866); *Chicago Tribune Magazine,* Feb. 22, 1922 (Sarah Rutledge Saunders to Katherine Wheeler); undated statement by Sarah Saunders enclosed in J. R. Saunders to Mary Saunders, Sisquoc, Calif., May 14, 1919, Saunders Papers, Illinois State Historical Library, Springfield. Sarah's information is based on what her mother and sister Nancy told her.); Reep, 76; Flindt; letter from A. M. Prewitt to Miss J. E. Hammand, Nov. 7, 1921, for the Decatur Lincoln Memorial Collection.

17. Walsh, 136; Reep, 84 (based on information provided by Dr. Allen's daughter or granddaughter, Miranda Allen.); Herndon & Weik, 112.

18. Bergevin, et. al., 27; Walsh, 37 (based on recollection of James McGrady Rutledge); Drake, 97.

19. Wilson & Davis, 383 (Robert B. Rutledge to Ibid., Nov. 1, 1866); 325 (Benjamin F. Irwin to WHH, Aug. 27, 1866); Ibid., 80 (Lynn McNulty Greene to WHH, July 30, 1865); Ibid., 13 (Hardin Bale to WHH, May 29, 1865); Ibid., 557 (Elizabeth Abell to WHH, Feb. 15, 1867); Ibid., 21 (William G. Greene to WHH, May 30, 1865); Hertz, *HL* 273 (John Hill to WHH, June 6, 1865).

20. Sandburg, *AL*, 190; Thomas, 124; Wilson & Davis, 21 (William G. Greene to WHH, May 30, 1865); Ibid., 155–56 (Henry McHenry to WHH, Jan. 8, 1866).

21. *Lerna* (Ill.) *Eagle*, Sept. 19, 1930 (based on correspondence of Eliza Armstrong Smith, daughter of Hannah Armstrong); Reep, 77 (based on letter from Sarah Rutledge Saunders and an interview with Mary Rutledge Moore; dates not given).

22. Reep, 77; Wilson & Davis, 236 (G. U. Miles to WHH, March 23, 1866); Herndon & Weik, 113.

23. Reep, 78–9; Angle, 116-17.

24. Tarbell, *Footsteps,* 220; Herndon & Weik, 113-14; Browne, 129.

25. Walsh, 123-26; Judd Stewart Collection, Huntington Library, San Marino, Calif. (William G. Greene to Paul Hull, unidentified clipping, 1887).

26. Walsh, 128-29 (recorded in 1879 by Usher Linder, a longtime political friend of Lincoln; appears in Linder's *Reminiscences*).

CHAPTER 8:
"I WANT IN ALL CASES TO DO RIGHT."

Note: Traditional versions of the Lincoln-Todd courtship are no longer supported by the available evidence. The scenario presented in this chapter is based primarily on historian Douglas Wilson's recent analyses of contemporary documents, such as Mary Todd's own letters and those of her friends. For more information, see Wilson's *Honor's Voice* and his essays in *Lincoln Before Washington.*

1. Wilson & Davis, 610 (B. R. Vineyard to JWW, March 14, 1887); Basler, 1:117-19 (AL to Mrs. Orville H. Browning, April 1, 1838).

2. Ibid..

3. Onstot, 24.

4. Angle, *HL*, 119-20 (Mary Owens Vineyard to WHH, Weston, Mo., May 22, 1866); Wilson & Davis, 262 (Mary Owens Vineyard to WHH, July 22, 1866).

5. Wilson & Davis, 531 (Johnson Gaines Greene to WHH, 1866).

6. Basler, 1:78 (dated May 7, 1837).

7. Ibid., 1:94 (AL to Mary Owens, Aug. 16, 1837).

8. Basler, 1:117-19 (AL to Mrs. Orville H. Browning, April 1, 1838).

9. Wilson & Davis, 263 (Mary Owens Vineyard to WHH, July 22, 1866).

10. Lincoln Museum, Fort Wayne, Ind. (Clipping Collection, Edna Bell Howell to "My dear friend," Los Angeles, March 20, 1938).

11. Herndon & Weik, 148; Speed 21-2.

12. Herndon & Weik, 149.

13. Wilson & Davis, 470 (James H. Matheny to WHH, 1865 or 1866); Herndon & Weik, 151.

14. Herndon-Weik Collection, Library of Congress (WHH to James H. Wilson, Sept. 23, 1889); Hertz, *HL,* 112 (WHH to JWW, Dec. 10, 1885); Sandburg, *AL,* 158; Hertz, *HL,* 263 (WHH to JWW, Feb. 21, 1891). Herndon told Weik that "Mr. Lincoln had a double consciousness. . . . In one moment he was in a state of abstraction and then quickly in another state when he was social, talkative, and a communicative fellow."

15. Wilson & Davis, 719 (Joshua F. Speed to WHH, Jan. 5, 1889).

16. Herndon-Weik Collection, Library of Congress (WHH to JWW, Jan. 1891); Hertz, *HL,* 259.

17. Wilson & Davis, 431 (Joshua F. Speed to WHH, Nov. 30, 1866).

18. Letter from Dr. Henry to his wife, Feb. 18, 1863 (original at the Illinois State Historical Library, Springfield).

19. Oates, 33.

20. Wilson & Davis, 624–25 (William Jayne to WHH, Aug. 17, 1887).

21. Sandburg, *AL,* 159–60; Herndon & Weik, 165.

22. Wilson & Davis, 443 (Elizabeth Todd Edwards to WHH, 1865 or 1866).

23. Helm, 32.

24. Angle, "Here I Have Lived," 110; Beveridge, 1:271.

25. The amount of time Lincoln was out-of-town is estimated, based on Miers, *Lincoln Day By Day.*

26. Turners, 14-19 (based on her letter to Mercy Ann Levering of July 23, 1840, and James C. Conkling's letter to Mercy Ann Levering of Sept. 21, 1840); Sandburg & Angle, 172 (James C. Conkling to Mercy Ann Levering, Sept. 21, 1840); *Lincoln Day By Day* (states that AL was "still stumping the lower part of state" on Sept. 21 and by Sept. 30 was appearing in court in the central part of the state); Wilson, *Honors Voice,* 219.

27. Letter of Matilda Edwards to her brother Nelson, Nov. 30, 1840 (in the Ruth Painter Randall Papers, Library of Congress, and in the Edwards Family Papers, Knox College Library, Galesburg, Ill.); Wilson & Davis, 474 (Joshua Speed to WHH, 1865 or 1866); Wilson, *Honor's Voice,* 217.

28. Sandburg and Angle, 172 (James C. Conkling to Mercy Ann Levering, Sept. 21, 1840).

29. Wilson, *Honor's Voice,* 220; Nolan, 19:3.

30. James G. Randall Papers, Manuscript Division, Library of Congress (Jane D. Bell in Springfeld to Ann Bell in Danville, Ky., Jan. 27, 1841—Jane Bell, a

Kentuckian, was related by marriage to the proprietor of James Bell and Company, and his partner and cousin was Lincoln's close friend Joshua Speed); Wilson, *Lincoln Before Washington,* 110; Wilson & Davis, 474–75 (Joshua Speed to WHH, 1865 or 1866); Herndon & Weik, 168; Wilson, *Lincoln Before Washington,* 102–03.

31. Herndon & Weik, 169; Wilson & Davis, 475 (Joshua Speed to WHH, 1865 or 1866).

32. Wilson & Davis, 477 (Joshua Speed to WHH, 1865 or 1866); Herndon & Weik, 169.

33. James G. Randall Papers, Library of Congress; Wilson, *Lincoln Before Washington,* 110; Ida M. Tarbell Papers, Allegheny College Library (Mrs. Benjamin S. Edwards to Tarbell, Oct. 8, 1895).

34. Herndon & Weik, 167; Wilson & Davis, 443 (Elizabeth Todd Edwards to WHH, 1865 or 1866).

35. Wilson, *Honor's Voice,* 222–23, 230–31; Wilson & Davis, 251 (James H. Matheny to WHH, May 3, 1866); Ibid., 476 (Joshua Speed to WHH, 1865 or 1866).

36. Herndon & Weik, 159.

37. Wilson & Davis, 187-88 (Joseph Gillespie to WHH, Jan. 31, 1866).

38. Barton, *The Women Lincoln Loved,* 239; Turners, 20–2, 25–6. As noted in the manuscript, Joshua Speed, Ninian W. Edwards, Elizabeth Todd Edwards, and James Matheny all indicated Lincoln's love for Matilda Edwards. Other strong evidence exists. A niece of Matilda's, Alice Edwards Quigley, wrote: "Tradition tells us that Lincoln and Douglas were both in love with her" (reproduced in H. O. Knerr's "Abraham Lincoln and Matilda Edwards" in the Illinois State Historical Library). Ninian W. Edwards's son Albert said his "family thought that Lincoln was much taken with Matilda, but nothing came of it" (Stevens, *A Reporter's Lincoln,* 75). Sarah Rickard also remembered Lincoln's interest in Matilda (*St. Louis Globe-Democrat,* Feb. 9, 1907). Also, Octavia Roberts of Springfield interviewed many Lincoln acquaintances. Writing about Lincoln's rejection of Mary Todd, he reported that his grandmother, who was Mrs. Lincoln's contemporary, always told her family that "it was due to Matilda Edwards, who won Lincoln's love" (Octavia Roberts, "We All Knew Abraham," *Abraham Lincoln Quarterly* 4, March 1946, page 27).

39. Wilson & Davis, 133 (Ninian W. Edwards to WHH, Sept. 22, 1865). Mary Todd and Ninian and Elizabeth Edwards all attested to Speed's pursuit of Matilda Edwards.

40. Wilson, *Lincoln Before Washington,* 125; Wilson & Davis, 431 (Joshua Speed to WHH, Nov. 30, 1866); Ibid., 443 (Elizabeth Todd Edwards to WHH, 1865 or 1866); Ibid., 133 (Ninian W. Edwards to WHH, Sept. 22, 1865).

41. Wilson & Davis, 592 (Elizabeth Todd Edwards to JWW, Dec. 20, 1883); Tarbell, *The Life of AL,* 1:174-80; Wilson, *Lincoln Before Washington,* 121.

42. Wilson & Davis, 342 (Joshua Speed to WHH, Sept. 17, 1866); Speed Papers, Illinois State Historical Library (Joshua F. Speed to Eliza J. Speed, March 12, 1841).

43. John Hay Papers, Brown University Library (O. H. Browning to John G. Nicolay, Springfield, June 17, 1875)—Browning affirmed that Lincoln "fell desperately in love with [Matilda Edwards] and proposed to her, but she rejected him." See also Wilson & Davis, 133 (Ninian W. Edwards to WHH, Sept. 22, 1865).

44. Chicago Historical Society (Martinette Hardin to John J. Hardin, Jan. 22, 1841).

45. Wilson & Davis, 444 (Elizabeth Todd Edwards to WHH, 1865 or 1866); Nellie Crandal Sanford, *St. Louis Globe Democrat,* Feb. 9, 1907 (an interview with Sarah Rickard Barret; the clipping is in the Lincoln files, Illinois State Historical Library).

46. Basler, 1:228 (AL to John T. Stuart, Jan. 20, 1841).

47. John Hay Papers, Brown University Library (John Nicolay with Hon. O. H. Browning, June 17,1875); Sandburg and Angle, 178-79 (James Conkling to Mercy Levering, Jan. 24, 1841).

48. James G. Randall Papers, Library of Congress (Jane D. Bell to Ann Bell, Jan. 27, 1841; from a copy of the letter supplied to Professor John B. Clark of Lincoln Memorial University by Mrs. Henry Jackson, a relative of Jane Bell, and, in turn, supplied to Professor James G. Randall).

49. Wilson & Davis, 133 (Ninian Edwards to WHH, Sept. 22, 1865); Sandburg and Angle, 178-79 (James Conkling to Mercy Levering, March 7, 1841).

50. Burlingame, *An Oral History* (Orville H. Browning to Nicolay, June 17, 1875); Barton, *The Women Lincoln Loved,* 239.

51. Wilson & Davis, 444 (Elizabeth Todd Edwards to WHH [1865-66].

52. Basler, 1:260-61 (AL to Mary Speed, Sept. 27, 1841).

53. Ibid., 1:259-60.

54. Kincaid, 16.

55. Basler 1:269 (Lincoln to Joshua Speed, Feb. 13, 1842); Ibid., 1:282 (Lincoln to Speed, March 27, 1842).

56. Ibid., 1:288-89 (Lincoln to Speed, July 4, 1842).

57. Ibid., 1:292-96.

58. Browne, 185.

59. Linder, 66-7.

60. Onstot, 18; Burlingame, *An Oral History,* 25 (William Butler to John Nicolay, June, 1875); Herndon & Weik, 201; Burlingame, *An Oral History,* 185.

61. Turner, *MTL,* 296, 299.

62. Sanford, *St. Louis Globe-Democrat,* Feb. 9, 1907 (from an interview with Sarah Rickard Barret and her husband); Hardin Papers, Chicago Historical Society (Sarah E. Hardin to John J. Hardin, Jan. 26 [1841]); Wilson & Davis, 665 (Sarah Rickard Barret to WHH, Aug. 12, 1888).

63. Wilson & Davis, 665 (Sarah Rickard Barret to WHH, Aug. 12, 1888).

64. Ibid; Barton, *Women,* 259.

65. Sanford, *St. Louis Globe-Democrat,* Feb. 9, 1907; Herndon & Weik, 179.

66. Ida M. Tarbell Papers, Allegheny College Library (Mrs. John T. Stuart to Ida Tarbell); *Chicago Times-Herald,* Sept. 8, 1895, 40.

67. Burlingame, *An Oral History,* 2 (Orville H. Browning to John Nicolay, June 17, 1875); Wilson & Davis, 475 (Joshua F. Speed to WHH, 1865 or 1866); Ida M. Tarbell Papers, Allegheny College Library (Elizabeth Todd Grimsley to Ida Tarbell, Springfield, Ill., March 9, 1895).

68. Wilson & Davis, 444 (Elizabeth Todd Edwards to WHH, 1865 or 1866).

69. Temple, 27; Wilson & Davis, 666 (James H. Matheny to WHH, Aug. 21, 1888); Ibid., 251 (James H. Matheny to WHH, May 3, 1866); Ida M. Tarbell Papers, Allegheny College Library (Mrs. Benjamin S. Edwards to Tarbell, Oct. 8, 1895); Wilson & Davis, 444 (Elizabeth Todd Edwards to WHH, 1865 or 1866); Beveridge, 1:355.

70. Kunhardts, *Lincoln,* 64; Oates, 63; Wilson & Davis, 665 (James H. Matheny to JWW, Aug. 21, 1888); Herndon & Weik, 181.

71. Ida M. Tarbell Papers, Allegheny College Library (reminiscences of a Mr. Beck, son of the proprietress, in Effie Sparks, "Stories of Abraham Lincoln," 20–1); Carnegie, *Lincoln the Unknown,* 71–2 (Catherine Miles Early to her nephew Jimmy Miles to Carnegie).

72. John Hay Papers, Brown University Library (O. H. Browning confided to John G. Nicolay that Mary Todd was indeed the aggressor in the courtship, June 17, 1875); Turners, 293 (Mary Todd Lincoln to Josiah Holland, Dec. 4, 1865).

73. Basler, 1:305 (Lincoln to Samuel D. Marshall, Nov. 11, 1842).

74. Temple, 28; Browne, 201; Wilson & Davis, 251 (James H. Matheny to WHH, May 3, 1866).

CHAPTER 9:
"LINCOLN'S WIFE WAS A HELLION."

1. Baker, *MTL,* 107.

2. Wilson & Davis, 465 (Turner R. King to WHH [1865–66]); Ibid. 597 (Margaret Ryan to JWW, Oct. 27, 1886); Albert J. Beveridge Papers, Library of Congress (Hillary A. Gobin to Beveridge, South Bend, Ind., May 17,

1923; her father was a minister who lived a few doors away from the Lincoln house); *New York Times,* Feb. 6, 1938, sec. 2:1; Sandburg and Angle, 70-1 (based on WHH's notes of a conversation with Stephen Whitehurst in 1867; Whitehurst heard the story from a Mr. Barrett who allegedly observed it in 1856 or 1857).

3. Wilson & Davis, 445 (Elizabeth Todd Edwards to WHH, 1865 or 1866).

4. Ibid., 713-14 (James H. Matheny to WHH, January, 1887).

5. William E. Barton Papers, University of Chicago ("Notes of Interview With Mrs. Fanny Grimsley, July 27, 1926," by Paul M. Angle, enclosed in Angle to Barton, Springfield, Ill., Jan. 10, 1927); Wilson & Davis, 389-90 (John B. Weber to WHH, Nov. 1, 1866).

6. Unpublished paper by Elizabeth A. Capps, niece of Jabez Capps, Springfield's first shoemaker; Wilson & Davis, 692 (Jesse K. Dubois to JWW, between 1883 and 1889).

7. *New York Times,* Aug. 26, 1934 (based on interview with Victor Kutchin, who acquired the couch from Mason Brayman, to whom Lincoln entrusted the couch when he left Springfield in 1861); *Belvedere* (Ill.) *Standard,* April 14, 1868 (reminiscences of Page Eaton).

8. Lincoln Collection, Chicago Historical Society (WHH to Isaac N. Arnold, Springfield, Ill., Oct. 24, 1883); Jesse W. Weik Papers, Illinois State Historical Library (Harriet Chapman to JWW, undated).

9. Fiske, 494.

10. Donald, *Lincoln,* 160.

11. Wilson & Davis, 349 (David Davis to WHH, Sept. 20, 1866). Judge Davis presided over the Eighth Judicial District in Illinois. Lincoln practiced before him for more than ten years. Davis managed Lincoln's nomination effort for the presidency in 1860. In 1862 Lincoln appointed him to the U.S. Supreme Court.

12. Basler, 1:378 (AL to Andrew Johnston, April 18, 1846).

13. Whitney, 1:238; Carpenter, *Six Months,* 59.

14. Wilson & Davis, 350 (David Davis to WHH, Sept. 20, 1866); Ibid., 490 (Charles S. Zane to WHH [1865-1866]).

15. Ibid., 453 (James Gourley to WHH, 1865 or 1866); Ibid., 349 (David Davis to WHH, Sept. 20, 1866).

16. Hertz, *HL,* 141; *Quincy* (Ill.) *Whig,* May 5, 1847 (poem by AL); Walsh, 169.

17. Basler, 1:465 (AL to Mary Todd Lincoln, April 16, 1848).

18. Clines; an archeological report by Elizabeth Barthold O'Brien and Donna J. Seifert preceding construction of the Smithsonian Institution's new National Museum of the American Indian in 1999 and 2000. (Ms. Seifert unearthed

the dregs of Ms. Hall's brothel on the construction site east of the Air and Space Museum.)

19. Basler, 1:465–66 (AL to Mary Todd Lincoln, April 16, 1848); Turners, 36-8; Basler, 1:466 (AL to Mary Todd Lincoln, April 16, 1848).

20. Basler, 1:466.

21. Ibid., 1:477; John S. Richards, *Berks and Schuylkill Journal,* Feb. 8, 1851; Nolan, 292.

22. Findley, 124.

23. Herndon-Weik Collection, Library of Congress (undated statement of John T. Stuart); John Hay Papers, Brown University (Stuart to John G. Nicolay, Springfield, June 24, 1875); Ward Hill Lamon Papers, Henry E. Huntington Library, San Marino, Calif. (WHH to Lamon, Springfield, March 6, 1870); Basler, 2:19 (AL to C. U. Schlater, Jan. 5, 1849).

24. Basler, 2:96–7 (AL to John D. Johnston, Jan. 12, 1851).

25. Abraham Lincoln Papers, Library of Congress (John D. Johnston to AL, May 25, 1849).

26. Lincoln Museum, Fort Wayne, Ind. ("Anecdotes of Mrs. Lincoln" by "a neighbor of the family at the time of Lincoln's funeral," quoted in *The News,* no city indicated).

27. Wilson & Davis, 357, 359 (Mary Todd Lincoln to WHH, September, 1866); Donald, *Lincoln,* 109; Herndon Weik Collection, Library of Congress (WHH to JWW, Feb. 18, 1887).

28. Donald, *Lincoln,* 159; Abraham Lincoln Papers, Library of Congress (Gibson W. Harris to AL, Nov. 7, 1860); Hill, 164.

29. Goff, 32.

30. Herndon & Weik, 274-75.

31. Ibid.

32. Ibid., 276; *Decatur Gazette,* clipped in *Illinois State Register,* May 27, 1854.

33. Browne, 217-18.

34. Whitney, 20; Menz, Katherine B., "Furnishings Plan. . . The Lincoln Home," unpublished report to the National Park Service, U.S. Department of the Interior, 1983.

35. Wilson & Davis, 453 (James Gourley to WHH, 1865 or 1866); Chenery, *Illinois State Register,* Feb. 27, 1938; Arnold, 83.

36. Herndon & Weik, 326. Lincoln's vast knowledge of Scripture provided the source for his famous statement, "A house divided against itself cannot stand." He was paraphrasing Mark 3:24–5: "And if a kingdom be divided against itself, that kingdom cannot stand. And if a house be divided against itself, that house cannot stand."

37. Ibid., 327.

38. Sparks, *The Lincoln-Douglas Debates of 1858.*

39. Lorant, 79.

40. Kunhardts, *Lincoln,* 110.

41. C. M. Smith and John Williams Account Books, 1859, Illinois State Historical Society; Wilson & Davis, 452 (James Gourley to WHH, 1865 or 1866).

42. Kunhardts, *Lincoln,* 120; *New York Tribune,* July 17, 1882, page 5.

43. Basler, 4:87.

44. Putnam, 220–22; Baringer, 158; Kunhardts, *Lincoln,* 116.

45. Zane, 430–38; Randall, *Lincoln the President,* 1:173–74.

46. Ashmun; Basler, 4:75. A newspaperman, John Mason Haight, wrote to Lincoln about this incident. Haight was an active member of a temperance society. In a letter marked "Private and Confidential," Lincoln replied on June 11, 1860: "I think it would be improper for me to write, or say anything to, or for, the public, upon the subject of which you inquire. I therefore wish the letter I do write to be held as strictly confidential. Having kept house sixteen years, and having never held the 'cup' to the lips of my friends then, my judgment was that I should not, in my new position, change my habit in this respect. What actually occurred upon the occasion of the Committee visiting me, I think it would be better for others to say." Nearly thirty years later the letter was reprinted in the *New York Voice,* a prohibition publication.

47. Ward, 32 (recollection of Henry C. Bowen); Stevens, 60 (recollection of Judith A. Bradner).

48. Donald, *Lincoln,* 270–71 (quoting an Ohio cousin of Mary Lincoln).

49. Wilson & Davis, 137 (Augustus H. Chapman to WHH, Oct. 8, 1865).

50. For an analysis of the reliability of Cogdall's account of his conversation with Lincoln, see Walsh, 31-2, 53-7, 82-5.

51. Wilson & Davis, 517 (Grace Bedell to WHH, Albion, N.Y., Dec. 14, 1866).

52. Herndon & Weik, 393.

53. Wilson & Davis, 517 (Grace Bedell to WHH, Albion, N.Y., Dec. 14, 1866).

54. Tiffany, 333–34. (The information was based on a letter from Samuel Felton to Francis Tiffany, May 8, 1888.)

55. Pinkerton, 44, 47.

56. Ibid., 48.

57. Hertz, *AL: A New Portrait,* 1:248 (A. K. McClure to an unidentified correspondent); Pinkerton, 53; Cuthbert, 15-6 (from the Pinkerton Record Book).

CHAPTER 10:
"MRS. LINCOLN IS INVOLVED IN CORRUPT TRAFFIC."

Note: For an interesting and excellent summary of Lincoln's married life, including Mary's financial indiscretions, see Michael Burlingame's book, *The Inner World of Abraham Lincoln,* especially pages 268 to 355.

1. Springfield (Ill.) *Register,* Jan. 14, 1874 (quoting WHH); Wilson & Davis, 701 (Horace White to WHH, Jan. 26, 1891).

2. Keckley, 130–31, 128.

3. Carman & Luthin, 28–9; James G. Randall Papers, Library of Congress (WHH to Horace White, Springfield, Feb. 13, 1891).

4. Browne, 413–14.

5. Ibid.; Basler, 4:271 (from AL's First Inaugural Address).

6. Baker, *MTL,* 184; Crawford, entry for Nov. 3, 1861; *Washington Sunday Gazette,* 23, Jan. 1887.

7. Basler, 4:385 (AL to Ephraim D. and Phoebe Ellsworth, May 25, 1861); "Ellsworth," *Atlantic Monthly,* 8, July 1861.

8. Nicolay & Hay, 4:352–55; John G. Nicolay Papers, Library of Congress (statement by George P. Goff, enclosed in Goff to Nicolay, Washington, D.C., Feb. 9, 1899).

9. Keckley, 132–33.

10. Basler, 4:87; Nolan, 298; Ames, 237-38.

11. *Commercial Gazette,* New York, Jan. 9, 1887.

12. Ames, 237–38.

13. Baker, *MTL,* 184 ("Union" to Lincoln, Washington, June 26, 1861); *The Sky Rocket,* Primghar, Iowa, March 15, 1929 (the source was Lincoln King, who claimed he knew Mrs. Lincoln's lover "intimately" in New York); William E. Barton Papers, University of Chicago (King to Barton, Primghar, Iowa, Aug. 9, 1930); John G. Nicolay Papers, Library of Congress (Schuyler Colfax to Nicolay, South Bend, Ind., July 17, 1875).

14. Manton Marble Papers, Library of Congress (George W. Adams to David Goodman Croly, Washington, Oct. 7, 1867); Turners, 202 (Edward McManus to Thurlow Weed); Lincoln Collection, Brown University (Oswald Garrison Villard to Isaac Markens, New York, March 26, 1927— Villard apparently was referring to Henry Wikoff, who was an adventurer but not of Hungarian origin); *Newark Star,* March 3, 1951 (letter to Abram Wakeman seen by his daughter, who described it to her daughter, Elizabeth M. Alexanderson of Englewood, N.J.).

15. Baker, *MTL,* 234; S. L. M. Barlow Papers, Henry E. Huntington Library, San Marino, Calif. (Sam Ward to Barlow, Washington, Nov. 21, [1864?]).

16. Records of the Commissioner of Public Buildings, National Archives (Letters Sent, vols. 13, 14); Ward Hill Lamon Papers, Henry E. Huntington Library (bill from Watt to Lincoln, Feb. 1, 1863); Randall, *MTL*, 254–58.

17. Records of the U. S. Senate, Committee on Public Buildings, 37th Congress, Record Group 46, National Archives (Upperman to Caleb B. Smith, Washington, Oct. 21, 1861).

18. W. H. Seward Papers, University of Rochester Library, microfilm edition, reel 66 (Caleb B. Smith to Seward, Washington, Oct. 27, 1861); New York *Commercial Advertiser,* Oct. 4, 1867, 2 (based on statement by Thurlow Weed); David Davis Papers, Chicago Historical Society (Davis to his wife, St. Louis, Feb. 23, 1862); Manton Marble Papers, Library of Congress (New York *World,* Sept. 26, 1864; E. V. Haughwout & Co. to Marble, Sept. 26, 27, 28, 1864); Ibid. (George W. Adams to David Goodman Croly, Washington, Oct. 7, 1867); *Boston Post,* Oct. 11, 1867, 1.

19. John Hay Diary, Feb. 13, 1867 (Newton to Hay).

20. Benjamin Brown French Papers, Library of Congress (French to Pamela French, Washington, Dec. 24, 1861).

21. Ibid. (Benjamin French to Pamela French, Dec. 24, 1861); Cole and McDonough, 382; John Hay Diary; William E. Barton Papers, University of Chicago (O. H. Browning Diary, July 3, 1873, quoting David Davis).

22. Washington *Sunday Gazette,* Jan. 16, 1887.

23. Burlingame, *The Inner World,* 325; Thomas, *AL,* 91; Keckley, 125.

24. Ross, *Proud Kate,* 47.

25. Keckley, 124–26.

26. Judd Stewart Collection, Huntington Library, op. cit. ("Presidential Domestic Squabbles," Washington correspondence, not dated; Rochester *Union,* unidentified clipping; Lincoln Scrapbooks, 5:44).

27. Ross, *Proud Kate,* 140.

28. Donald, *Lincoln,* 482; Basler, 7:212–13 (Al to Salmon P. Chase, Feb. 29, 1864).

29. Phelps, 158–59.

30. Basler, 7:419 (AL to Salmon P. Chase, June 30, 1864); Phelps, 167–68.

31. *New York World,* Feb. 20, 1870.

32. Baker, *MTL,* 231–33; Horace Greeley Papers, New York Public Library (Adam Gurowski to Greeley, Washington, Oct. 1, 1861); *Missouri Republican,* Oct. 25, 1861 (John Hay's anonymous Washington dispatch); S. L. M. Barlow Papers, Henry E. Huntington Library (T. J. Barnett to S. L. M. Barlow, Washington, Oct. 27, 1862).

33. Smith, 284–89.

34. Browne, 644–45.

35. Ross, *Proud Kate,* 151.

36. Ibid., 78–9 (based on the story in Julia Taft Bayne's memoir, *Tad Lincoln's Father.*

37. Keckley, 101; Burlingame, *Inner World of AL* (J. W. Nesmith to his wife, Washington, D. C., Feb. 5, 1862).

38. Helen Nicolay, 132-33; Browne, 465-66.

39. Keckley, 105.

40. Illinois State Historical Library, Springfield (reminiscences of Mary Miner Hill, daughter of the Rev. Dr. Noyes W. Miner, 1923); Rankin, 176-79.

41. MacKaye, 1:105-06 (MacKaye was told this story by his mother, who heard it from Francis B. Carpenter, an artist who, while living in the White House, overheard Mary and Lincoln).

CHAPTER 11:
"HER LETTER HAD BEEN CAREFULLY TREASURED BY HIM."

1. Keckley, 118.

2. Basler, 5:403-04 (from AL's Meditation on the Divine Will, Sept. 2, 1862).

3. Segal, 171-73; Basler, 5:278-79 (from AL's remarks to Progressive Friends, June 20, 1862); New York *Herald,* June 21, 1862.

4. Welles, 1:143.

5. Basler, 7:281 (AL to A. G. Hodges, Washington, D.C., April 4, 1864).

6. Braithwaite, 28-9; Mott, 307; Bullard, 10.

7. Mott, 308; Livermore, 550, 560.

8. Mott, 309.

9. Braithwaite, 31; Mott, 308, 313.

10. Ibid., 313-15.

11. Ibid., 316-17; Basler, 7:535; Mott, 318–21.

12. Bullard, 12.

13. Robertson, 73.

14. Browning, 1:600-01; Brooks, 57-8.

15. Keckley, 147; Sandburg & Angle, 110–12.

16. Beveridge, 1:536-37.

17. John Hay Papers, Library of Congress (Hay to John G. Nicolay, Washington, D.C., June 20, 1864). Lincoln chose Nicolay as his chief private secretary during his presidential campaign. Bavarian-born, Nicolay had been a newspaper editor. Nicolay then recruited John Hay as junior secretary. Hay, a recent graduate of Brown University, studied law in his uncle's office in Springfield

and was admitted to the bar two weeks before accompanying Lincoln to Washington. The two young men had known each other since 1851. They performed their jobs with great ability. Hay later became ambassador to England (1897) and secretary of state (1898) and earned a reputation as one of the country's leading writers. With Nicolay, he wrote the monumental ten-volume study, *Abraham Lincoln: A History* (1890).

CHAPTER 12:
"THE BEST ABUSED MAN OF OUR NATION"

1. Herr & Spence, 266; Basler, 4:519 (Lincoln to Mrs. John C. Fremont, Washington, Sept. 12, 1861).

2. McPherson, 108; Harper Collection, Henry E. Huntington Library (Anna E. Dickinson to [Elizabeth Cady Stanton?], Philadelphia, July 12, 1864).

3. Massey, 157.

4. Basler, 5:382; Blackwell, 47 (Edward Bates to Anna Ella Carroll, April 15, 1862, Washington, D.C.); *Chicago Times-Herald* clipping dated only 1895.

5. Blackwell, 52 (O. H. Browning to Anna Ella Carroll, Sept. 17, 1873, Quincy, Ill.).

6. Browning, 1:659 (entry for Feb. 6, 1864); John G. Nicolay Papers, Library of Congress (Nicolay's interview with Lot M. Morrill, probably Sept. 20, 1878); Livermore, 568.

7. *Littell's Living Age,* Feb. 6, 1864.

8. Segal, 372 (Joshua F. Speed to WHH, Jan. 12, 1866).

9. Ibid., 372–73.

10. Basler 6:256; 10:187.

11. Welles, 1:364.

12. Basler, 6:283, 471.

13. John Hay, 110; *New York World,* April 19, 1865.

14. Helm, 230–31.

15. Ibid., 225–26; Browning, 651.

16. Ibid.

17. Leonard, 89 (from Official Records, Ser. 2, Vol. 5, p. 567).

18. John G. Nicolay Papers (Nicolay to John Hay, Washington, Jan. 18, 29, 1864); Helen Nicolay, 191–92.

19. Simon, *The Papers of U. S. Grant,* 10:422; Carpenter, 283; Keckley, 133–34; Porter, 216–23.

20. Cramer, 64.

21. Keckley, 149–50.

22. General Ethan Allen Hitchcock Papers, Library of Congress (Hitchcock to Mary Mann, July 14, 1864).

23. Mabee, *Sojourner Truth: Slave, Prophet, Legend,* 74.

24. Ibid., 116.

25. Ibid., 122 (letter from Sojourner Truth to Rowland Johnson, a New Jersey Quaker, Nov. 17, 1864; published in the *National Anti-Slavery Standard,* Dec. 17, 1864). Note: The additional quotations from the meeting with Lincoln are taken from this letter.

26. Mabee, *New England Quarterly,* 527; Mabee, *Slave, Prophet, Legend,* 122-28.

27. Quarles, 256-57.

28. Keckley, 121.

29. Basler, 8:116-17.

30. Eagle, 603.

31. Ibid., 604 (quoting from Vinnie Ream Hoxie's 1893 speech, "Lincoln and Farragut").

32. *The Midland Monthly,* Nov. 1897; *Topeka State Journal,* July 4, 1903, page 13.

33. "Vinnie Ream an Interesting Page in Her History," *The Brooklyn Union,* Nov. 8, 1872; Eagle, 603.

34. Hall, 58-9; Turners, 387.

35. *Washington Evening Star,* Jan. 26, 1871.

CHAPTER 13:
"THAT WOMAN IS PRETENDING TO BE ME!"

1. Pfanz, 4; Porter, chapters 26–7 provide a full account of the visit; Arnold, 423 (based on General Sherman's recollection and statement).

2. Randall, *MTL,* 372–74; Badeau, 358–60.

3. Badeau, 358–60.

4. Keckley, 166–67.

5. Ibid., 172; Herndon-Weik Papers, Library of Congress, undated manuscript in Herndon's hand; Ishbel Ross, 232.

6. Ishbel Ross, 235.

7. Keckley, 177.

8. Hanchett, *TLMC,* 37.

9. Lamon, *Recollections,* 115–18.

10. Turners, 219.

11. Ibid., 257.

12. Chase, *Diary,* 268; Storey, 464; Welles, *Lincoln & Johnson,* 526–27; Thomas & Hyman, 357–58; Welles, *Diary,* 2:283; Flower, 271–72.

13. Bishop (based on Lincoln's remarks to John G. Nicolay).

14. Hanchett, "Booth's Diary," 40.

15. Wilson & Davis, 360 (Mary Lincoln to WHH, Sept. 1866); Turners, 283–85.

16. Storey, 464; Bates, 366–67; Donald, *Lincoln,* 594.

17. Donald, *Lincoln,* 594; Bates 367; Crook, *Through Five Administrations,* 66–7; Roscoe, 21–2.

18. Grant, 380; Bates, 392; Kunhardt, *Twenty Days,* 54.

19. Crook, *Memories of the White House,* 39.

20. Randall, *ML,* 382; Roscoe, 23.

21. Annie F. F. Wright, 113–14.

22. Donald, *Lincoln,* 599. Note: After the assassination, scores of women, many of them respectable ladies, were arrested and grilled by the Army Provosts on Stanton's orders, but, apparently, none of John Wilkes Booth's "lady friends" was pursued, even though numerous informants reported them. Among them were Nellie Starr, his former Washington favorite; "Jenny," his Canadian attachment; his large New York harem; harlot Ella Turner, his Washington mistress who tried to kill herself on the night of the assassination by covering her face with a towel soaked in chloroform (*New York Herald Tribune,* April 17, 1865); and his betrothed, Lucy Hale, whose name was kept secret for sixty-five years. Lucy was whisked to Spain soon after the assassination by her father, Republican Sen. John P. Hale, who had been appointed minister to Spain. See Roscoe, 322–26.

23. Lattimer, 32; Letter of Elizabeth Dixon, dated May 1, 1865, in *Surratt Society News* 7 (March 1982), 3–4; Bryan, 189.

24. Keckley, 192.

25. Julian, 255, 257; Chandler Papers in the Library of Congress (Zachariah Chandler to Mrs. Chandler, April 22, 1865); Bryan, 383.

26. Keckley, 197.

27. Ibid., 190; Kunhardts, *Lincoln,* 386.

Selected Bibliography

Alford, Terry, "The Silken Net: Plots to Abduct Abraham Lincoln During the Civil War" (Annandale, Va.: unpublished paper, April 21, 1987).

Allen, John W., "Story of Ann Rutledge Has Ties in Henderson, Ky., Enfield, Ill." (Carbondale, Ill.: Southern Illinois University, undated).

Ames, Mary Clemmer, *Ten Years in Washington—Life and Scenes in the National Capital—As a Woman Sees Them* (Hartford: A. D. Worthington & Co., 1874).

Angle, Paul M. (ed.), The Lincoln Reader (New Brunswick: Rutgers University Press, 1947).

———, *"Here I Have Lived": A History of Lincoln's Springfield 1821-1865* (New Brunswick: Rutgers University Press, 1950).

——— (ed.), *Herndon's Life of Lincoln: The History and Personal Recollections of Abraham Lincoln as Originally Written by William H. Herndon and Jesse W. Weik* (Cleveland: World, 1942).

Arnold, Isaac N., *The Life of Abraham Lincoln* (Chicago: Jansen, McClurg, & Co., 1885).

Asbury, Herbert, *A Methodist Saint: The Life of Bishop Asbury* (New York: Alfred A. Knopf, 1927).

Ashmun, George, "Abraham Lincoln at Home" in *Springfield* (Mass.) *Daily Republican* (May 23, 1860).

Badeau, Adam, *Grant in Peace: From Appomattox to Mount McGregor* (Hartford: S. S. Scranton & Co., 1887).

Baker, Jean H., *Mary Todd Lincoln* (New York: W. W. Norton & Co., 1987).

———, "Not Much of Me: Abraham Lincoln as a Typical American" at the Louis A. Warren Lincoln Library and Museum, Fort Wayne, Ind. (1988).

Baringer, William E., *Lincoln's Rise to Power* (Boston: Little, Brown & Co., 1937).

Barton, William E., "Abraham Lincoln and New Salem" in the *Journal of the Illinois State Historical Society,* 19 (1926-27).

——, "Sister of Lincoln's Sweetheart Recalls Romance Death Ended" in *San Diego Sun* (Jan. 11, 1922).

——, *The Paternity of Abraham Lincoln* (New York: George H. Doran C., 1920).

——, *The Women Lincoln Loved* (Indianapolis: Bobbs-Merrill,1927).

Basler, Roy P. et. al. (eds.),*The Collected Works of Abraham Lincoln* (Springfield, Ill.: Abraham Lincoln Association, 1953), 8 vols.

Bates, David Homer, *Lincoln in the Telegraph Office* (New York: D. Appleton-Century Co., 1907).

Bayne, Julia Taft, *Tad Lincoln's Father* (Boston: Little, Brown & Co., 1931).

Bergevin, Charlotte; Daisy Sundberg; and Evelyn Berg, "Camerons, Westward They Came" (Peoria, Ill.: unpublished paper, 1983).

Beveridge, Albert J., *Abraham Lincoln 1809–1858* (Boston & New York: Houghton Mifflin, 1928).

Bigelow, John (ed.), *Letters and Literary Memorials of Samuel J. Tilden* (New York: Harper & Brothers, 1908).

Bishop, Jim, *The Day Lincoln Was Shot* (New York: Harper & Brothers, 1955).

Blackwell, Sarah Ellen, *A Military Genius, Life of Anna Ella Carroll* (Washington, D.C.: Judd & Detweiler, 1891).

Bogue, Allan G., *The Congressman's Civil War* (Cambridge: Cambridge University Press, 1989).

Boritt, Gabor S. and Adam Boritt, "Lincoln and the Marfan Syndrome: The Medical Diagnosis of a Historical Figure" in *Civil War History,* 29 (Sept. 1983).

Bowman, John S. (ed.), *Who Was Who in the Civil War* (New York: Crescent Books, 1994).

Braithwaite, Joseph Bevan, *Memoirs of Eliza Paul Gurney and Others* (Philadelphia: Henry Longstreth, 1883).

Bray, Robert, "The Cartwright-Lincoln Acquaintance" in *The Old Methodist,* 13 (Summer, 1987).

Brockett, Linus P., and Mary C. Vaughan, *Woman's Work in the Civil War: A Record of Heroism, Patriotism, and Patience* (Philadelphia: Zeigler, McCurdy, 1867).

Brooks, Noah, *Washington in Lincoln's Time* (New York: The Century Co., 1896).

Brown, Pearl, *"Marian": Modern Pioneer Woman* (Springfield: publisher unknown, 1957), copies of various chapters provided by genealogist C. Vale Mayes of Shell Knob, Mo., to Ralph E. Winkler about 1985).

Browne, Francis Fisher, *The Every-Day Life of Abraham Lincoln* (Minneapolis: Northwestern Publishing Company, 1887).

Browning, Orville H., *The Diary of Orville Hickman Browning*, edited by Theodore Calvin Pease and James G. Randall (Springfield: Illinois State Historical Society, 1925, 1933) 2 vols.

Bryan, George S., *The Great American Myth* (New York: Carrick & Evans, 1940).

Bullard, F. Lauriston, "Lincoln and the Quaker Woman" in *Lincoln Herald,* 46:2 (June, 1944).

Burba, Howard, "A Story of Lincoln's Boyhood" in *American Boy* (Feb. 1905).

Burlingame, Michael (ed.), *An Oral History of Abraham Lincoln: John G. Nicolay's Interviews and Essays* (Carbondale, Ill.: Southern Illinois University Press, 1996).

———, *The Inner World of Abraham Lincoln* (Urbana & Chicago: University of Illinois Press, 1994).

Burt, Silas W., "Lincoln On His Own Story Telling" in *Century Magazine* 73 (Feb. 1907).

Carman, Harry J. and Reinhard H. Luthin, *Lincoln and the Patronage* (New York: Columbia University Press, 1943).

Carnegie, Dale, *Lincoln the Unknown* (New York: Perma Giants, 1932).

———, *The Unknown Lincoln* (New York: Pocket Books, 1952).

Carpenter, Francis B., *Six Months at the White House with Abraham Lincoln* (New York: Hurd and Houghton, 1866).

Cartwright, Peter, *Autobiography of Peter Cartwright* (Nashville: Abingdon Press, 1984).

Chandler, Josephine, "New Salem: An Early Chapter in Lincoln's Life" in *Journal of the Illinois State Historical Society* (Jan. 1930).

Chenery, William, "Mary Lincoln Should be Remembered for Many Kind Acts" in *Illinois State Register* (Feb. 27, 1938).

Clines, Francis X., "Discretion a Hallmark of Bordello in Capital" in *The New York Times* (April 18, 1999).

Cole, Donald B. and John J. McDonough (eds.), *Witness to the Young Republic* (Hanover: University Press of New England, 1989).

Coleman, Charles H., *Abraham Lincoln and Coles County, Illinois* (New Brunswick: Scarecrow Press, 1955).

———, "The Half-Faced Camp in Indiana—Fact or Myth?" in *Abraham Lincoln Quarterly* 7 (Sept. 1952).

Collier, Robert Laird, Moral Heroism: Its Essentialness to the Crisis. A Sermon, Preached to the Wabash Ave., M. E. Church, Chicago, Sabbath Evening, Aug. 3, 1862.

Conway, W. Fred, *Young Abe Lincoln, His Teenage Years in Indiana* (New Albany, Ind.: FBH Publishers, 1992).

Cook, Florita, "Ann Rutledge Figured Prominently in Life of Abraham Lincoln" in *Lompoc Record* (Feb. 12, 1967).

Coryell, Janet L., *Neither Heroine nor Fool: Anna Ella Carroll of Maryland* (Kent, Ohio: Kent State University Press, 1990).

Cramer, John Henry, *Lincoln Under Enemy Fire* (State University Press, Louisiana, 1948).

Crawford, Martin (ed.), *William Howard Russell's Civil War: Private Diary and Letters, 1861-62* (Athens: University of Georgia Press, 1991).

Crook, William H., "Lincoln's Last Day," in *Harper's* (Sept. 1907).

———, *Memories of the White House: The Home Life of Our Presidents from Lincoln to Roosevelt* (Boston: Little, Brown, & Co., 1911).

———, *Through Five Administrations* (New York: Harper & Brothers, 1907).

Cuthbert, Norma B. (ed.), *Lincoln and the Baltimore Plot, 1861: From Pinkerton Records and Related Papers* (San Marino: Henry E. Huntington Library, 1949).

Davis, James E., *Frontier Illinois* (Bloomington: Indiana University Press, 1998).

Davis, J. M., "Lincoln as a Storekeeper and as a Soldier in the Black Hawk War" in *McClure's* (Jan. 1896).

Davis, Rodney O. (ed.), *A History of Illinois From Its Commencement as a State in 1818 to 1847* (Urbana & Chicago: University of Illinois Press, 1995).

Donald, David Herbert, *Lincoln's Herndon* (New York: Alfred A. Knopf, 1948).

———, *Lincoln* (New York: Simon and Schuster, 1995).

Doster, William E., *Lincoln and Episodes of the Civil War* (New York: G. P. Putnam & Sons, 1915).

Drake, Julia A., *Flame O' Dawn* (New York: Vantage Press, 1959).

Duncan, Kunigunde, and D. F. Nickols, *Mentor Graham: The Man Who Taught Lincoln* (Chicago: University of Chicago Press, 1944).

Eagle, Mary (ed.), *The Congress of Women* (Chicago: International Publishing Co., 1894).

Erickson, Gary, "The Graves of Ann Rutledge and the Old Concord Burial Ground" in *Lincoln Herald* (Fall, 1969).

Findley, Paul, *A. Lincoln: The Crucible of Congress* (New York: Crown Publishers, 1979).

Fiske, A. Longfellow, "A Neighbor of Lincoln" in *Commonweal* 2 (March 1932).

Flindt, Margaret, "Lincoln as a Lover" (interview with Nancy Rutledge Prewitt, sister of Ann Rutledge), in *Chicago Inter-Ocean* (Feb. 12, 1899).

Flower, Frank Abial, *Edwin McMasters Stanton: The Autocrat of Rebellion, Emancipation, and Reconstruction* (New York: Western W. Wilson, 1905).

Foner, Philip S., (ed.), *The Complete Writings of Thomas Paine* (New York: Citadel Press, 1945).

Fowler, William Worthington, *Woman on the American Frontier* (Hartford: S.S. Scranton, 1877).

Freedman, Russell, *Lincoln: A Photobiography* (New York: Clarion Books, 1987).

Garrison, Webb, *The Lincoln No One Knows* (Nashville: Rutledge Hill Press, 1993).

Goff, John S., *Robert Todd Lincoln: A Man in His Own Right* (Norman: University of Oklahoma Press, 1969).

Grant, Ulysses S., *Personal Memoirs* (New York: C. L. Webster & Co., 1885-86).

Gridley, Eleanor, *The Story of Abraham Lincoln* (Chicago: Monarch, 1902).

Hall, Gordon Langley, *Vinnie Ream, The Story of the Girl Who Sculptured Lincoln* (New York: Holt, Rinehart & Winston, 1963).

Hammand, Jane E., *Memoirs of the Rutledge Family of New Salem, Illinois* (typescript, collects documents at the Library of Congress), compiled for the Decatur Lincoln Memorial Collection (1921).

Hanchett, William, *The Lincoln Murder Conspiracies* (Urbana: University of Illinois Press, 1983).

——, "Booth's Diary" in *Journal of the Illinois State Historical Society* 72 (Feb. 1979).

Hay, John, *Inside Lincoln's White House, The Complete Civil War Diary of John Hay*, edited by Michael Burlingame and John R. Turner Ettlinger (Carbondale: Southern Illinois University Press, 1997).

Hay, William D. (ed.), "... *A matter of history*..." (Carmi, Ill.: The White County Historical Society, 1996).

Helm, Katherine, *The True Story of Mary, Wife of Lincoln* (New York: Harper & Brothers, 1928).

Hendrick, Burton J., *Lincoln's War Cabinet* (Boston: Little Brown, 1946).

Herndon, William, *Lincoln and Ann Rutledge and the Pioneers of New Salem* (Herrin, Ill.: Trovillion Press, 1945).

—— and Jesse W. Weik *Herndon's Life of Lincoln* (New York: Da Capo Press, 1983).

Herr, Pamela and Mary Lee Spence (eds.), *The Letters of Jessie Benton Fremont* (Urbana: University of Illinois Press, 1993).

Hertz, Emanuel, *Abraham Lincoln: A New Portrait* (New York: Boni and Liveright, 1931), 2 vols.

—— (ed.), *Lincoln Talks, An Oral Biography* (New York: Bramhall House, 1986).

—— (ed.), *The Hidden Lincoln, From the Letters and Papers of William Herndon* (New York: Viking, 1938).

Hill, Frederick T., *Lincoln the Lawyer* (New York: Century Co., 1906).

Holland, J. G., *The Life of Abraham Lincoln* (Springfield, Mass.: Gurdon Bill, 1866).

Howells, W. D., *Life of Abraham Lincoln* (Springfield, Ill.: Abraham Lincoln Association, 1938).

Janney, John Jay, "Talking with the President: Four Interviews with Abraham Lincoln" in *Civil War Times Illustrated*, 26 (Sept. 1987).

Jones, Lewis P., *South Carolina, A Synoptic History for Laymen* (Lexington, S.C.: The Sandlapper Store, 1981).

Jordan, Philip D., "The Death of Nancy Hanks Lincoln" in *Indiana Magazine of History* 40 (June 1944).

Julian, George W., *Political Reflections, 1840 to 1872* (Chicago: Jansen, McClurg & Co., 1884.

Kane, Harnett T., *Spies for the Blue and Gray* (Garden City: Hanover House, 1954).

Keckley, Elizabeth, *Behind the Scenes. . . or Thirty Years a Slave, and Four Years in the White House* (New York: G. W. Carleton, 1868).

Kincaid, Robert L., *Joshua Fry Speed: Lincoln's Most Intimate Friend* (Harrogate: Lincoln Memorial University, 1943).

Kunhardt, Dorothy Meserve and Philip B. Kunhardt, *Twenty Days* (New York: Harper & Row, 1965).

Kunhardt, Jr., Philip B.; Philip B. Kunhardt, III; and Peter W. Kunhardt, *Lincoln* (New York: Alfred A. Knopf, 1991).

Lair, John, *Songs Lincoln Loved* (New York: Duel, Sloan, 1954).

Lamon, Ward Hill, *Life of Abraham Lincoln, from His Birth to His Inauguration as President* (Boston: Osgood, 1872).

———, *Recollections of Abraham Lincoln, 1847–1865*, edited by Dorothy Lamon Teillard (Chicago: A. C. McClurg & Co., 1895).

Land, Margaret, "The Seven Mile Prairie Settlement" (Carmi, Ill.: unpublished paper in the Carmi Public Library, circa 1960).

———, "Enfield Township" (Carmi, Ill.: unpublished paper in the Carmi Public Library, circa 1960).

———, Letter to Georgia Archives (Jan. 12, 1954).

Lattimer, Dr. John K., *Kennedy and Lincoln: Medical and Ballistic Comparisons of Their Assassinations* (New York: Harcourt Brace Jovanovich, 1980).

Leech, Margaret, *Reveille in Washington: 1860 to 1865* (New York: Harper & Row, 1941).

Leonard, Elizabeth D., *All the Daring of the Soldier* (New York: W. W. Norton & Co., 1999).

Leslie, Frank, *Heroic Incidents* (New York: publisher unknown, 1862).

Lincoln, Waldo, *History of the Lincoln Family* (Worcester: 1923).

Linder, Usher, *Reminiscences of the Early Bench and Bar of Illinois* (Chicago: Legal News Co., 1879).

Livermore, Mary A., *My Story of the War* (Hartford: A. D. Worthington, 1889).

Lomask, Milton, *Andrew Johnson: President on Trial* (New York: Farrar, Strauss and Giroux, 1960).

Lorant, Stefan, *Life of Abraham Lincoln* (New York: Harper & Brothers, 1952).

Mabee, Carleton, "Sojourner Truth and President Lincoln" in *The New England Quarterly* 61 (Dec. 1988).

————, *Sojourner Truth: Slave, Prophet, Legend* (New York: New York University Press, 1993).

MacKaye, Percy, *Epoch: The Life of Steele MacKaye, Genius of the Theater* (New York: Boni and Liveright, 1927).

Maltby, Charles, *The Life and Public Services of Abraham Lincoln* (Stockton, Calif.: Daily Independent Steam Power Print, 1884).

Manfrina, Myra, "Lincoln-Rutledge Romance Recalled by Memoirs of Lompoc Resident" in *News-Press,* Santa Barbara, Calif. (Feb. 12, 1952).

Massey, Mary Elizabeth, *Women in the Civil War* (Lincoln, Neb.: University of Nebraska Press, 1966).

Masters, Edgar Lee, *Lincoln the Man* (Columbia, S.C.: The Foundation for American Education, 1997).

McCoy, Susan Hatton, *A Frontier Wife* (New York: Ballantine Books, 1988).

McPherson, James M., *The Struggle for Equality: Abolitionists and the Negro in the Civil War and Reconstruction* (Princeton: Princeton University Press, 1964).

Mearns, David C. (ed.), *The Lincoln Papers* (Garden City: Doubleday, 1948).

Miers, Earl Schenck (ed.), *Lincoln Day By Day,* 3 (Washington: Lincoln Sesquicentennial Commission, 1960), 3 vols.

Miller, R.D., *Past and Present of Menard County, Illinois* (Chicago: Clarke, 1905).

Milton, George F., *The Age of Hate, Andrew Johnson and the Radicals* (Hamden: Archon Books, 1965).

Moorhead, James H., *American Apocalypse: Yankee Protestants and the Civil War* (New Haven: Yale University Press, 1978).

Mott, Richard F. (ed.), *Memoir and Correspondence of Eliza P. Gurney* (Philadelphia: J. B. Lippincott & Co., 1884).

Murphy, Alice Purvine, T*he Rev. John Miller Camron and Descendant 1790–1962* (privately published, 1962).

Murr, J. Edward, "Lincoln in Indiana" in *Indiana Magazine of History* 14 (March 1918).

Nevins, Allan, *The War for the Union* (New York: Charles Scribner's Sons, 1959).

Nicolay, Helen, *Lincoln's Secretary: A Biography of John G. Nicolay* (New York: Longmans, Green & Co., 1949).

Nicolay, John, *A Short Life of Abraham Lincoln* (New York: Century Co., 1902).

Nicolay, John, and John Hay, *Abraham Lincoln: A History* (New York: Century Co., 1891).

Nolan, J. Bennett, "Of a Tomb in the Reading Cemetery and the Long Shadow of Abraham Lincoln" in *Pennsylvania History,* 19:3 (July 1952).

Oates, Stephen B., *With Malice Toward None* (New York: HarperPerennial, HarperCollins, 1994).

Oldroyd, Osborn H., *The Assassination of Abraham Lincoln: Flight, Pursuit, Capture and Punishment of the Conspirators* (Washington, D.C: privately published, 1901).

Onstot, T. G., *Pioneers of Menard and Mason Counties* (Peoria, Ill.: J. W. Franks & Sons, 1902); reprinted (Havana, Ill.: Members of the Church of Jesus Christ of Latter-day Saints, 1986).

Ostendorf, Lloyd, *Abraham Lincoln, The Boy, The Man* (Springfield, Ill.: Phillip H. Wagner, Wagner Office Systems, 1962).

Pfanz, Donald C., *The Petersburg Campaign, Abraham Lincoln at City Point, March 20-April 9, 1865* (Lynchburg, Va.: H. E. Howard, 1989).

Phelps, Mary Merwin, *Kate Chase Dominant Daughter* (New York: Thomas Y. Crowell Co., 1935).

Pickard, Samuel, *Autobiography of a Pioneer* (Church and Goodman, 1866).

Pinkerton, Allan, *The Spy of the Rebellion: Being a True History of the Spy System of the United States Army During the Late Rebellion* (New York: G. W. Carleton, 1883; Toronto: Rose Publishing Company, 1884).

Pond, Fern Nance, "Abraham Lincoln and David Rutledge" in *Lincoln Herald* (June 1950).

———, "Intellectual New Salem in Lincoln's Day," an address delivered at Lincoln Memorial University, Harrogate, Tenn., Feb. 12, 1938.

———, "The Memoirs of James McGrady Rutledge" in *Journal of the Illinois State Historical Society* (April 1936).

Porter, David W., *Incidents and Anecdotes of the Civil War* (New York: D. Appleton, 1885).

Porter, Horace, *Campaigning With Grant* (New York: Century Co., 1897).

Pratt, Harry E., "Lincoln in the Black Hawk War" in *Bulletin of the Abraham Lincoln Association,* No. 54 (Dec. 1938).

Putnam, George Haven, "The Speech that Won the East for Lincoln" in *Outlook* 130 (Feb. 8, 1922).

Quarles, Benjamin, *The Negro in the Civil War* (New York: Da Capo Press, 1989; Boston: Little, Brown & Co. 1953).

Randall, James G., "Sifting the Ann Rutledge Evidence" in *Lincoln the President* (New York: Dodd, Mead & Co., 1945).

————, *Lincoln the President: Springfield to Gettysburg* (New York: Dodd, Mead & Co., 1946).

Randall, Ruth, *Mary Lincoln: Biography of a Marriage* (Boston: Little, Brown, & Co., 1953).

————, *Lincoln's Sons* (Boston: Little, Brown, & Co., 1955).

Rankin, Henry, *Personal Recollections of Abraham Lincoln* (New York: G. P. Putnam & Sons, 1916).

Reep, Thomas, *Lincoln at New Salem* (Petersburg: New Salem Lincoln League, 1927, 1918).

Rice, Allen Thorndike (ed.), *Reminiscences of Abraham Lincoln* (New York: North American Review, 1888).

Richardson, Albert D., *The Secret Service, the Field, the Dungeon, and the Escape* (Hartford: American, 1865).

Robertson, James I., Jr., *Civil War! America Becomes One Nation* (New York: Alfred A. Knopf, 1992).

Roscoe, Theodore, *The Web of Conspiracy* (Englewood Cliffs: Prentice-Hall, 1959).

Ross, Harvey, *Early Pioneers and Pioneer Events in the State of Illinois* (Chicago: Eastman, 1899).

Ross, Ishbel, *The President's Wife, Mary Todd Lincoln* (New York: G. P. Putnam & Sons, 1973).

————, *Proud Kate* (New York: Harper & Brothers., 1953).

Rouse, Parke S., Jr., *The Great Wagon Road* (Richmond, Va.: The Dietz Press, 1995).

————, *Planters and Pioneers: Life in Colonial Virginia* (New York: Hastings House, 1968).

Rutledge, James McGrady, "The Memoirs of James McGrady Rutledge, 1814-1899" in *Journal of the Illinois State Historical Society* XXIX, No. 1 (April 1936).

Sandburg, Carl, *Abraham Lincoln, the Prairie Years* (New York: Harcourt, Brace & Co., 1926).

Sandburg, Carl, and Paul M. Angle, *Mary Lincoln: Wife and Widow* (New York: Harcourt, Brace, & Co., 1932).

Saunders, James Rutledge, *The Rutledge Family of New Salem, Illinois* (Sisquoc, Calif.: unpublished, Jan. 1922), compiled from the Rutledge family Bible and other family records.

Segal, Charles M. (ed.), *Conversations With Lincoln* (New York: G. P. Putnam & Sons, 1961).

Shelton, Vaughan, *Mask for Treason: The Lincoln Murder Trial* (Harrisburg: Stackpole Books, 1965).

Shere, Doc, "Story of Ann Rutledge As Illinoisans Were Told It By Their Grandmothers" in unidentified clipping (circa 1940).

Sheridan, Philip H., *The Personal Memoirs of P. H. Sheridan* (New York: Da Capo Press, 1992; New York: C. L. Webster, 1888).

Sherwood, Glenn V., *Labor of Love, The Life and Art of Vinnie Ream* (Hygiene, Col.: Sunshine Press Publications, 1997).

Shutes, Milton H., *Lincoln's Emotional Life* (Philadelphia: Dorrance, 1957).

Simon, John Y., "Abraham Lincoln and Ann Rutledge" in *Journal of the Abraham Lincoln Association,* II (1990), pp. 13-33.

——— (ed.), *The Papers of Ulysses S. Grant* (Carbondale, Ill.: Southern Illinois University Press, 1982).

Smith, Don, *Peculiarities of the Presidents: Strange Facts Not Usually Found in History* (Van Wert, Ohio: Wilkinson Press, 1938).

Smith, Matthew Hale, *Sunshine and Shadow in New York* (Hartford: J. B. Burr, 1868).

Sparks, Edwin E. (ed.), *The Lincoln-Douglas Debates of 1858* (Springfield, Ill.: Illinois State Historical Library Collection, 1908).

Speed, Joshua Fry, *Reminiscences of Abraham Lincoln and Notes of a Visit to California* (Louisville: John P. Morgan, 1884).

Stanton, Elizabeth Cady; Susan B. Anthony; and Matilda Joslyn Gage (eds.), *History of Woman Suffrage* (Rochester: Charles Mann, 1889).

Stevens, Walter B., *A Reporter's Lincoln* (St. Louis: Missouri Historical Society, 1916).

Stoddard, William O., *Inside the White House in War Times* (New York: Charles L. Webster & Co., 1892).

Storey, Moorfield, "Dickens, Stanton, Sumner, and Storey" in *Atlantic Monthly* 145 (April 1930).

Strozier, Charles, *Lincoln's Quest for Union: Public and Private Meanings* (New York: Basic Books, 1982).

——— and Stanley H. Cath, et. al. (eds.), "Lincoln and the Fathers: Reflections on Idealization" in *Fathers and Their Families* (Hillsdale, N.J.: Analytic Press, 1989).

Swinton, William, *Campaigns of the Army of the Potomac* (New York: Charles B. Richardson, 1866).

Tarbell, Ida M., *The Early Life of Abraham Lincoln,* reprint of 1896 edition (New York: Barnes, 1974).

———, *The Life of Abraham Lincoln* (New York: Lincoln Memorial Association, 1900), 2 vols.

———, "Lincoln's First Love" in *Collier's* 8 (Feb. 1930).

———, "Ann Rutledge" in *In the Footsteps of the Lincolns* (New York: Harper & Brothers, 1924).

Temple, Wayne C., *Abraham Lincoln From Skeptic to Prophet* (Mahomet, Ill.: Mayhaven Publishing, 1995).

Thomas, Benjamin P., *Abraham Lincoln: A Biography* (New York: Alfred A. Knopf, 1952).

———, *Lincoln's New Salem,* revision of 1934 and 1954 editions (Carbondale, Ill.: Southern Illinois University Press, 1987).

———, and Harold M. Hyman, *Stanton: The Life and Times of Lincoln's Secretary of War* (New York: Alfred A. Knopf, 1962).

Thompson, Ernest Trice, *Presbyterians in the South 1607–1871* (Richmond, Va.: John Knox Press, 1963).

Tiffany, Francis, *Life of Dorothea Lynde Dix* (Boston: Houghton Mifflin Co., 1890).

Townsend, William H., *Lincoln and Liquor* (New York: Press of the Pioneers, 1934).

Turner, Justin G. and Linda Levitt Turner, *Mary Todd Lincoln: Her Life and Letters* (New York: Alfred A. Knopf, 1972).

Verduin, Paul H., "Lincoln's Tidewater Virginia Heritage: The Hidden Legacy of Nancy Hanks Lincoln," unpublished address to the Lincoln Group of the District of Columbia (Oct. 17, 1989).

———, "New Evidence Suggests Lincoln's Mother Born in Richmond County, Va., Giving Credibility to Planter-Grandfather Legend" in *Northern Neck of Virginia Historical Magazine* 38 (Dec 1988), pp. 4354–89.

Voss, Veronica, "Seven Mile Community" in *Carmi Times* (Feb. 8 1966).

Walsh, John Evangelist, *The Shadows Rise, Abraham Lincoln and the Ann Rutledge Legend* (Urbana & Chicago: University of Illinois Press, 1993).

Ward, William Hayes (ed.), *Abraham Lincoln: Tributes from His Associates: Reminiscences of Soldiers, Statesmen and Citizens* (New York: Thomas Y. Crowell, 1895).

Warren, Louis A., *Lincoln's Parentage and Childhood* (New York & London: The Century Company, 1926).

———, *Lincoln's Youth* (New York: Appleton, Century, Crofts, Inc., 1959).

Warren, Mary Bondurant, *Citizens and Immigrants—South Carolina, 1768* (Danielsville, Ga.: Heritage Papers, 1980).

Weeks, Stephen Beauregard, "Confederate Textbooks: A Preliminary Bibliography," Report of the U. S. Commissioner of Education, 1898-99, Vol. II (Washington, D.C.: 1900).

Weichmann, Louis J., *A True History of the Assassination of Abraham Lincoln and of the Conspiracy of 1865,* edited by Floyd E. Risvold (New York: Alfred A. Knopf, 1975).

Weik, Jesse W., *The Real Lincoln* (Boston: Houghton Mifflin, 1922).

Welles, Gideon, *Diary of Gideon Welles,* edited by John T. Morse, Jr. (Boston:

Houghton Mifflin Co., 1911).

——, "Lincoln and Johnson," *Galaxy* 13 (April 1872).

Whipple, Wayne, *The Story of Young Abraham Lincoln* (Chicago: Goldsmith Company, 1934).

Whitney, Henry C., *Life on the Circuit With Lincoln* (Boston: Estes and Lauriat, 1892).

Wilson, Douglas, "Abraham Lincoln, Ann Rutledge, and the Evidence of Herndon's Informants" in *Civil War History* (Dec. 1990).

——, *Lincoln Before Washington: New Perspectives on the Illinois Years* (Urbana & Chicago: University of Illinois Press, 1997).

—— and Rodney O. Davis (eds.), *Herndon's Informants: Letters, Interviews, and Statements About Abraham Lincoln* (Urbana & Chicago: University of Illinois Press, 1997).

——, *Honor's Voice, The Transformation of Abraham Lincoln* (New York: Alfred A. Knopf, 1998).

Wright, Annie F. F., "The Assassination of Abraham Lincoln" in *Magazine of History* 9 (Feb. 1909).

Wright, Richardson, *Forgotten Ladies: Nine Portraits from the American Family Album* (Philadelphia: J. B. Lippincott, 1928).

Zane, Charles S., "Lincoln as I Knew Him" in *Sunset Magazine* 29 (Oct. 1912).

Index